Mariusz Załucki

Wills Formalities versus Testator's Intention

Functional model of effective testation for informal wills

Nomos

The book is part of a research project funded by the National Science Centre (Poland), agreement No. UMO-2018/29/B/HS5/00361.

The Deutsche Nationalbibliothek lists this publication in the Deutsche Nationalbibliografie; detailed bibliographic data are available on the Internet at http://dnb.d-nb.de

ISBN   978-3-8487-7082-3 (Print)
         978-3-7489-2472-2 (ePDF)

British Library Cataloguing-in-Publication Data
A catalogue record for this book is available from the British Library.

ISBN   978-3-8487-7082-3 (Print)
         978-3-7489-2472-2 (ePDF)

Library of Congress Cataloging-in-Publication Data
Załucki, Mariusz
Wills Formalities versus Testator's Intention
Functional model of effective testation for informal wills
Mariusz Załucki
204 pp.
Includes bibliographic references.

ISBN   978-3-8487-7082-3 (Print)
         978-3-7489-2472-2 (ePDF)

Scientific review:
Prof. Rita Lobo Xavier, Universidade Católica Portuguesa, Portugal
Prof. Fryderyk Zoll, Universität Osnabrück, Germany
and Jagiellonian University, Poland

1st Edition 2021

Published by
Nomos Verlagsgesellschaft mbH & Co. KG
Waldseestraße 3–5 | 76530 Baden-Baden
www.nomos.de

Production of the printed version:
Nomos Verlagsgesellschaft mbH & Co. KG
Waldseestraße 3–5 | 76530 Baden-Baden

ISBN   978-3-8487-7082-3 (Print)
ISBN   978-3-7489-2472-2 (ePDF)
DOI   https://doi.org/10.5771/9783748924722

Onlineversion
Nomos eLibrary

Table of Contents

Introduction

There is always a need to take an interest in succession law and the instruments it provides for the *mortis causa* disposal of property when society undergoes changes.[1] Therefore, the development of succession law is not uniform. From time to time, events occur that intensify the changes in this area.[2] The political transformation in the Eastern European countries more than thirty years ago may serve as an example,[3] since it led to a different view of private property relations[4] and also to an increase in inheritance problems.[5] At that time, the legislators and practice of the individual states in this area saw a gradual increase in the number of cases involving problems that had not existed before. Similarly, one can try to assess the issue of individual technological revolutions and their impact on the availability and enforceability of individual legal inheritance instruments.[6] In recent years in particular, as a result of the very rapid development of various technologies, the phenomenon of so-called informal wills has appeared on a large scale in the practice of succession law.[7] These are wills made by testators who, when disposing of their assets in the event of their death, do

---

1 *Cf.* Anne Röthel, *Ist unser Erbrecht noch zeitgemäß?* (C H Beck 2010) 9 ff.
2 Germain Brière, 'Le projet de réforme du droit des successions' (1984) 15 Revue générale de droit 405, 406 ff.
3 Olivier Moreteau, 'A Summary Reflection on the Future of Civil Codes in Europe ' in P Apathy and others (eds), *Festschrift fur Helmut Koziol zum 70. Geburtstag* (2010) 1139–1149.
4 *Cf.* Peter Gardos, 'Recodification of the Hungarian Civil Law' (2007) 2007 European Review of Private Law 707.
5 Paul Terner, 'Perspectives of a European Law of Succession' (2007) 14 Maastricht Journal of European and Comparative Law 147.
6 Salvatore Patti, 'Il testamento olografo nell'era digitale' (2014) 2014 Rivistra di dirittio civile 992.
7 See, e.g.: Bruce H Mann, 'Formalities and Formalism in the Uniform Probate Code' (1994) 142 University of Pennsylvania Law Review 1033; Kevin White, 'Dispensing Powers. Validating Testamentary Intentions in the Absence of Formal Compliance' [2000] Law Society Journal 56; Ben Mceniery, 'Succession Law Keeping Pace with Changes in Technology and Community Expectations – Informal Wills' (2014) 12 Journal of New Business Ideas & Trends 1; Susan Gary, 'Harmless Error: History of the Doctrine and Recent Cases from the U.S. and Australia', *Oregon State Bar CLE seminar Advanced Estate Planning 2019* (Oregon State Bar 2019); Francois du Toit, 'Remedying Formal Irregularities in Wills: A Comparative Analy-

not make use of the forms of will provided for by the law or use them incorrectly. This is most often the result of ignorance or confusion as to the admissibility of a particular method of disposing of assets in the event of their death, and also reflects the needs of the testator who, in this instance, trusts other means of preserving his last intention than those provided for by the law.[8] Despite the testator's relatively obvious intentions, this type of legal act does not generally lead to the legal effects desired by the testator. In the light of the relevant provisions, at least from the perspective of most European countries, such a will is frequently invalid. Despite clear and convincing evidence and testation intentions, the testator's last will does not produce any legal effects regarding his estate, as it was expressed in a manner contrary to the law. The inappropriateness of this kind of solutions was shown, among others, during the COVID-19 pandemic, when the need for making last wills has increased significantly, and has rarely been executed in a manner consistent with the formalities.[9]

The functioning of such a solution in practice seems to be unsatisfactory for a number of reasons. Above all, it is a contradiction with a fundamental premise of modern succession law, i.e. the desire to reflect at all costs the last intentions of the deceased when determining the circle of beneficiaries of the succession estate.[10] Such an assumption is today not only at the heart of dispositions of property upon death, but is also, for example, the basic guideline for the drafting of the provisions on the statutory succession, where it is indicated that the aim is to shape it in such a way that the statutory succession reflects the statistical will of the hypothetical testator.[11] The influence of the last intent of the deceased on the succession law and its particular instruments is therefore considerable, so it seems that also the basic tools reflecting this intent, such as wills, should make it pos-

---

sis of Testamentary Rescue in Canada and South Africa' (2020) 20 Oxford University Commonwealth Law Journal 139.

8 Mariusz Załucki, 'A Few Remarks about the Future of Provisions on Making a Will Contrary to the Testamentary Formalities Law' (2020) 13 Cadernos de Dereito Actual 20.

9 Kelly Purser, Tina Cockburn and Bridget J Crawford, 'Wills Formalities beyond COVID-19; An Australian-United States Perspective' (2020) 9 UNSW Law Journal Forum 1.

10 John H Langbein, 'Substantial Compliance with the Wills Act' (1975) 88 Harvard Law Review 489.

11 Susan Gary, 'Adapting Intestacy Laws to Changing Families' (2000) 18 Law & Inequality: A Journal of Theory and Practice 1.

sible to preserve this value and not be rigorously formal.[12] Reflecting the intent of a testator, sometimes expressed informally, seems to be more important value of the law of succession than respecting the formalities.

Such assumptions have already appeared in the succession law of some countries over the years. The voices of the doctrine,[13] the case-law[14] and, before that, the society,[15] have in some places brought about certain changes, including legislative changes, which today can be described as those on the side of a liberal approach to this issue. According to these solutions, fulfilling the intent of a testator at the expense of formalities is a "cure", and therefore it is possible to validate a last will and to respect testator's intentions despite the existence of certain formal defects in last wills.[16] However, there are also places in the world, and these places include most European countries, where the traditional approach to the formalities of succession law prevails, with the result that a testator's failure to comply with the statutory model during a testamentary act renders it invalid.[17] Time is moving inexorably on, however, and positive law is subject to constant change and development, which must also apply to the issue of last wills. For legal institutions come into being, change and disappear. Among other things, this is what links them to the fate of human beings, for when we come into the world, at some point we become aware of the inevitability of our passing. Then we can make a conscious choice to make a last will in the event of death or leave the order of succession and the de-

---

12   David Hayton, 'By-Passing Testamentary Formalities' (1987) 46 Cambridge Law Journal 215.

13   The most momentous text in this regard is that published by John H. Langbein back in 1975, a must-read for all reformers of this area of law. See: Langbein, 'Substantial Compliance with the Wills Act' (n 10).

14   Against this background, there have been many examples over the years of judgments referring to the problem of undue formal rigour. See: Mariusz Załucki, 'About the Need to Adjust the Regulations Regarding the Form of Will to the Modern Requirements' (2019) 6 The European Journal of Economics, Law and Politics 1.

15   It is difficult to present the views of the public in one place, especially as these are always diversified. Nevertheless, attention should be drawn to a number of statements on Internet forums, for example, indicating the need to modernise the law in this area. This can also be seen in the research of various scientific institutes. See, e.g.: British Columbia Law Institute, *Wills, Estates and Succession: A Modern Legal Framework* (2006).

16   Anne Breuer, 'Pellegrini v. Breitenbach. Power to Reform Innocent Mistakes in Wills' (2012) 26 Quinnipac Probate Law Journal 46.

17   Antoni Vaquer Aloy, 'La relajación de las solemnidades del testamento' (2016) 3 Revista de Derecho Civil 9.

cision in this matter to the legislature.[18] But does today's law allow for a free and discretionary construction of the declaration of the last will and the shaping of legal relations *mortis causa*? Do the instruments available in this regard guarantee a proper reflection of the testator's instructions? How far should succession law remain from the often emerging and disappearing solutions based on devices used in everyday *inter vivos* practice? Is there a room in succession law for the Internet, social media, smart phones and other benefits of new technologies? Are existing forms of estate disposition coherent with the technological opportunities created by the emergence in recent years of a range of technological devices in almost every household? The answers to these questions are not the easiest ones and require taking into account a number of factors, both subjective and objective in nature. They can also affect and influence the shape of normative regulation in this area.

With this in mind, and observing the wide influence of technological innovation on various areas of legislation,[19] as well as noticing the potential vulnerability of succession law to this kind of interference, I decided to explore the tools used by the testator to dispose of property upon death. The current state of affairs, including the normative state of affairs in the various European countries has given rise to a need to search for an instrument which would make it possible to reconcile the traditional approach with the modern one, the current formalism with the increasingly frequent practice of preparing informal wills. I have therefore turned my attention to the question of the form of a will and its current and possible future image.

For this reason I considered it necessary to examine whether it is possible to design provisions on the form of a will in such a way as to meet contemporary needs in the context of the dysfunctions of these provisions,[20] which emphasise the form rather than the content of a specific disposition in the event of death. In my view, it is the content of the will and not the manner in which it is preserved that should be decisive in the context of assessing whether, in a given case following the testator's death, there is an effectively made declaration of intent in the event of death that has an ef-

---

18 Gerry W Beyer, *What If Your Parrot Outlives You? Preparing for Your Bird's Future* (Phoenix Landing Foundation 2020).

19 Ricardo Berti and Simone Zanetti, 'La trasmissione mortis causa del patrimonio e dell'identità digitale: strumenti giuridici, operativi e prospettive de iure condendo' [2016] Law and Media Working Paper Series 1.

20 *Cf.* Rudolf Welser, 'Die Reform des österreichischen Erbrechts', *Zivilrechtsgesetzgebung heute Festschrift Gerhard Hopf zum 65. Geburtstag* (Manz 2007).

fect on the deceased person's property interests. The form of a will, understood as the manner in which the declaration is made and the vehicle of its content,[21] should be merely a means of recording the testator's will, and not a mechanism conditioning its effectiveness. Without observance of any form, a testator's declaration of intent containing his instructions in the event of death could not survive until after his death and thus produce any legal effects. In my opinion, however, it does not matter whether the form is oral, written or any other,[22] as long as it is capable of recording the testator's last will in such a way that it can be reproduced some time after his death. Therefore, the main objective of this work is to design such a normative solution which could function in the provisions of succession law as one that constructs the legal figure of the form of a will, giving it characteristics enabling it to reflect the testator's last intention irrespective of the manner in which it was made and irrespective of the manner in which it was recorded. In my opinion, it is possible to dissociate the provisions on the form of a will from the indication of the specific manner in which the testator made his last will, just as it is possible to dissociate these provisions from the indication of the specific manner in which the testator's last will was recorded. This is why I present the functional model of effective testation for informal wills and propose its implementation by individual European legislators. After its introduction to the law, all the future wills will be formal.

In the light of this, my main objective is to demonstrate that it is possible, justified by the needs of the practice of drawing up wills, to give the provisions on the form of a will a wording which makes them technologically independent, allowing the testator's declaration of last intent, made in any manner whatsoever, recorded by means of any method enabling the testator's last intent to be reflected after his death, to produce legal effects *mortis causa*. For it is not in all the current formalities and methods of testation indicated by individual legislators, but in the reflection of the testator's intentions that the most important value underpinning modern succession law lies.[23]

---

21 Instead of many, see: Philippe Malaurie and Claude Brenner, *Droit des successions et des libéralités* (8th edn, LGDJ Lextenso 2018) 241 ff.

22 Reinhard Zimmermann, 'Testamentsformen: »Willkür« oder Ausdruck einer Rechtskultur?' (2012) 76 Rabels Zeitschrift für ausländisches und internationales Privatrecht 471; Mariusz Załucki, 'Współczesne tendencje rozwoju ustawodawstwa testamentowego' (2012) 22 Roczniki Nauk Prawnych 23.

23 Francesca Cristiani, 'Nuove tecnologie e testamento: presente e futuro' [2013] Diritto dell'informazione e dell'informatica 559.

This thesis is accompanied by the hypothesis that one of the main tasks of modern succession law is to link the available legal constructions to the shape of property relations in society and to favour solutions ensuring the best possible use of the testator's estate after his death, which is achieved, among other things, by provisions on the form of a will. Moreover, the analysis of freedom of testation in the light of the existing legal basis for the disposition of property upon death in the face of increasing social expectations in the context of attempts to draw up wills in contravention of the provisions on the form (informal wills) also aims to discover the links between the social and technological changes that have taken place in recent years and their impact on the legal situation of the heir and the legal relationships *mortis causa*.[24] Carrying out the research tasks defined in this way allows, in my opinion, a critical assessment to be made of the legal instruments provided by the current law for the testator to dispose of his estate upon his death, particularly as regards the provisions concerning the form of a will. It also entitles to a theoretical explanation of the challenges posed by the changing reality to the law of succession, as well as to new theses and hypotheses in the context of the possibility of using more universal solutions for legal inheritance purposes.

The above assumptions shape the layout of the work. The work consists of five chapters. The first chapter consist of recalling the basic legal solutions functioning in the world in the area of disposing of property upon death by means of a last will and the objections against them, resulting primarily from the observation of the practice of applying the law of succession (in the area of testamentary formalities). This must be the starting point for all critical analyses of the current state of affairs, without which further comments would be detached from the actual normative state and its basic solutions. Hence, this chapter serves as an introduction to further discussion. That is why I am presenting the evolution of legal regulations related to wills formalities, the actual consequences of failure to comply with wills formalities and the search for legal mechanisms whose task was to relax the rigour of the wills formalities regulations.

Chapter two of the book is devoted to present the ideas for validation of wills executed against the regulations on the wills formalities. A will as a tool to reflect the testator's real intention proved not to be foolproof, as it happened many times in practice that the testator was not able to effective-

---

24 Jens Beckert, 'The Longue Durée of Inheritance Law. Discourses and Institutional Development in France, Germany, and the United States since 1800' (2007) 48 European Journal of Sociology 79.

ly prepare a will according to the formal expectations of the legislator. For a long time it has been recognised that strict observance of the formal requirements of wills may lead to the harm of testamentary heirs and challenge the testator's freedom to dispose of his estate upon death. This became the basis for the theories that mitigated the formal rigor of dispositions made in the event of death. They then became the basis for legislative changes or changes in the practice of law in some countries. Before analysing how these theories work in practice, it is necessary to present their foundations. This is what I do in this chapter.

The chapter three of the book is therefore a presentation of the practice. It is worthwhile to look at how the chosen mechanisms for maintaining the testator's last will are applied in practice, to determine what problems the courts faced and how they dealt with them. The exploration concerns four basic current models of relaxing the formal rigours of a will: the *substantial compliance* approach, the *dispensing power* approach, the *harmless error* approach and the *favor testamenti* approach. This path allows for an analysis of current solutions and their possibilities, and provides a basis for further discussion. This further discussion takes place in the chapter four of the book, where I consider the functions that are performed by the provisions on the form of wills, including in the context of mechanisms relaxing formal rigour. It is only through such an analysis that we can properly understand what the point of the legislation on wills formalities is, whether it is an area susceptible to change, and what the objectives of the legislation in this area should be in concrete cases.

Against this background, in the chapter five of the book I consider the need for changes to the current normative situation, consider the desired structure of the provisions on the form of a will and present my own proposal of the functional model of effective testation for informal wills. The proposed model is designed so that it can be implemented in the succession laws of the various countries as a universal model. This is why, in this part of the book, I also justify this proposal and reflect on the future of succession law taking this proposal into account. The book ends with conclusions and recommendations, which are a synthesis of the most important findings of my research.

The book is based on the basic scientific tools used in legal studies, i.e. dogmatic analysis, the comparative law method and the analysis of case law. Due to the rather specific subject matter of the need to make succession law more flexible and a certain restraint on the part of individual legislators, my deliberations were directed primarily at those legislators who have so far faced this type of challenges. Therefore, I have referred not only to the universally acknowledged canons of civil law (I am focusing mainly on German, French, Spanish, Austrian and Dutch law), but I have also devoted a number of comments to solutions being part of the *common law* system (especially Australia, the United States of America, New Zealand and Canada), where the flexibility of particular solutions and possibilities for intervention in the judicial application of law to respect the principle of *favor testamenti* are much greater than in continental Europe. Since it is not possible to analyse all legal systems in one book, my focus is aimed at those legal systems that usually serve as a paradigm for changes. This is why I do not analyse the legislation of all European countries. I have also made a number of references to Polish law, which is close to me. The work has, however, a universal character and should not be treated as a dogmatic analysis of one legal order.

These methods allowed me to obtain research material which made it possible to formulate theoretical and legal conclusions relating to the private law regulations governing the disposal of property upon death (wills formalities), to evaluate the practice against the background of these regulations in the light of the tendencies prevailing in the legal science and to draw *de lege ferenda* conclusions relating to the *mortis causa* disposal of property by a testator in the face of current and future challenges.

* * *

Many people have supported the preparation of this book. It is difficult to list them all here. However, there are some without whom this book would never have been written. They certainly include Professor John H. Langbein, whom I met during a scientific conference in Iowa City, and who inspired me to re-discuss the issue of testamentary formalities. I had such a discussion on parts of this book with, among others, Prof. Prue Vines from the University of New South Wales, Prof. Doug Surtees from the University of Saskachewan and Prof. Piotr Stec from the University of Opole. These were very fruitful discussions, for which I would like to thank. I would also like to thank the book's reviewers - Prof. Rita Lobo Xavier from the Catholic University of Porto and Prof. Fryderyk Zoll from the University of Osnabrück and the Jagiellonian University - for their pertinent comments, which forced me to reconsider several points. I would also like to thank Ewa Horan for her linguistic consultations. I am also sure that my family deserves a word of appreciation. They still put up with me and wait for me to "finish writing". Thank you !

(1) Development of provisions on the wills formalities in modern legal systems

1. Introductory remarks

Making dispositions of property, both *inter vivos* and *mortis causa*, is natural today. The freedom granted to an individual in this field, derived from the private law principle of the autonomy of the will of the law subjects,[25] has a long legal tradition and is now one of the attributes of an individual as an owner and holder of other rights of a proprietary nature.[26] The evolution of legislation in this area has resulted over the years in the development of at least several instruments for property dispositions, the effect of which occurs upon the death of the bequeather, who is the subject of these rights.[27] These instruments include, in particular, codicilles and last wills, succession agreements and trust constructions (characteristic in particular of Anglo-American legislation).[28] Therefore, a last will is one of the basic titles of succession, which has emerged over the years through development of the law in this field and is now believed to be the most popular of these instruments, most frequently used in practice.[29]

---

25 Nicolas Coumaros, *Le rôle de la volonté dans l'acte juridique* (Librarie du Recueil Sirey 1931) 46; Marek Safjan, *System prawa prywatnego, vol. 1, Prawo cywilne - część ogólna* (Marek Safjan ed, C H Beck 2007) 237; Jan Schapp, *Methodenlehre und System des Rechts* (Mohr Siebeck 2009) 109.

26 In principle, it is the economic rights that are transferred to other persons as a result of the death of the subject of those rights. *Cf.* Józef Stanisław Piątowski and Bogudar Kordasiewicz, *Prawo spadkowe. Zarys wykładu* (Lexis Nexis 2011) 34; Hans Brox and Wolf-Dietrich Walker, *Erbrecht* (C H Beck 2018) 5 ff; Peter T Wendel, *Wills, Trusts, and Estates* (Wolters Kluwer 2018) 78 ff.

27 Shelly Kreiczer-Levy, 'The Mandatory Nature of Inheritance' (2008) 53 The American Journal of Jurisprudence 105; Mark Glover, 'A Social Welfare Theory of Inheritance Regulation' (2018) 2018 Utah Law Review 411; Maria Gigliola di Renzo Villata (ed), *Succession Law, Practice and Society in Europe across the Centuries* (Springer 2018) passim.

28 Thomas E Atkinson, *Handbook of the Law of Wills and Other Principles of Succession: Including Intestacy and Administration of Decedents' Estates* (West Academic Publishing 1953) passim.

29 It should be pointed out that in individual countries in the world there are no statistics on the popularity of specific mortis causa instruments. However, observation of the practice and analysis of some of the available statistics indicates that

In the world, the term "last will" (or briefly a "will" or a "testament" – in English all of these forms are used interchangeably) is not a uniformly understood concept.[30] It is true that, in general, doctrine consistently indicates some of its essential features, but it differs in the assessment of the legal nature of some of these features.[31] This is due to the fact that in different legal systems succession law was developing with varying intensity which was based on different patterns and because of that the current shape of the laws in this area is different in many countries. Regardless of these differences, the successful drafting of a last will depends on a number of factors, which in a given legal system are determined by statutory provisions. In general, the legislators provide for the validity of a last will that the testator must have testamentary capacity, make dispositions intentionally and freely, and must respect a certain statutory form and express his or her last will within this form.[32] The first two of these requirements can be referred to as substantive requirements for the validity of a last will, and the last two as formal requirements for the validity of a last will.[33]

Therefore, one of the basic requirements imposed by legislators on last wills is the necessity to prepare them in a special way, described in the law. This leads to general acceptance of the position, according to which a last will is a formal legal act.[34] This view is accepted not only in *civil law*

---

it is necessary to recognise that last will (testament) is the main alternative to statutory inheritance.

30 *Cf.*, e.g.: Irma Sasso, 'Will Formalities in the Digital Age: Some Comparative Remarks' (2018) 4 Italian Law Journal 169.

31 *Cf.* Kenneth GC Reid, Marius J De Waal and Reinhard Zimmermann (eds), *Comparative Succession Law. Testamentary Formalities* (Oxford University Press 2011); Anna Pabin, 'Testament jako akt sformalizowany - uwagi w sprawie przyszłego kształtu regulacji dotyczących formy rozrządzeń testamentowych' (2016) 2016 Studia Prawnicze 91.

32 *Cf.* Michał Niedośpiał, *Testament. Zagadnienia ogólne testamentu w polskim prawie cywilnym* (Polski Dom Wydawniczy 'Ławica' 1993) 9 ff.

33 Mariusz Załucki, *Videotestament. Prawo spadkowe wobec nowych technologii* (CH Beck 2018) 22–36.

34 Ashbell G Gulliver and Catherine J Tilson, 'Classification of Gratuitous Transfers' (1941) 51 Yale Law Journal 1, 5 ff.

states,[35] but also in *common law* countries.[36] Individual legal systems provide for regulations according to which the disposition of property upon death by a testator may take place only within the framework of instruments designed by the legislator.[37] These instruments are commonly referred to as the form of a last will, which should be understood as a form of a legal act (as such a last will should be considered, obviously in systems which separate such a theoretical construction), i.e. the way in which this act, and specifically the declaration of intent constituting it, is expressed externally.[38]

According to the classic view, which today can be described as rigorous, the testator's declaration of last will cannot therefore be made in any way, but must take one of the forms provided for by the law.[39] In this respect, the *numerus clausus* principle prevails in individual legal systems.[40] The range of possible solutions in this respect is wide, with the proviso, however, that some forms of last wills are more common than others.[41] It is emphasised that the formalism of a last will is intended to protect, on the one hand, the testator and, on the other, the security of legal transactions. According to the doctrine, solutions providing for formal requirements for dispositions of property upon death create a "safe harbour" allowing for the protection of succession property against the routine of applying legal mechanisms, also in exceptional circumstances.[42] A lawmaker who wants to introduce the principle that the intention of the person preparing a last will should be implemented to the fullest possible extent must seek to en-

---

35 Peter Breitschmid, 'Revision der Formvorschriften des Testaments – Bemerkungen zur Umsetzung der «Initiative Guinand»' (1995) 1995 Zeitschrift des Bernischen Juristenvereins 179; Zimmermann (n 22); Mariusz Załucki, 'Forma testamentu w perspektywie rekodyfikacji polskiego prawa spadkowego. Czas na rewolucję?' (2017) 72 Państwo i Prawo 31.

36 *Cf.* Mann (n 7); Bridget J Crawford, 'Wills Formalities in the Twenty-First Century' (2019) 2019 Wisconsin Law Review 269.

37 Robert H Sitkoff and Jesse Dukeminier, *Wills, Trusts and Estates* (10th edn, Wolters Kluwer 2017) 147; Dirk Olzen, *Erbrecht* (De Gruyter 2005) 73.

38 JK Maxton, *Formalities, Mistake and Construction in the Law of Wills* (Uniersity of Canterbury 1982) 9 ff.

39 Maura Tampieri, 'Formalismo testamentario e testamento olografo' (1998) 1998 Rivista del Notariato 119.

40 Sylwester Wójcik, *System prawa cywilnego, vol. IV, Prawo spadkowe* (Józef Stanisław Piątowski ed, Ossolineum 1986) 191.

41 Reid, De Waal and Zimmermann (n 31) 432–472.

42 John H Langbein, 'Excusing Harmless Errors in the Execution of Wills: A Report on Australia's Tranquil Revolution in Probate Law' (1987) 87 Columbia Law Review 1, 4.

sure that only the real intention of that person is respected.[43] Therefore, in individual legal systems there are regulations on testamentary formalities.

The form of declarations in the event of death was already highlighted in Roman law, then in customary laws and first codifications.[44] This is how it has remained until today.

Despite the often unformalized legal circulation *inter vivos*, the *mortis causa* circulation often had and still has a much more stringent dimension. One could even say that over the years, the formalism of the *mortis causa* circuit has reached its limits.[45] Regardless of the needs of society, until recently, many countries still considered that the rules on the form of last wills should be observed very strictly.[46] For this reason, according to the various legal provisions, failure to comply with the formal requirements of last wills, and therefore failure to comply with the rules on the form of last wills, has generally (and often still does) lead to the invalidity of a will.[47]

Fortunately, the rigor of form resulting from the one-sidedness of last wills and its *mortis causa* nature is sometimes mitigated.[48] This is particularly noteworthy in recent times, as some legal systems have found few solutions to maintain a will in force (as a valid will) despite being prepared in contravention of the provisions of the law on testamentary formalities, or providing only for the possibility of the optional invalidation of a will at

---

43 Jan Gwiazdomorski, 'Formy testamentu' (1966) 22 Nowe Prawo 713.

44 *Cf.* Franciszek Longchamps de Bérier, *Law of Succession. Roman Legal Framework and Comparative Perspective* (Wolters Kluwer 2011) 151; Dieter Leipold, 'Europa und das Erbrecht' in Gerhard Köbler, Meinhard Heinze and Wolfgang Hromadka (eds), *Europas universale rechtsordnungspolitische Aufgabe im Recht des dritten Jahrtausends. Festschrift für A. Söllner zum 70. Geburtstag* (C H Beck 2000) 648.

45 Mariusz Załucki, 'Evidentiary Function of the Provisions on the Form of Wills in the Contemporary Succession Law. Is the Complete Abandonment of Formalism Possible?' (2020) 26 Trusts & Trustees 814.

46 Cf, e.g.: Aloy (n 17); Richard Hedlund, 'Introducing a Dispensing Power in English Succession Law' (2019) 25 Trusts & Trustees 722.

47 Załucki, 'Evidentiary Function of the Provisions on the Form of Wills in the Contemporary Succession Law. Is the Complete Abandonment of Formalism Possible?' (n 45).

48 Jesús Delgado Echeverría, '¿Qué reformas cabe esperar en el derecho de sucesiones del código civil? (Un ejercicio de prospectiva)' (2009) 3 El Cronista del Estado Social y Democrático de Derecho 26; Maciej Rzewuski, 'Formalisation of the Testament in the Light of the Favor Testamenti Principle' (2013) 2013 Míľníky Práva v Stredoeurópskom Priestore 978; Natalie M Banta, 'Electronic Wills and Digital Assets: Reassessing Formality in the Digital Age' (2020) 71 Baylor Law Review 547.

the request of a person having a legal interest in it.[49] This is a model characteristic of the Anglo-American countries in particular[50], although it is probably too early to speak of a trend in all these countries towards easing the formal requirements of wills, but surely a lot has happened in this area over the last years. As one might think, a lot is still to come. The last can be mainly referred to the European countries, where, despite rather classic legal solutions, the need for a more liberal approach to the problems discussed here is becoming increasingly apparent.[51] The current solutions are criticised and changes are postulated, which sometimes become provisions of the new law. The last intensive activities of individual legislators in this respect took place in the initial phase of the COVID-19 pandemic, when some legislators decided to significantly ease the formal requirements for wills.[52] These issues still remain relevant.

The form of a last will, in the opinion of many, as a mechanism for ensuring the authenticity of a last will and its reflection, should undergo transformations. As it usually happens in such cases, the impulse for scientific discourse and the legislative action that follows it, is the practice of law. In many cases it is the unsatisfactory effects of the application of the law of succession that have become the source and driving force of change.[53] The classic approach to the problems of the form of a will has not worked for a long time.

The reasons for this should be sought precisely in the different shape of the needs of the practice and statutory regulations, which do not keep up with the former.[54] There is a reason to believe that a will, as an instrument to reflect the testator's intent, should be an instrument that is more flexi-

---

49 Załucki, 'About the Need to Adjust the Regulations Regarding the Form of Will to the Modern Requirements' (n 14); Crawford (n 36).

50 Juliet Brook, 'To Dispense or Not to Dispense? A Comparison of Dispensing Powers and Their Judicial Application' (2018) 2018 Private Client Business 205.

51 Aloy (n 17).

52 David Horton and Reid Kress Weisbord, 'COVID-19 and Formal Wills' [2020] Stanford Law Review Online 1; Mariusz Załucki, 'Preparation of Wills in Times of COVID-19 Pandemic - Selected Observations' (2020) 45 Journal of Modern Science 143, 143 ff.

53 Pierre Ciotola, 'Le testateur et son clone inavoué, le juge : clone difforme ou conforme dans la recherche des intentions du testateur : le juge et l'interprétation des volontés du testateur' (2005) 107 La Reveue du Notariat 239.

54 Doron Menashe, 'Relaxed Formalism: The Validation of Flawed Wills' (2007) 40 Israel Law Review 119.

ble than it is usually described.[55] It is therefore necessary to look at the current trends in the development of the law in this field, against the background of standards known in succession law for many years. Such an analysis may only allow for a further search for the optimal shape of the testamentary inheritance.

For this reason, before presenting possible solutions taking into account the needs of society in terms of the form of wills, it is necessary to recall the basic legal solutions functioning in the world in the area of disposing of property upon death by means of a last will and the objections against them, resulting primarily from the observation of the practice of applying the law of succession (in the area of testamentary formalities).

2. Wills formalities and the evolution of legal regulations related to it

Further consideration should begin with a reminder that it is the law that regulates *mortis causa* acts. This is not only the case in *civil law* systems, but also in *common law* states, where, as it is known, statutory regulations do not cover all types of legal relationships. *Mortis causa* actions, including last wills, are therefore those legal acts whose functioning is regulated by law and which must be executed in practice under this law.[56] It is in this area that the testator must operate, otherwise the legal act conducted by the testator may not have the intended legal effects, which, after all, are to occur only after his death.[57] For this reason alone, the issue of formal requirements for dispositions of property upon death seems to be exceptional.[58] The regulations should be shaped in such a way that it is possible to reconstruct the content of a declaration of last will made before the testator's death, which usually takes place within a relatively long time period, as the testator usually makes such a declaration many years before his death (ac-

---

55 Judy Martin, 'La pertinence de l'article 714 du Code civil du Québec ou le paradoxe d'un formalisme sujet à la libre interprétation des tribunaux' (2018) 113 Revue du notariat 431; Kelly Purser and Tina Cockburn, 'Wills Formalities in the Twenty-First Century – Promoting Testamentary Intention in the Face of Societal Change and Advancements in Technology: An Australian Response to Professor Crawford' (2019) 2019 Wisconsin Law Review Forward 46.

56 Marco Echeverria Esquivel and Mario Echeverria Acuna, *Derecho sucesoral* (Universidad Libre 2011) 35 ff.

57 Bernhard Eccher, *Erbrecht* (Verlag Österreich 2016) 47–93.

58 Reid K Weisbord, 'Wills for Everyone: Helping Individuals Opt Out of Intestacy' (2013) 53 Boston College Law Review 877.

cording to the available statistics, it can be assumed that a large part of last wills is made even about a decade before the death of their author).[59] For this reason, when designing regulations on the form of wills, individual legislators pay attention primarily to two issues: the manner of making a declaration of last will and the manner of preserving a declaration of last will. This is to guarantee the existence of the testator's real last will, its authenticity and freedom of undertaking, as well as to allow for the belief that the testator has acted with full awareness of the dispositions made.[60] The legislator must protect the testator's and his heirs' personal interests, but also the public interest, including in particular counteracting falsification of the testator's last will. If there are property incentives and succession matters are precisely such matters, there are many temptations which should be counteracted in the public interest. At the same time, assuming generally that a proper reflection of the testator's last will is the most important value of the succession law,[61] it is also necessary to create such mechanisms which will allow for this and consider the testator's last will as an important indication for shaping the succession order.[62] It is not without reason that the statutory succession, which is the main construction of inheritance acquisition in many countries, is considered to be nothing more than a hypothetical will of the bequeather.[63] This is why a testamentary succession, the main alternative to it,[64] should reflect this will but on

---

59 As an example, the results of research conducted in Poland on the records of succession cases covering the years 1984-2004 can be quoted, where the issues of making holographic wills were analysed and it was found that more than 7% of wills were made more than 3 years before the testator's death. On the other hand, a study conducted in the State of California in 2008-2009 found that, on average, wills were made about a decade before the testator's death. See: Katarzyna Liżyńska, *Badanie autentyczności testamentu holograficznego* (Cyfrowa Biblioteka Prawnicza 2008) 16–17; David Horton, 'Wills Law on the Ground' (2015) 62 UCLA Law Review 1094, 1129–1133.

60 Judith Solzbach, *Formstrenge bei Testamenten im deutsch–US–amerikanischen Vergleich* (Friedrich-Alexander- Universität Erlangen-Nürnberg 2016) 146–152.

61 This is generally believed in the doctrine of succession law, *cf.*, e.g.: Stefan Grundmann, 'Favor Testamenti: Zu Formfreiheit und Formzwang bei bei privatschriftlichen Testamenten' (1987) 187 Archiv Für Die Civilistische Praxis 429, 429–476.

62 Rzewuski, 'Formalisation of the Testament in the Light of the Favor Testamenti Principle' (n 48).

63 Brigitte Keuk, *Der Erblasserwille post testamentum und die Auslegung des Testaments* (Röhrscheid 1965) 80.

64 Michael Albery, 'Coincidence and the Construction of Wills' (1963) 26 Modern Law Review 353, 357 ff.

an individualized basis.[65] Therefore, individual legislators, observing these phenomena and responding to different social transformations and needs, over the years of development of the law in this field, have developed different legal solutions in their legal systems to meet such needs and challenges.[66]

As it is known, some of the first last wills, known as early as in Roman times, were essentially simple, although often strongly formalised.[67] An example of this is the last will described as the *calatis comitis testament*, which was a solemn public act and could only be executed twice a year, during the people's assemblies in Rome,[68] or the evolved last will *par aes et libram*, made in the presence of five witnesses and a person watching over the ceremony of the formal transfer of property (*mancipatio*).[69] Already at that time the emphasis was placed on the observance of the ceremonial correctness of a last will,[70] and any omissions in this respect could have resulted in the invalidity of the disposition.[71] The law was shaped in a similar way in the pre-codification era, after the birth of the European legal science (12th century),[72] although it was then that the turn towards recognizing in the later science the competence of subjects to freely shape legal property relationships has started to occur, which in the context of last wills, resulted in the recognition that the regulations on the form of wills may have other functions than ceremonial ones.[73] In practice, this meant, among other things, noticing that e.g. the presence of witnesses at the act of testation does not have to be treated only as an element confirming the fact of testation, but may also be a source of proof of the testator's intentions. Such assumptions were, among others, the basis for the adoption by the

---

65 *Cf.* Solzbach (n 60) 187.
66 *Cf.* Mariusz Załucki, 'Attempts to Harmonize the Inheritance Law in Europe: Past, Present, and Future' (2018) 103 Iowa Law Review 2318, 2319–2338.
67 Hans Wieling, *Testamentsauslegung im Römischen Recht* (C H Beck 1972) 7 ff.
68 Ulrike Babusiaux, *Römisches Erbrecht* (Böhlau Verlag 2015) 15 ff.
69 Carlos Sánchez-Moreno Ellart, 'The Late Roman Law of Inheritance: The Testament of Five or Seven Witnesses' in Béatrice Caseau and Sabine R Huebner (eds), *Inheritance, Law and Religions in the Ancient and Mediaeval Worlds* (Association des amis du Centre d'histoire et civilisation de Byzance 2014) 229–257.
70 Francois du Toit, 'The Impact of Social and Economic Factors on Freedom of Testation in Roman and Roman-Dutch Law' (1999) 10 Stellenbosch Law Review 232.
71 Yaakov Stern, 'The Testamentary Phenomenon in Ancient Rome' (2000) 49 Historia: Zeitschrift für Alte Geschichte 413, 413–428.
72 Bérier (n 44).
73 Rudolpf Huebner, *History of Germanic Private Law* (1918) 740 ff.

Parliament of the United Kingdom of the *Wills Act* (1837), where an important role for witnesses of the act of last will was provided for.[74]

The great codifications that emerged in the nineteenth and twentieth centuries, as well as the regulations of Anglo-American countries based on the *Wills Act* (1837), provided for specific legal solutions regulating the form of a will and became important inspirations for contemporary legal regulations. *Code civil des Français* (1804), *Allgemeines Bürgerliches Gesetzbuch* (1811), *Wills Act* (1837) *Bürgerliches Gesetzbuch* (1896) and *Zivilgesetzbuch* (1907) introduced or confirmed the possibility of making wills in several types of forms.[75] These include, in particular, wills made by handwriting (holographic wills), wills in the presence of witnesses and wills made in the presence of a public person,[76] which continue to operate in many legal systems in the world and which are still the most common legal constructions used in this area.[77] French, Austrian, British, German and Swiss legislations are the models for many other codifications,[78] whether in European countries, Asia, Australia or the Americas.[79] For many years, the development of the law in this field has been extremely traditional, and it was believed that the solutions developed over the centuries seem to be sufficient for the needs of society. It is only in the last few decades that the voices of the doctrine about the necessity to modernise the law of succession in the context of the form of a will have appeared.[80] First of all, solutions related to technological progress have been proposed,

---

74 George W Keeton and LCB Gower, 'Freedom of Testation in English Law' (1934) 20 Iowa Law Review 326.

75 Załucki, *Videotestament. Prawo spadkowe wobec nowych technologii* (n 33) 51–56.

76 These laws also knew other forms, including those which could only be prepared under special conditions. Their practical role today, however, is not significant.

77 These forms are, of course, differently formulated in different national regulations, but in principle a common paradigm can be identified.

78 George A Pelletier Jr and Michael Roy Sonnenreich, 'A Comparative Analysis of Civil Law Succession' (1966) 11 Villanova Law Review 323.

79 *Cf.* Francois du Toit, 'Roman-Dutch Law in Modern South African Succession Law' (2014) 2014 Ars Aequi 278.

80 *Cf.*, e.g., Langbein, 'Substantial Compliance with the Wills Act' (n 10); Maxton (n 38); Grundmann (n 61); James Lindgren, 'The Fall of Formalism' (1992) 55 Albany Law Review 1009; Brigitte Lefebvre, 'L'accroissement du pouvoir discrétionnaire du juge en matière de validation d'un testament informe : les enseignements de la cour d'appel' in Brigitte Lefebvre (ed), *Mélanges Roger Comtois* (Éditions Thémis 2007); Karlheinz Muscheler, 'Das eigenhändige Testament – Gestern , Heute und Morgen' (2014) 2014 Successio – Zeitschrift für Erbrecht 24; Aloy (n 17); Załucki, 'About the Need to Adjust the Regulations Regarding the Form of Will to the Modern Requirements' (n 14).

including, among others, a videotestament or an electronic will.[81] The need to use blockchain technology in this area was also pointed out.[82] Some solutions even met with the recognition of legislators. For example, in the U.S. state of Nevada in 2001, for the first time in the world, the form of an electronic will was introduced into the provisions of the act (§ 133.085 *Nevada Revised Statutes*).[83] On the other hand, e.g. the Swiss legislature from 2016 is considering the possibility of introducing a videotestament (to change § 506 of *Zivilgesetzbuch*).[84] Other legislators have also taken initiatives to reform and modernise succession law.[85] Discussions in this area have taken place in many countries, essentially on all continents,

---

81 *Cf.*, e.g.: Gerry W Beyer, 'Video Requiem: Thy Will Be Done' (1985) 7 Trust & Estates 24; JC Sonnekus, 'Videotestamente naas skriftelike testamente' (1990) 1990 Tydskrif vir die Suid-Afrikaanse Reg 114; Emily V. Sanchez, 'Are We Ready for Electronic Wills' (2006) 206 Notes on Business Education 1; Gerry W Beyer and Claire G Hargrove, 'Digital Wills: Has the Time Come for Wills to Join the Digital Revolution' (2007) 33 Ohio NUL Rev. 865; Silvia Barrera Ibañez and others, *Testamento digital* (Ricardo Oliva Leon and Sonsoles Valero Barcelo eds, Juristas con Futuro 2016); Paige Hall, 'Welcoming E-Wills into the Mainstream: The Digital Communication of Testamentary Intent' (2019) 20 Nevada Law Journal 339; Philippe Ropenga, 'Testament by SMS' (2020) 2020 Alacriter - blog - Insights into contracts, intenational law, trusts and estates 1; Banta (n 48).

82 Bridget J Crawford, 'Blockchain Wills' (2020) 95 Indiana Law Journal 735; Jainam Chirag Shah and others, 'Crypto-Wills: Transferring Digital Assets by Maintaining Wills on the Blockchain' in Jagdish Chand Bansal and others (eds), *Communication and Intelligent Systems* (Springer 2020) 407–416.

83 Adam J Hirsch, 'Technology Adrift: In Search of a Role for Electronic Wills' (2020) 61 Boston College Law Review 828.

84 Report: Bundesamt für Justiz BJ z 10.5.2017 r., Änderung des Zivilgesetzbuches (Erbrecht). Berichtüberdas Ergebnis des Vernehmlassungsverfahrens, https://www.bj.admin.ch/.

85 *Cf.*, e.g.: Brière (n 2); Dieter Leipold, 'Ist unser Erbrecht noch zeitgemäß?' (2010) 65 Juristen Zeitung 802; Antoni Vaquer Aloy, 'La protección del testador vulnerable' (2015) 68 Iuris Dictio 327; Załucki, 'About the Need to Adjust the Regulations Regarding the Form of Will to the Modern Requirements' (n 14).

including Europe (Germany,[86] Austria,[87] Switzerland,[88] France,[89] England,[90] Scotland,[91] Spain,[92] Poland[93]), North America (United States of

---

86 *Cf.* Grundmann (n 61); Röthel (n 1); Peter Breitschmid, 'Bericht zu den Konturen eines "zeitgemässen Erbrechts" zu Handen des Bundesamtes für Justiz zwecks Umsetzung der "Motion Gutzwiller"' (2014) Sonderheft Not@lex/succesio 7.

87 *Cf.* Martin Spitzer, 'Neues ze letzwilligen Verfügunen. Ein Beitrag zu Nottestament und Testierfähigkeit' (2006) 2006 Österreichische Notariats Zeitung 77, 77 ff; Rudolf Welser, 'Die Reform des österreichischen Erbrechts' (2012) 144 Österreichische Notariat Zeitung 249, 249 ff; Rudolf Welser, 'Reformbedarf bei den letztwilligen Verfügungen' in Reinhold Geime, Rolf A Schütze and Thomas Garber (eds), *Europäische und internationale Dimension des Rechts: Festschrift für Daphne-Ariane Simotta* (Lexis Nexis 2012) 669 ff.

88 *Cf.* Jean-Philippe Dunand, 'Le testament oral en droit suisse et dans l'ancien droit neuchâtelois' in Jean Kellerhals, Dominique Manaï and Robert Roth (eds), *Pour un droit pluriel: études offertes au professeur Jean-François Perrin* (Helbing & Lichtenhahn 2002) 33 ff; Michelle Cottier, 'Ein zeitgemässes Erbrecht für die Schweiz: Bericht zur Motion 10.3524 Gutzwiller "Für ein zeitgemässes Erbrecht" zuhanden des Bundesamtes für Justiz' (2014) Sonderheft Not@lex/succesio 29.

89 In France, this has led, among other things, to the adoption of a new law: *Loi n ° 2015-177 du 16 février 2015 relative à la modernisation et à la simplification du droit et des procédures dans les domaines de la justice et des affaires intérieures.* The law relaxes the requirements for drawing up a notarial will. *Cf., e.g.,* Jean-François Sagaut, 'Présentation de la loi réformant le droit français des liberalités et des successions' (2010) 14 Electron. J. Comp. Law 1; Henri D Richemont, *Projet de loi portant réforme des successions et des libéralités (Rapport No. 343)* (Sénat de la République Française 2006).

90 *Cf.* Gareth Miller, 'Reforming the Formal Requirements for the Execution of a Will' (1993) 8 Denning Law Journal 71, 71 ff; Steve Evans, 'Testators' Wishes; Dead or Alive: Is There a Difference?' (2013) 2013 Conveyance and Property Lawyer 481, 481 ff; Hedlund (n 46).

91 *Cf.* Fiona Burns, 'Surviving Spouses, Surviving Children and the Reform of Total Intestacy Law in England and Scotland: Past, Present and Future' (2013) 33 Legal Studies 85.

92 *Cf.* Echeverría (n 48); María Elena Cobas Cobiella and Christian de Joz Latorre, 'La modernización del derecho de sucesiones. Algunas propuestas' (2007) 7 Cuestiones de Interés Jurídico 1; F Ramón Fernández, 'El testamento y la futura reforma del código civil en materia de discapacidad: Algunas reflexiones' (2009) 10 Actualidad Jurídica Iberoamericana 346; J Silverio Sandoval, 'El testamento ológrafo en soporte digital y la firma biométrica' (2019) 2019 Boletín del Ministerio de Justicia 1.

93 Załucki, 'Współczesne tendencje rozwoju ustawodawstwa testamentowego' (n 22); Konrad Osajda, 'Prawo spadkowe (w) przyszłości. Perspektywy rozwoju prawa spadkowego' (2019) 2019 Monitor Prawniczy 66.

America,[94] Canada[95]), South America (Brazil[96]), Australia (Australia,[97] New Zealand[98]), Africa (Republic of South Africa[99]) or Asia (Japan, [100] China[101]). This process is still ongoing.

The multiplicity of types of will forms can and generally means the realization of the principle of freedom of testation, another important value

---

94 Beyer and Hargrove (n 81); Mann (n 7); John H Langbein, 'Absorbing South Australia's Wills Act Dispensing Power in the United States: Emulation, Resistance, Expansion' (2017) 38 Adelaide Law Review 1; Ryan M Tucker, 'How Substantial Is Substantial? Compliance with the Louisiana Civil Code' s Requirements for Notarial Testaments' (2018) 92 Tulane Law Review 969.

95 *Cf.* Averie Mc Nary, *The New Alberta Wills and Succession Act—What's In It?...And What's Out* (Legal Education Society of Alberta 2011); William H Hurlburt, 'Electronic Wills and Powers of Attorney: Has Their Day Come', *The Uniform Law Conference of Canada, Proceedings of 83rd Annual Meeting* (The Uniform Law Conference of Canada 2001); Katherine S Melnychuk, 'One Click Away: The Prospect of Electronic Wills in Saskatchewan' (2014) 77 Saskatchewan Law Review 27.

96 *Cf.* Zeno Veloso, 'Testamentos – Nocoes Gerais, Formas ordinarias' in Domingos Franciulli Netto, Gilmar Ferreira Mendes and Ives G da Silva Martins Filho (eds), *O novo Codigo Civil: Estudos em Homenagem ao Prof Miguel Reale* (LTr 2003); Reid, De Waal and Zimmermann (n 31).

97 *Cf.* Rosalind F Croucher, 'Statutory Wills and Testamentary Freedom – Imagining the Testator's Intention in Anglo-Australia Law' (2007) 7 Oxford University Commonwealth Law Journal 241; David Haines, 'Informal Wills and the Uniform Legislation', *The Law Society of South Australia Succession Law Conference 2007* (The Law Society of Australia 2007).

98 *Cf.* Nicola Peart, 'Where There Is a Will, There Is a Way - A New Wills Act for New Zealand' (2007) 15 Waikato Law Review 26; Nicola Peart and Greg Kelly, 'The Scope of the Validation Power in the Wills Act 2007' (2013) 2013 New Zealand Law Review 73.

99 *Cf.* Sonnekus (n 81); Sizwe Snail and Nicholas Hall, 'Electronic Wills in South Africa' (2010) 7 Digital Evidence and Electronic Signature Law Review 67; Francois Du Toit, 'Testamentary Condonation in South Africa: A Pyrrhic Victory for Private Autonomy over Mandatory Formalism in the Law of Wills?' in Alain-Laurent Verbeke and others (eds), *Confronting the Frontiers of Family and Succession Law. Liber Amicorum Walter Pintens* (Intersentia 2012).

100 *Cf.* Masayuki Tamaruya, 'Japanese Wealth Management and the Transformation of the Law of Trusts and Succession' (2019) 33 Trust Law International 147.

101 *Cf.* Hao Wang, Michael W Galligan and Jeffrey B Kolodny, 'Modern Inheritance Develops in China' (2013) 2013 New York Law Journal 2; Frances H Foster, 'Dark Side of Trusts: Challenges to Chinese Inheritance Law, The' (2003) 2 Washington University Global Studies Law Review 151.

formed over the years of development of law in this field.[102] Today it is expressed in principle in all democratic countries. A kind of guardians of this principle are precisely the regulations on the form of wills, which, apart from the public interest, are supposed to secure the possibility of preparing a valid act of last will by a testator. The primary purpose of the wills form regulations is therefore to give the testator's declaration of last will a form in which the last will persists until it is restored, i.e. sometime after the death of a testator. The method of preservation depends on whether the testator's declaration of will is made orally or otherwise.[103] In the context of testamentary succession, it may be tempted to assess that the most popular method is the use of a written document for this purpose,[104] while the admissible method of preserving the testator's last will depend on the current imagination of a given legislator.

This approach, over the years, has led the doctrine to believe that the wills formalities regulations have four functions: evidentiary function, channeling function, cautionary (ritual) function, protective function.[105] The implementation of the first of these functions in the area of the wills formalities is aimed at providing reliable evidence of the testator's intentions and the circumstances in which the will was created. The channeling function of the provisions on the form, in turn, serves to unify the process of passing the inheritance estate to the heirs. The cautionary function is intended to make the testator aware of the seriousness of the action performed. The creation of a protection mechanism, on the other hand, is primarily aimed at protecting the testator from external pressures and enabling him/her to create a last will freely.[106] Traditionally, it is claimed that it is precisely these functions that the regulations on wills formalities are designed to fulfil. However, the significance of each of these functions is

---

102 du Toit, 'The Impact of Social and Economic Factors on Freedom of Testation in Roman and Roman-Dutch Law' (n 70); Frances Hannah and Myles Mcgregor-Lowndes, *From Testamentary Freedom to Testamentary Duty: Finding the Balance* (Queensland University of Technology 2008); Erik Jayme, 'Party Autonomy in International Succession and Family Law: New Tendencies' (2009) 11 Yearbook of Private International Law 1.

103 Reid, De Waal and Zimmermann (n 31).

104 Tampieri (n 39); Patti (n 6); Carolos Espino Bermell, *El testamento ológrafo. La importancia de la escritura y la firma del testador. El cotejo pericial de letras (La prueba caligráfica)* (Universidad de Córdoba 2016).

105 Gulliver and Tilson (n 34) 1–39; Gerrit Ponath, *Die Beschränkungen der Testierfreiheit durch das Testamentsrecht* (Zerb Verlag 2006) 442; Załucki, *Videotestament. Prawo spadkowe wobec nowych technologii* (n 33) 167–196.

106 Gulliver and Tilson (n 34).

different, as is its place in individual countries' legislations on succession. The greatest criticism so far, has been levelled at the protective function, which has been accused, among other things, of being difficult to justify in modern times.[107] In general, the criticism did not mean the uselessness of this function in practice, but rather a signal that deviations from formal rules in favour of the functionalism of the law of succession are possible and even desirable. This is because in the law of succession, solutions that will allow the testator's will to be reconstructed after his death, while maintaining the safety of testation (i.e. counteracting the occurrence in practice of dispositions of uncertain origin, counteracting the dispositions made in unclear circumstances and counteracting the dispositions with doubts as to their authorship) are desirable. The task of the provisions on wills formalities, as may be believed, is primarily to ensure that the testator's will is properly reflected (and preserved). This can also be the case for types of *mortis causa* dispositions which potentially jeopardise the realisation of this value. The conflict between the freedom of testation and its reflection *versus* the safety of legal circulation should be resolved with due respect taking into consideration that it is not a compliance with formal requirements but the execution of the testator's will that is important enough to pursue its realization, sometimes precisely against formal requirements.[108]

The above indicates an important problem that individual legislators have been struggling with for many years. The need to strictly comply with the provisions on the form of wills has often led to the invalidation of wills executed against the provisions on the form of wills.[109] For this reason, it has already been stressed many times that a flexible approach to formal requirements in this area is necessary in order to keep the *mortis causa* disposition valid after the death of a testator. However, such views have been and still are received with varying degrees of enthusiasm. However, in order to take a closer look at them, it is first necessary to present the consequences of the testator's failure to comply with the wills form requirements when making a last will. Only then it will be possible to illustrate the problem outlined here.

---

107 ibid 9–10; Richard Lewis Brown, 'The Holograph Problem - The Case Against Holographic Wills' (2005) 74 Tennessee Law Review 93, 93–128.
108 Breuer (n 16).
109 *Cf.* Langbein, 'Excusing Harmless Errors in the Execution of Wills: A Report on Australia's Tranquil Revolution in Probate Law' (n 42).

3. The consequences of failure to comply with wills formalities

The requirement for a testator to comply with wills formalities, which is common in all democratic legal systems of today, is a requirement which, if not complied with, generally results in the sanction of invalidity of the will. This means that the execution of a will in a manner incompatible with legal formalities will not result in legal effect desired by the testator and that such a will cannot constitute a succession title.[110] Such a rule was developed over the years, was present in Roman law, has reached the great codifications and is still present today.[111] Its classic approach, which today can be called rigorous, means that any failure to comply with the regulations on the form of a will is a failure that results in no legal effect of such legal act.[112] Therefore, while in private law the principle of freedom of form of legal transactions is usually applied, in the law of succession it can be said that there is an obligation to keep the form of legal acts performed *mortis causa*.[113]

The reason for the introduction of such measures by individual legislators is the care for the public and private interest, which is manifested as already mentioned, and can be supplemented in detail by an indication that this is also demonstrated, among others, in such elements as abolition of doubts as to the submission of a declaration of last will, facilitation of evidence, protection against ill-considered decisions, or the possibility of subsequent control.[114]

The requirement of compliance with form for legal acts is, of course, known not only in succession law.[115] As it is known, there are generally three types of rigors of form restriction for a given legal act: *ad solimnitatem, ad probationem, ad eventum*.[116] The first of these rigours means restriction of form under order of invalidity, the second one means the existence of evidentiary limitations to prove the content of a given legal act,

---

110 Sitkoff and Dukeminier (n 37).

111 Zimmermann (n 22).

112 Alexander Wingerter, *Die eigenhändige letztwillige Verfügung im Spannungsverhältnis zwischen Form und der Verwirklichung des Erblasserwillens* (Bayerischen Julius-Maximilians-Universität 1998) 135 ff.

113 Anne Röthel, 'Testamentsformen' (2014) 5 Juristische Ausbildung 475.

114 Załucki, *Videotestament. Prawo spadkowe wobec nowych technologii* (n 33) 29 ff.

115 Stephen Darwall, 'The Value of Autonomy and Autonomy of the Will' (2006) 2006 Ethics 263.

116 Mateusz Grochowski, *Skutki braku zachowania formy szczególnej oświadczenia woli* (C H Beck 2017) 85 ff.

while the third one means that failure to comply with the form is connected with the lack of certain legal effects of a given legal act.[117] In succession law, the rigour of form is generally restricted *ad solemnitatem*, although there are also other solutions aimed at restricting the form of a will only *ad probationem*.[118] However, the rule is a restriction made *ad solemnitatem*. This rigour can, in turn, have two sanctions under all circumstances: absolute invalidity and relative invalidity (voidability). The sanction of absolute invalidity is typical for the regulations on the form of wills.[119] In principle, therefore, over the years of development of the law in this area, the sanction of absolute invalidity has developed as a sanction of the testator's failure to observe the provisions on the form of wills. Therefore, according to this concept, a will prepared contrary to the provisions on the form of wills is absolutely null and void.[120] It has no legal effect. Therefore, the concepts of the law of succession of these states which apply such solutions are referred to as "*strict compliance*" because of the strict observance of testamentary formal requirements.[121]

In modern private law such solutions have become a standard. They have existed in great codifications, and nowadays they exist in most of the law on successions.[122] The regulations are generally designed in such a way that the law on successions contains a rule according to which deviations from the form known by the law, when making a will, mean its invalidity. As an example, Polish law may be indicated here, where the provision of Article 958 of *Kodeks cywilny* states that a will prepared in violation of the provisions on form is invalid.[123] A similar path is followed by, for example, the Austrian law, which provides in § 601 of the *Zivilgesetzbuch*, if a mandatory formal requirement was not complied with when a final will was drawn up, the last will is invalid. A corresponding provision is also contained in the Spanish *Código Civil*: the will in whose execution the formali-

---

117 Katarzyna Górska, *Zachowanie zwykłej formy pisemnej czynności prawnych* (C H Beck 2007).

118 Załucki, 'About the Need to Adjust the Regulations Regarding the Form of Will to the Modern Requirements' (n 14) 5.

119 Peter Breitschmid, 'Testament und Erbvertrag - Formprobleme: Die Einsatzmöglichkeiten für die Nachlassplanung im Lichte neuerer Rechtsentwicklungen' in Peter Breitschmid (ed), *Testament und Erbvertrag* (Haupt 1991).

120 Sasso (n 30) 177.

121 *Cf.*, e.g.: Mark Glover, 'The Therapeutic Function of Testamentary Formality' (2012) 185 Kansas Law Review 139.

122 Peter T Wendel, 'Wills Act Compliance and the Harmless Error Approach: Flawed Narrative Equals Flawed Analysis?' (2017) 95 Oregon Law Review 339.

123 Mariusz Załucki (ed), *Kodeks cywilny. Komentarz* (C H Beck 2019) 1996.

ties respectively established have not been observed shall be null and void (Article 687 of the *Código Civil*). Also in German law, a will made contrary to the requirements of form is not valid (§ 125 of the *Bürgerliches Gesetzbuch*). This kind of solution is also known in English law (it indicates in the content of Section 9 of *Wills Act* (1837): "no will shall be valid unless"), American (e.g. the Indiana Code indicates several times in the content of § 29-1-5-3 what is necessary for a will to be considered as "a valid will") or Australian (e.g. it indicates in Section 8 of South Australia *Wills Act* (1936) "no will is valid unless"). Other legal systems also contain similar solutions.[124] However, there are also solutions which provide only for the will to be declared invalid (voidability). This approach is known, for example, from Italian law, which differentiates between sanctions of nullity. In the case of some defects the will is completely invalid, in the case of others only voidable (Article 606 of the *Codice Civile*).[125] The idea of voidability of testamentary formal errors also occurs, for example, in Hungary.[126]

As can be assumed, in the course of the evolution of the law in this field, the dilemma that arises against the background of two conflicting values has been repeatedly resolved: the rigor of formal wills and the reflection of the testator's last will made in the event of a *mortis causa* disposition prepared contrary to the regulations on the formalities.[127] Certainly the practice of making wills has developed differently in different countries, but it is worth recalling that private wills, especially holographic wills, have played an important role in the European tradition and so far are still very popular.[128] In principle, only in some countries has it been customary to consult a lawyer when drawing up such wills, which must have had an im-

---

124 Reid, De Waal and Zimmermann (n 31).

125 *Cf.* Carlo Cicala, 'Il formalismo testamentario. Il documento' in Giovanni Bonilini (ed), *Trattato di diritto delle successioni e delle donazioni. La successione testamentaria* (Giuffrè 2009) 1235; Pietro Rescigno, 'Ultime volontà e volontà della forma' (1987) 38 Vita Notarile 17.

126 *Cf.* Reid, De Waal and Zimmermann (n 31) 267. However, these are not remedies based on a search for testamentary intent as the primary factor in recognising the validity of a will and shall therefore not be further discussed.

127 Kelly A Hardin, 'An Analysis of The Virginia Wills Act Formalities and The Need For a Dispensing Power Statute in Virginia' (1993) 50 Washington & Lee Law Review 1145.

128 Reginald Parker, 'History of the Holograph Testament in the Civil Law' (1943) 3 Jurist 1; Patti (n 6).

pact on their content and the problems of interpretation associated with it.[129] This was and still is a completely different issue in Anglo-American countries, where there is a well-established practice of using legal professional knowledge in the design of dispositions of property upon death.[130] This does not mean, however, that in the practice of these countries wills made contrary to the rules on the form do not exist.[131] Succession courts have had to deal with imperfections of *mortis causa* dispositions made in practice on many occasions and have repeatedly declared them invalid.[132] This has often led to misunderstandings in society, even though the testator's will expressed in case of death was clear and legible. This must have given rise to and, of course, raised doubts about the practical aspects of applying the provisions on the form of wills.[133] It was noted that strict adherence to the formal requirements (*strict compliance*) is not always fair and can lead to harm of the heirs.[134] It has certainly also led to the order of the succession against the will expressed by the testator. For this reason, the search for an instrument that would mitigate this formal rigor has begun.

4. *Criticism of legal regulations concerning the wills formalities*

In the light of the above, it is not surprising that in individual legal systems there have been relatively frequent calls for consideration to be given to the legitimacy of the functioning of the provisions on the form of wills which are strictly observed (*strict compliance*). It has been argued many times, among others, that the current formal rigour does not correspond to modern times, not even taking into account the opportunities created by new technologies, which has been stressed especially in recent years.

---

129 Brown (n 107); Stephen Clowney, 'In Their Own Hand: An Analysis of Holographic Wills and Homemade Willmaking' (2008) 43 Real Property, Probate and Trust Journal 27.

130 Albery (n 64); Thomas Gray, 'Succession Law: Reflections and Directions' (2019) 40 Adelaide Law Review 331.

131 Jane B Baron, 'Irresolute Testators, Clear and Convincing Wills Law' (2016) 73 Washington & Lee Law Review 3.

132 Pamela R Champine, 'My Will Be Done : Accommodating the Erring and the Atypical Testator' (2014) 80 Nebraska Law Review 388.

133 Weisbord (n 58).

134 Jeffrey A Dorman, 'Stop Frustrating the Testator's Intent: Why the Connecticut Legislature Should Adopt the Harmless Error Rule' (2016) 30 Quinnipiac Probate Law Journal 36.

The imperfection of this system can be seen, for example, in the case of a handwritten will, where it is rather commonly accepted that this type of will must be preserved on a durable medium, which in the opinion of the vast majority of the debaters (at least in the countries of continental Europe, where the form of a will is generally treated rigorously) makes it impossible to consider a will written on a tablet as valid will.[135] In a place where succession law is entering the digital world, there are, moreover, a number of doubts, and traditional instruments from this area are not able to meet today's requirements.[136] These are not only observations of today when attempts are made to make an act of last will by means of SMS (text) messages,[137] leaving a file in the memory of a computer,[138] sending an e-mail[139] or using a webcam for this purpose,[140] but also known examples found in succession law textbooks, including an attempt to make a will by means of recording on a gramophone record, [141] cassette tape,[142] floppy disk[143] or DVD, [144] most of which ended negatively for the testator and did not have legal effects after his death. This state of affairs seemed and still seems unsatisfactory to many.

---

135 *Cf.*, e.g.: Sylwester Wójcik and Fryderyk Zoll, 'Testament' (2006) 2006 Studia Prawa Prywatnego 83. However, see: Kyle B Gee, 'Beyond Castro's Tablet Will: Exploring Electronic Will Cases Around the World and Re-Visiting Ohio's Harmless Error Statute' (2016) 26 Probate Journal of Ohio 149, 149.

136 Thomas Hoeren, 'Der Tod und das Internet. Rechtliche Fragen zur Verwendung von E-Mail- und WWW-Acounts nach dem Tode des Inhabers' (2005) 2005 Neue Juristische Wochenschrift 2113.

137 Nichol v. Nichol, [2017] Queensland Supreme Court 220.

138 MacDonald v. The Master, [2002] South African Law Reports 64.

139 Mahlo v. Hehir. [2011] Queensland Supreme Court 243.

140 Estate of Sheron Jude Ladduhetti, Supreme Court of Victoria, 20.9.2013, unreported.

141 In its judgment of 18.7.1935, the German Reich Supreme Court, in the context of a will recorded on a gramophone record, ruled that even if the authenticity of a declaration of intent made in this way was not in doubt, the will could not be prepared by means of other media, because only by the legislature itself and only the legislature could make a different decision.*Cf.* Deutsche Juristenzeitung 1935, 78.

142 The Supreme Court of Wyoming, in a judgment of 12.1.1983, held that the possible use of such recordings for the purposes of succession law is a decision that belongs to the legislature and not to the court, which cannot go beyond the applicable law and thus create new forms of will. *Cf.* Estate of Robert G. Reed, [1981] 672 P.2d 829 (WY).

143 Rioux v. Coulombe, [1998] 19 Estates and Trust Reports (2d) 201.

144 Mellino v. Wnuk, [2013] Queensland Supreme Court 336.

In applying the law of succession, the courts have repeatedly stressed the need for a different approach than formalistic one. As early as 1853, in the USA, the Supreme Court of Victoria, when examining an informal will, justified its ruling: "Upon the whole, there had been a reasonable substantial, if not a literal, compliance with the requirements of the statute shown in this case, sufficient for all practical purposes, and which in favor of the testamentary right ought to be sustained. To reject the will, would be, to sacrifice substance to form, and this ends of justice to the means by which they are to be accomplished."[145] In an another well-known case, in 1924, the Supreme Court of Pennsylvania held that the letter written to decedent's sons that conclude with dispositions of his property "IF ENNY THING HAPPENS" exhibited testamentary intent and ordered it to probate as a holographic will, assuming that the will of the testator should be taken into account and not the exact formalities.[146] A similar position, although many years later (1981), was taken by Pennsylvania first-instance court, who, in assessing a will drawn up without a proper signature, has indicated that "the intent of the testator was plain", and "no useful purpose can be served by destroying the will he created by a technical adherence to the *Wills Act*, the principal purpose of which is to make certain that the intent of a testator is effectuated."[147] The same views were also stressed on other continents.

This happened for example in Germany, among others, where LG Hamburg (in 1938) pointed to the need to respect the will of the testator by accepting the validity of the last will despite the fact that under the holographic form the place and date had not been inserted by hand but were imprinted on the letterhead[148] (however, the decision was eventually overturned on appeal and the last will was declared void.)[149] This informal trend was also the case, for example, in South Africa, where the court in 2010 admitting an informal will has stated, that "failure to comply with the formalities prescribed by the act should not frustrate or defeat the gen-

---

145 Sturdivant v. Birchett, [1853] 51 Virginia Supreme Court (10 Gratt.) 67.
146 Kimmel's Estate, [1924] 278 Pa. 435.
147 Kajut, [1981] 2 Pa. Fiduc. 2d 197, 204.
148 LG Hamburg, 27.11.1937, [1938] Deutsche Juristenzeitung 199.
149 KG, 3.2.1938, [1938] Deutsche Juristenzeitung 428. According to some, it even became the cause of the German law reform. *Cf.* Burkhard Hess, *Intertemporales Privatrecht* (Mohr Siebeck 1998) 101; Lothar Gruchmann, 'Die Entstehung des Testamentss-gesetzes vom 31. Juli 1938. Nationalsozialistische „Rechtserneuerung" und Reformkontinuität' (1985) 7 Zeitschrift für Neuere Rechtsgeschichte 53.

uine intention of testators".[150] It also happened many times in Australia, for example in the case decided in 2018 by the Supreme Court of Victoria, in which the court wondered about the validity of the, so-called, do-it-yourself will, a part of a "will kit", and have accepted that "the court can give effect to the testator's true testamentary intentions, despite the fact that a will has not been validly executed".[151] Similar situations and problems have occurred in many other countries. The court rulings have repeatedly drawn attention to the problem of the current regulations and have also advocated changes. That was, for example, the case in Spain. The judiciary there has invoked the principle of *favor testament* and postulated "the reduction to the essential minimum of the requirement of testamentary formalities that cannot be governed", and emphasized "a clear tendency of simplification of formalities".[152]

However, there are also a number of court rulings where, despite clear and convincing testator's intention evidence, the courts have denied the validity of the will. The following can serve as an example. In 1971 in Israel the court has refused as a valid will an unsigned and undated writing found among the decedent's papers after his death, even though the writing said: "In the case of death my brother inherits from me."[153] In another case, also the Israeli court in 1982 refused to probate a purported holographic will that lacked the testator's signature and date, even though a series of unsigned and undated notes in the woman's handwriting were found with a disposition that her estate should go to her brothers rather than to her husband.[154] Of course this has occurred also in other countries. For example in Australia (Queensland), in the case decided in 1985, where the testator had his daughter-in-law attest his will when the two of them were alone, hence not in the joint presence of the second witness, the court said that "since presence is most important .... it is difficult therefore to say that... there has been substantial compliance with the formalities."[155] In Poland, the Supreme Court in 2005 has ruled that a notarial will does not meet the formal requirements if the testator presents the future contents of the will (draft) to a notary, and then another notary using this draft has started the procedure of preparation of the will from reading this

---

150 Van der Merwe v. Master of the High Court & Another, [2010] ZASCA 99.
151 Willis v. McKenzie, [2018] VSC 325.
152 STSJ Cataluña, 4.9.2006 [2007] RJ 6176.
153 *Gitah*, Estate 39/70, [1971] 76 P.M. 156 (Dist. Ct.).
154 Koenig v. Cohen, [1982] 36(3) Israeli Supreme Court 701.
155 McIlroy, [1985] 1 Queensland Reports 514.

draft and then the last will was only confirmed by the testator (and not declared before this second notary). The court has explained that "in consideration of the importance of this act, which is a formalised act, it does not comply with the provisions on the form of wills, which are of a mandatory nature, and therefore the will is invalid."[156]

Such judgements have been made many times in the US, as for example, in one of the rulings made by the Supreme Court of New Jersey in 1987, where the will was declared invalid because the witness who signed the will was not present when the testator himself signed this will.[157] Similar were the circumstances of the invalidation of the will in England, where the frequently quoted old case law recalls a judgement from 1902, when one of the witnesses of the last will was distracted by another person, and therefore did not see the testator signing the will and did not sign the last will at the same time as the testator did (he added his signature later).[158] This has also happened more frequently, for example in the case decided in England in 2011, where the claimant has successfully challenged the validity of the will, saying that it had not been validly attested because the two witnesses were not being present at the same time despite the attestation clause saying they had been.[159]In 2013 a case from Sweden was reported, where one of the Swedish courts of appeal has invalidated a will send by SMS-messages, "because the SMS was not signed by the testator".[160] Certainly there are also many other examples of such judgements cited in the literature. As many may think, such rulings seems doubtful.

The doctrine of succession law, in connection with these and similar decisions, has repeatedly pointed out the need for a different approach to the problems of wills formalities.[161] A large part of the statements advocated reducing the formal requirements, which, among other things, could be

---

156 Supreme Court, 13.1.2005, IV CK 428/04, [2005] Legalis 84460.
157 In re Estate of Peters, [1987] 107 N. J. 263, 526 A.d2 1005.
158 Brown v. Skirrow, [1902] P 3.
159 Re Singh, [2011] EWHC 2907.
160 T 11306-12.
161 *Cf.*, e.g.: Melissa Essary, 'Wich v. Fleming The Dilemma of a Harmless Defect in a Will' (1983) 35 Baylor Law Review 903; Michael W McCrum, 'Wills – Execution – Witnesses' Signatures Located Only after Self-Proving Affidavit Do Not Satisfy Attestation Requirements' (1983) 15 St. Mary's Law Journal 219; Mary Ann Glendon, 'Fixed Rules and Discretion in Contemporary Family Law and Succession Law' (1986) 60 Tulane Law Review 1165.

achieved through a rational interpretation of the applicable laws.[162] These statements often criticised the case-law following the principle of *strict compliance*, indicating the invalidation of the testator's last will despite convincing evidence of this will. It was argued that it is necessary to take into account the testator's intention. However, the discussion also included the opposite voices, emphasizing the need to leave the wills formalities unchanged.[163]

The legislators observing it, although not all of them, have over the years tried various types of legislative solutions to solve the above mentioned problem. At least two trends can be observed in this respect. The first one consists in mitigating, in some legal systems, the formal requirements for wills. The second one is an attempt to adjust the law of succession through the introduction of solutions whose effect is to keep a wills' disposition incompatible with formal requirements in force (as valid wills). The first of these solutions, i.e. easing the formal requirements for *mortis causa* dispositions, is not at all exceptional and extraordinary. In world literature, the discussion of this subject on a wider scale has been going on for more than eighty years.[164] The first legislative proposals have also appeared. For example, as early as 1969 the *Uniform Probate Code* proposed a solution which primary objective was to keep the will "wherever possible" which has reduced the formal requirements of a holographic will to the "necessary minimum".[165] A trend of this kind can therefore be seen in later years in individual state legislations. It is also not unfamiliar to the *civil law* systems. It manifests itself on many different levels. One of the most important measures in this direction is the German regulation, i.e. § 2232 in conjunction with § 2233 of *Bürgerliches Gesetzbuch*, according to which an illiterate person may express his will in any way that is acceptable, as long as

---

162 *Cf.*, e.g.: Jane B Baron, 'Gifts, Bargains, and Form' (1998) 64 Indiana Law Journal 155; James Lindgren, 'Abolishing the Attestation Requirement for Wills' (1990) 68 North Carolina Law Review 541.

163 *Cf.*, e.g.: Lawrence S Friedmann, 'The Law Of The Living, The Law Of The Dead: Property, Succession, And Society' (1966) 1966 Wisconsin Law Review 340; Lloyd Bonfield, 'Reforming the Requirements for Due Execution of Wills: Some Guidance from the Past' (1996) 70 Tulane Law Review 1893; John V. Orth, 'Wills Act Formalities: How Much Compliance Is Enough?' (2008) 43 Real Property, Probate and Trust Journal 73.

164 Gulliver and Tilson (n 34) 3–13.

165 Opinion of the Uniform Law Commission contained in the commentary to § 2-502 of the Uniform Probate Code 1969 according to which: "formalities for a written and attested will are kept to a minimum".

this is understood by the notary drawing up the will.[166] As far as the validity of decisions that do not meet the formal criteria is concerned, the provision of Article 714 of the *Civil Code of Quebec*, for example, is interesting. According to it, a holographic or witnessed will that does not meet all the formal requirements is valid if it satisfies the essential requirements and unquestionably and unequivocally contains the last wishes of the deceased.[167] Similar solutions are also found in the laws of European countries, including, for example, Italy[168] and Hungary,[169] as already mentioned. Although this is not a common direction, and even the opposite solutions do happen, such as the new regulations of the Dutch *Burgerlijk Wetboek* on the form of wills, often pointed out in the literature as very strict, due to - and this should be recalled - the construction providing only for the notarial form of wills (Article 4:94 of the *Burgerlijk Wetboek*),[170] the problem of unsatisfactory legislative solutions in the area of regulations concerning the form of wills exists. This is a simple relationship. The less formal requirements there are in the regulations of individual acts, the less final will decisions that are invalid for purely technical reasons.[171] More liberal forms of wills to a greater extent guarantee the possibility of testation until the last days of the testator's life, but at the same time, due to the greater ease of falsifying or distorting their content, they may pose a greater threat to the certainty of legal transactions.[172] The requirements of the security of legal circulation are best met by those legal acts for which restrictive requirements are provided. Excessive formalism may, however, make testation impossible.[173]

With this in mind, it should also be pointed out that an important direction that can be observed in individual legal systems, which is the implementation of the second of the above mentioned trends, is the search for solutions allowing to keep in force the *mortis causa* disposition, which, although it does not meet all the requirements for this type of legal actions,

---

166 Martin Avenarius, *BGB Kommentar* (Hans Prütting, Gerhard Wegen and Gerd Weinreich eds, Wolters Kluwer 2010) para 2233.
167 Martin (n 55).
168 Reid, De Waal and Zimmermann (n 31) paras 128–138.
169 ibid 267.
170 Johan Du Mongh, 'Het erfrecht van de langstlevende echtgenoot: de "Wet-Valkeniers" van 22 April 2003' (2004) 2004 Rechtskundig Weekblad 1521.
171 Baron (n 131) 12.
172 Jan Rudnicki, 'Rola formy testamentu. Uwagi na tle porównawczym' (2013) 2 Forum Prawnicze 35, 36.
173 Rudnicki (n 172).

is - as one may think in the given circumstances - disposition of the testator in case of death. It is connected with the acceptance of the principle of protecting the testator's intention as one of the most important, if not the most important, value protected by the law of succession. Thus, the doctrine of *"strict compliance"* (characterised by a strict formalism) is increasingly often abandoned in favour of the doctrine of *"substantial compliance"* and its variations, according to which the fulfilment of the testator's last will is the most important, and therefore the testator's wishes and intentions must be respected despite certain formal errors in the will. This concept, based on observations of jurisprudence and some normative solutions of selected countries was extensively presented in the doctrine of succession law in 1975 by John H. Langbein.[174] It now appears in some legal systems as a basis for normative solutions to protect the testator's last will, which significantly allows for its fuller reflection. It is at its basis that selected legislators refer to the construction of a *"harmless error"* of the testator or "clear and convincing evidence" of testation.[175] These solutions oscillate around the intentions of the testator, who wanted to dispose of the estate in case of his death, but was unable to do so in a manner dictated by the provisions of the applicable law. Such constructions occur primarily in *common law* systems, which is most probably due to the fact that until recently the various legislations in this circle approached the formal requirements of wills very rigorously, as well as perhaps because these systems are based on a wide discretionary power of the judge, which makes it somewhat easier to implement them in such realities.[176] The law of succession is also familiar with other constructions whose effect is similar. As one may think, individual legislators have not yet said the last word in this respect.

This means that over the years the regulations on the form of a will have undergone some evolution. Today's view of succession law through this prism indicates at least a few interesting mechanisms that have been or are still in use and whose main task was to counteract the excessive formalism of *mortis causa* dispositions. In order to consider the legitimacy of their application it is necessary to take a closer look at these solutions and determine what was the direct cause of their appearance in the legal space. It is necessary not so much to further outline the problem of excessive formalism in succession law, but to indicate the instruments whose task was and is to reflect the testator's last will. This will be the subject of further considerations.

---

174 Langbein, 'Substantial Compliance with the Wills Act' (n 10).
175 Horton, 'Wills Law on the Ground' (n 59).
176 Baron (n 131).

(2) The search for a mechanism to relax the rigour of the wills formalities regulations

1. *Departure from strict formalism*

The concept of a will as a formal legal act has long been present in the law of succession, as indicated above, and covers virtually all legal systems. Originally, in the most exemplary succession laws that have influenced the shape of legislation in other countries in this area, this concept was found as a result of the perception of the wills formalities through the prism of a tool to ensure that a declaration of testator's intent is made effectively and without pressure.[177] However, as it has turned out over the years of application of the law in this area, strict compliance with the provisions on the form of wills - as was the case in most countries at the time - has often had unsatisfactory results.[178] A will as a tool to reflect the testator's real intention proved not to be foolproof, as it happened many times in practice that the testator was not able to effectively prepare a will according to the formal expectations of the legislator.[179] Such effects of applying the law in this area gave rise to a need to look at the formal requirements of wills from a slightly different perspective, i.e. from the standpoint of achieving the effects of a testation act while maintaining formalism. For a long time it has been recognised that strict observance of the formal requirements of wills may lead to the harm of testamentary heirs and challenge the testator's freedom to dispose of his estate upon death.[180] This became the basis for the theories that mitigated the formal rigor of dispositions made in the event of death. They then became the basis for legislative changes or changes in the practice of law in some countries. These concepts and the effects of their application gave rise to various comments, from deep acceptance to strong criticism. As some of them had an impact on the current

---

177 Hayton (n 12).
178 *Cf.*, e.g., Randall Friedman, 'Proof and Effect of Mistake as to the Provisions of Wills' (1973) 38 Missouri Law Review 48.
179 Langbein, 'Substantial Compliance with the Wills Act' (n 10) 489 ff.
180 *Cf.*, e.g.: Andrew G Lang, 'Formality v. Intention - Wills in an Australian Supermarket' (1985) 15 Melbourne University Law Review 82.

legislation, it is worth looking at the stages of the search for the golden mean in this area.

2. Ideas for the validation of wills executed against the regulations on the wills formalities

Socially unacceptable statutory solutions in the area of succession law are not something new, coming up only recently. This is why these remarks can start with the observation that in the opinion of many, the unsatisfactory statutory solutions can be seen, for example, as early as the German law adopted in 1896 came into force. Among other things, the *Bürgerliches Gesetzbuch* introduced a rule according to which a will must be drawn up in the form of "a declaration, specifying the place where, and the day when, it had been made, and written and signed by the testator in his own hand" (§ 2231 subsection 2 of *Bürgerliches Gesetzbuch*). The failure of the declaration of last will to comply with the formal requirements outlined above meant that the entire disposition was invalid (§ 125 *Bürgerliches Gesetzbuch*). Despite the fact that the doctrine considered that the requirements laid down by it appeared to be "so straightforward and so easy to be complied with, that no testator has to worry about invalidity",[181] it soon became apparent that the application of this provision in practice raises important questions. As Reinhard Zimmermann have noticed recently, the generally accepted area of interpretation for the German courts was that the requirements laid down in § 2231 subsection 2 of *Bürgerliches Gesetzbuch* for holograph wills had to be taken seriously.

This has led to a situation where countless wills eventually failed, even though there could be no doubt that they reflected the real intention of the testator.[182] It was estimated that up to 25 % of the wills made in practice were invalid.[183] These solutions were therefore criticised, while pointing out the need for reform.[184] Such reform took place through the adop-

---

181 Erler Busch and Michaelis Lobe, *Das Bürgerliche Gesetzbuch mit besonderer Berücksichtigung der Rechtsprechung des Reichsgerichts* (De Gruyter 1928) para 2231 n 3.

182 Reid, De Waal and Zimmermann (n 31) 188.

183 Weyer, 'Das eigenhändige Testament - Gedanken und Erfahrungen eines Nachlassrichters' (1935) 1935 Deutsche Notar-Zeitschfirt 348, 348.

184 Fritz von Hippel, *Formalismus und Rechtsdogmatik: dargestellt am beispiel der 'errichtung' des zeugenlosen schrifttestaments (eigenhändiges testament; testament olographe)* (Hanseatische Verlagsanstalt 1935) 121 ff.

tion in 1938 of the *Testamentsgesetz*[185] amending the BGB, the provisions of which were finally incorporated into the *Bürgerliches Gesetzbuch* (in 1953).[186] The key provision of the *Testamentsgesetz* was § 21 dealing with holograph wills. It was now no longer necessary for a testator to indicate in his will the date when and the place where it had been made. According to the wording incorporated into *Bürgerliches Gesetzbuch* (§ 2247 subsection 5), where a will does not contain any information about the time when it was made and where this causes doubts about its validity, the will is to be deemed to be valid only if the necessary ascertainments about the time when it was made can be established in some other manner. The same applies with the necessary modifications to a will that does not contain any information about the place where it was made. These provisions are therefore an example of the admission in legal circulation of wills drawn up in a manner contrary to the formal requirements. They may serve as a basis for taking into account the testator's last will, even though it was expressed in a manner inconsistent with the law.

The practice in Germany has therefore changed the existing legal provisions, which in part have had the effect of increasing the number of valid wills in practice. However, before the statutory changes took place, the idea of keeping informal wills as valid wills came also from the German doctrine. These concepts are still valid today, also against the background of the current legal regime, although they are not very popular and are not applied in practice. There are at least three main trends in the viewpoint that aim to take into account the testator's last wishes at the expense of formal requirements for *mortis causa* dispositions.

Firstly, in this respect, it should be noted that as early as 1909 Erich Danz advocated the so-called theory of achieving a result.[187] According to this position, once the result of a form has been achieved, no importance should be attached to form and its observance. A judge should therefore ignore formal defects if the purpose of a formal requirement is achieved even without compliance with the form. According to this theory, a will drawn up informally could be regarded as valid, since the provision of § 125 of *Bürgerliches Gesetzbuch* does not apply to it (by achieving the result

---

185 Gesetz über die Errichtung von Testamenten und Erbverträgen, Reichsgesetzblatt 1938, No. 123.
186 Under the law: Gesetz zur Wiederherstellung der Gesetzeseinheit aufdem Gebiete des bürgerlichen Rechts, Bundesgesetzblatt 1953, No. 8.
187 Erich Danz, 'Können Testamente mit Formfehlern aufrecht erhalten werden?' (1909) 1909 Deutsche Juristen Zeitung 281.

of the purpose of form).[188] However, this view was not very popular in the system there.[189] It was referred to many years later by Stefan Grundmann, an advocate of a liberal approach to the rules on the form of wills, who stressed that a will should not be considered invalid if the objectives of the formal requirements were achieved and if the denial of formal invalidity did not create a new form.[190] In his opinion, this may apply in cases where the application of a formal requirement is not met, but the testator's intention can be proven to be authentic and final. However, these views are also not widely accepted in Germany.

Secondly, in that legal system, for the purpose of keeping informal wills in force, the so-called theory of equity was also invoked. According to this position, the limitation of formal invalidity may be necessary in individual cases for reasons of equity. The formal invalidity of wills drawn up in contravention of the rules on the form of wills on the basis of § 125 of *Bürgerliches Gesetzbuch* is therefore subject to the stipulations set out in § 242 of *Bürgerliches Gesetzbuch*. According to the latter provision, good faith and customary practice must be taken into consideration when assessing the validity of a legal transaction. For example, in 1965, Helmut Coing considered this in the context of testamentary formalities.[191] According to this theory it is necessary to limit the effect of invalidity on the basis of good faith. The invalidity of a will should not take place if it leads, from the point of view of good faith, to results that are simply not acceptable to the general perception of the law. In balancing individual cases from the point of view of good faith, it is necessary to take into account the objectives of the form of wills.[192]

Although there appear to be important reasons for the supporters of this theory, this theory is not generally applied in practice, as the theory of achieving a result. In Germany, it is usually considered that for reasons of equity, there can be no justification for relaxing or not applying formal re-

---

188   Solzbach (n 60) 180.
189   Gert Reinhart, *Das Verhältnis von Formnichtigkeit und Heilung des Formmangels im bürgerlichen Recht* (Universität Heidelberg 1969) 154 ff.
190   Grundmann (n 61) 429 ff.
191   Helmut Coing, 'Form und Billigkeit im moderne Privatrecht' (1965) 1965 Deutsche Notar-Zeitschfirt1 29, 33 ff.
192   ibid 48.

quirements.[193] Therefore this theory has been rejected by practice.[194] Against this background, it is generally stressed that there is a need for formal control over the testator's actions and that balancing the testator's interests individually could reduce legal certainty. Attempts to derogate from the formal requirements based on the equity principle are therefore rejected.[195]

Thirdly, there are also views in that doctrine that the well-known interpretative rule of *favor testamenti* should be applied not only to the interpretation of the testator's last will statements, but also towards a form of *mortis causa* dispositions. In this context, it is a question of examining the testator's actual intention and reflecting it without the need to take into account the form of the instrument reflecting that intention. Thus, it has sometimes been postulated, for example, that the will may be supplemented on the basis of evidence existing outside its content.[196] In this regard, it has also been suggested that, since such an approach seems to contradict the requirement as to the form of a will, only those results of interpretations that are somehow, although imperfectly, expressed or suggested in the will document should be taken into account.[197] The requirement of form should not be understood as an obstacle to making dispositions of property upon death, but as protecting the freedom to declare one's last will. In this regard, the need to protect the so-called negative freedom, i.e. the possibility for the testator to decide not to make a will, was also stressed. However, this theory has also not become widespread and has not become a common way to keep informal wills in force.

Regardless of the positions taken in the German legal sciences, the practice of applying the law in this country has not yet developed a clear mechanism to move away from strict compliance with the rules on the form of wills. However, some doctrine generally emphasises this desire and need, as can also be seen in the German case law. However, in practice, if there is no doubt as to the authenticity of the testator's last will, it is often difficult for the courts to disapply the rules on form and sometimes reluctant to declare them valid. Thus, a trend can be identified in the German jurispru-

---

193 Ludwig Häsemeyer, *Die gesetzliche Form der Rechtsgeschäfte – objektive Ordnung und privatautonome Selbstbestimmung im formgebundenen Rechtsgeschäft* (Athenaeum 1971) 295.

194 Uwe Beinke, *Der Formzwang beim privatschriftlichen Testament* (Philipps Universität Marburg 1988) 37 ff.

195 Solzbach (n 60) 181.

196 Brox and Walker (n 26) 201.

197 Solzbach (n 60) 188.

dence to take into account the *mortis causa* intention at the expense of formal requirements. The common feature of the views expressed in this regard is the view that the formal requirements for dispositions of property upon death constitute an irritating obstacle to reflect the testator's last will.[198] However, this is not a commonly accepted position.

When analysing the problem of testamentary formalities against the background of German law, it should also be mentioned that German law is one of the *ius civile* systems in which there is a general basis for a so-called conversion of invalid legal transactions.[199] According to § 140 of *Bürgerliches Gesetzbuch*, if an invalid legal act satisfies the requirements of another legal act, then the latter is valid if it can be assumed that the parties would have wanted the other legal act to be valid if they had known of the invalidity.[200] The position under German law is generally accepted that an "invalid legal act" can be maintained as another legal act if it meets the requirements of the validity of the other legal act. This also applies to succession law.[201] The purpose of the conversion in this regard is to make the testator's will come true. This statutory rule can therefore also be an instrument to keep an informal will in force as a valid will.

Measures aimed at keeping a flawed last will in force have also appeared in practice in other countries. A very interesting example of a system solution that allows to maintain an informal will is the instrument introduced into the Israeli law in 1965. As it is often indicated, it was the first statutory provision in the world to give courts a power to excuse flaws in wills formalities.[202] The provision was based on the Talmudic doctrine of *mitzvah* (to carry out the wishes of the deceased)[203] and was presented for public debate already in 1952 (*Israel Misrad ha-Mishpatim*).[204] The preparation of

---

198 ibid 193–194.

199 Helmut Heiss, *Formmängel und ihre Sanktionen. Eine privatrechtsvergleichende Untersuchung* (Mohr Siebeck 1999) 214 ff.

200 Thomas Zerres, *Bürgerliches Recht* (Springer 2019) 91 ff.

201 Röthel (n 113) 482.

202 As it can be judged today, it was the first *substantial compliance* approach to the wills formalities, since only minor defects could have been cured by the court.

203 However see: Samuel Flaks, 'Excusing Harmless Error in Will Execution: The Israeli Experience' (2010) 3 Estate Planning and Community Property Law Journal 27, 35 ff.

204 Israel Misrad ha-Mishpatim, A Succession Bill for Israel: Text and Explanatory Notes, translated in Harvard Law School-Israel Cooperative Research on Israel's Legal Development (1952).

the bill was influenced by American scholars.[205] The bill was passed in 1965 as the *Israeli Succession Law* (חוק הירושה)[206] and contained the Section 25 (prepared already in 1952) that allowed a court to probate a will that had a defect in the formalities required by law. According to its original wording, where the court has no doubt as to the genuineness of a will, it may grant probate thereof notwithstanding any defect with regard to the signature of the testator or of the witnesses, the date of the will, the procedure set out in Sections 20, 22, 23, or the capacity of the witnesses. The mentioned Sections 20, 22 and 23 of the *Succession Law* were related to other than holographic (Section 19) forms of will known in that system (attested wills, notarial wills and oral wills).

As it is noticed by the doctrine, the drafters of this law believed that wills formalities have no absolute value in themselves.[207] They argued that will formalities only exist to assure the authenticity of the decedent's will and of guarding against forgeries and fraudulent designs.[208] This was also emphasized in one of the first rulings of the Israeli Supreme Court based on this Section. The court deciding upon formal requirements of the will have described the doctrine of *mitzvah* as the major "guide-line" of the law of wills and have explained that where the intent of the testator is expressed in a will, and no doubt exists as to the genuineness of the will, then his intentions should be ascertained in order to uphold the wishes of the deceased and not to frustrate them merely for formal defect.[209] This provision therefore made it possible in practice to reflect the testator's last will at the expense of formal requirements.[210] However, against the background of this provision, there were some doubts about omissions in holographic wills,[211] which resulted in a legislative change in 1985. A new subpart was added to this Section that empowered courts to dispense with an omission of a signature or date in a holographic will. According to this subpart, if the court has no doubt as to the authenticity of a holographic will and as to the testamentary intent of the testator, it may, in special cir-

---

205 Amihai Radzyner, 'Inheritance from Uncle Sam: The American Influence on Israeli Succession Law' (2016) 4 Comparative Legal History 19, 19 ff.
206 Israeli Succession Law 5725-1965.
207 Israel Misrad ha-Mishpatim, A Succession Bill for Israel: Text and Explanatory Notes, translated in Harvard Law School-Israel Cooperative Research on Israel's Legal Development (1952) 67.
208 ibid 66.
209 Brill [1977] 31(1) Israeli Supreme Court 98.
210 Flaks (n 203) 40.
211 Koenig v. Cohen, [1982] 36(3) Israeli Supreme Court 701.

cumstances, admit the will to probate even if the signature or date required by Section 19 is lacking.[212] The amendment made it possible for the courts, even in the absence of a signature and a date, to probate the will as written if the court has no doubt as to the authenticity of the document and as to the testamentary intent of the testator, and there are special circumstances justifying such action.[213]

These provisions lasted until 2004. They were modified then and in this modified version they are applicable until today.[214] According to the present wording of Section 25 of the *Israeli Succession Law* (חוק הירושה): if the fundamental parts of a will are present, and the court has no doubt that the will represents the true and free wishes of the testator, the court may, in a reasoned judgment, grant probate thereof, notwithstanding any defect with regard to an element or procedure detailed in Sections 19, 20, 22, 23, or with regard to the capacity of the witnesses, or due to the absence of one of these elements or procedures. "The fundamental parts of a will" are: (i.) in a handwritten will, as detailed in Section 19-the entire will is in the testator's handwriting; (ii.) in a witnessed will, as detailed in Section 20-the will is in writing and the testator brought it before two witnesses; (iii.) in a will made before the authority, as detailed in Section 22-the will was voiced before an authority, or presented to an authority, by the testator himself; (iv.) in an oral will, as detailed in Section 23-the will was voiced by the testator himself, before two comprehending witnesses, while he was on his deathbed or when he considered himself, justifiably considering the circumstances, to be facing death.[215]

The 2004 amendment of section 25 ended the era of a court's full dispensing power in Israel. On the background of this regulation the concepts of *"static formalities"* and *"dynamic formalities"* were born. The first ones are those who are indispensable and are called in the present law as the fundamental parts of a will. The second ones are those that could possibly be dispensed with, and therefore are not treated as the fundamental ones. This distinction may be understood as a path to rectify any flawed will that meets the fundamental parts criterium. The statute requires *strict compliance* with the listed fundamental parts of a will, but empowers courts to exercise a full dispensing power for less important formalities.[216]

---

212 Succession Law (Amendment No. 7) 1985, (1985) SH 1140.
213 Flaks (n 203) 42.
214 Succession Law (Amendment No. 11) 2004, 5764-2004.
215 Menashe (n 54) 125.
216 Flaks (n 203) 44.

The fundamental parts of a will serve as safeguards necessary to establish true testamentary intent. If a *static formality* is executed in a faulty manner or is completely lacking, then it cannot be corrected. However, if a *dynamic formality* is faulty or lacking, then it can be dispensed, in order to fulfil the goal of executing the will of the deceased.[217]

The Israeli legal system thereby provides for a mechanism that allows for a departure from the formal requirements for *mortis causa* dispositions, the aim of which is to seek to reflect the real intention of a testator. A bequeather who draws up a will contrary to formal requirements can nevertheless achieve the desired result. The invalidity of the will is limited by the regulation of the aforementioned provision. However, it has to be mentioned that the prevailing view in the Israeli case law interprets this section literally. Therefore, a beneficiary wishing to probate the will must prove his case "beyond any doubt".[218] The recent Israeli cases indicate that courts applying the rules of Section 25 of the *Israeli Succession Law* usually arrive at results that reasonably protect the authentic testamentary intent of the testator.[219]

One of the most frequently cited solutions in the doctrine of succession law for the validation of informal wills is the solution that was developed in South Australia, enacted in 1975. The roots of this solution go back to the Report of the Law Reform Committee of South Australia on intestacy and wills,[220] prepared in 1974, where it was noticed that there are a number of situations in which legislation should be enacted to cure deficiencies in the binding law. One of such situations (as mentioned in this Report) was the requirement of the South Australian *Wills Act* (1936) that the signature of the testator must be placed at the foot or end of the will (Section 8 of *Wills Act*) what caused a number of cases in which a testator did not do it so, and because of this mistake died intestate.[221] The Committee has observed that in all cases where there is a technical failure to comply with the *Wills Act*, there should be a power given to the court to declare that the will in question is a good and valid testamentary document if the court is satisfied that the document does in fact represent the last will and testament of the testator and that he then had the requisite testamentary capaci-

---

217 ibid 45.
218 Menashe (n 54) 127.
219 See a survey of case law presented by Samuel Flaks: Flaks (n 203) 47 ff.
220 Law Reform Committee of South Australia, *Twenty-Eight Report of the Law Reform Committee of South Australia to the Attorney-General Relating to the Reform of the Law on Intestacy and Wills* (1974).
221 ibid 10.

ty.[222] Similar solution, according to this Report, should also be enacted in order to maintain a will made without the requirement of two witnesses being present at the testation act. "There should be a general provision that of the document produced without doubt represents the last will of the deceased and the court is satisfied that for some good sufficient reason it was impossible or impracticable to obtain witnesses to that will then the court should have power to declare that the will is valid in those circumstances".[223]

In 1975 this recommendation was enacted as Section 12(2) of the South Australia *Wills Act*. According to its wording, a document purporting to embody the testamentary intentions of a deceased person shall, notwithstanding that it has not been executed with the formalities required by this act, be deemed to be a will of the deceased person if the court, upon application for admission of the document to probate as the last will of the deceased, is satisfied that there can be no reasonable doubt that the deceased intended the document to constitute his will.[224] However, as noticed it the doctrine, this Section was rather accidental and surprising also for its creators.[225] One of the authors of the 1974 Report, Howard Zelling (an active judge), deciding one of the cases based on the enacted provisions has written that he had "no idea that section 12(2), which came from one of the ideas incorporated in the Report, would produce the amount of case law that it has".[226] Regardless of that kind of assessment, it has to be recalled that under Section 12(2) of the *Wills Act* the court could validate a defectively executed will only if persuaded that there was "no reasonable doubt" that the decedent intended it to be his will. As noticed by the doctrine, this "beyond-reasonable-doubt standard" originated in the criminal law, where it served the special purpose of tilting the scales in favour of liberty for an accused who is threatened with penal sanctions.[227] Usually it is said that this is the highest standard of proof known to the law.[228] For this reason, its application in private law is interesting.

---

222 ibid 11.
223 ibid.
224 Wills Act Amendment Act (No. 2) of 1975, 8 South Australia Statutes 665.
225 Langbein, 'Excusing Harmless Errors in the Execution of Wills: A Report on Australia's Tranquil Revolution in Probate Law' (n 42) 10.
226 Kelly, [1983] 34 S.A. State Reports 370, 380.
227 Langbein, 'Excusing Harmless Errors in the Execution of Wills: A Report on Australia's Tranquil Revolution in Probate Law' (n 42) 34.
228 Kelly, [1983] 34 S.A. State Reports 370, 384

The first case decided upon Section 12(2) of the South Australia *Wills Act* was the so-called case of *Graham*. In the proceedings, it was found that the will was signed by the testatrix and by two witnesses. However, the testatrix did not sign or acknowledge the will in the presence of the witnesses. Instead, having signed the will, the testatrix handed it to a relative and asked him to "get it witnessed". The relative took the will to two neighbours who knew the testatrix, and they both signed as witnesses. In these circumstances the court held on the evidence that there was "not the slightest doubt that the deceased intended the document to constitute her will" and accordingly ordered that the will be admitted to probate.[229] The statutory change has therefore achieved the goal of maintaining a flawed will.[230]

During a similar period as in South Australia, preparations for reforming the succession law of another Australian state, Queensland, began. The Queensland legislation resulted from a large-scale review of Queensland succession law that the Queensland Law Reform Commission commenced in 1973 and published its results in 1978.[231] As indicated there, the Commission have given careful consideration to attractive arguments which have been raised with the object of reducing the formalities. The two cases decided in 1972[232] and in 1974,[233] where the wills were refused admission to probate have raised the Commission doubts about the utility of the formal requirements.[234] The Commission highlighted that some formal requirements are necessary, however there is a need for uniformity of practice throughout Australia, especially that this is an area of law where unqualified persons sometimes feel competent to exercise themselves.[235] In the opinion of the Commission, there was more a need for uniformity, than for a law reform. However, the Commission has noticed "different

---

229 In the Estate of Graham, [1978] 20 S.A. State Reports 198.
230 Stephanie Lester, 'Admitting Defective Wills to Probate, Twenty Years Later: New Evidence for the Adoption of the Harmless Error Rule' (2007) 42 Real Property, Probate and Trust Journal 577.
231 Queensland Law Reform Commission, *The Law Relating to Succession. Report No. 22* (1978).
232 In re Colling, [1972] 1 WLR 1440, where a will was refused admission to probate because one of the attesting witnesses left the presence of the testator when he was half way through writing his signature.
233 Re Beadle, [1974] 1 ALL ER 493, where a will was refused to admission to probate on the grounds that it has not been signed at the foot or end thereof.
234 Queenstead Law Reform Commission, *The Law Relating to Succession. Report No. 22* (n 231) 7.
235 ibid.

criticism of the working rules relating to the formalities prescribed for the execution of wills, and that is the criticism not of the formalities them-selves, but of the rigid attitude of the courts respecting compliance with them".[236] Understanding the criticism, the Commission has decided to re-commend "that some relaxation in the court's standard should be permit-ted", especially when "the instrument presented for probate represents the testamentary intention of the maker of it".[237] This gave grounds for the adoption of § 9(a) of the Queensland Succession Act (1981). The provision of this article was formulated as follows: the court may admit to probate a testamentary instrument executed in substantial compliance with the for-malities prescribed (by law) if the court is satisfied that the instrument ex-presses the testamentary intention of the testator.[238] As it is believed, this wording was drafted by W.A. Lee, who was influenced by the article pre-pared in 1975 by John H. Langbein[239].

This provision was slightly different than the South Australian one. As it was estimated in the first comments on this provision made in the litera-ture, in practice it may occur that despite the differences of wording, the sorts of defects of execution which have been overlooked under the South Australian jurisdiction would be seen as coming within the scope of the Queensland jurisdiction.[240] However, as the case law shows, it was not go-ing to happen. The three cased decided in 1985, as already noticed in the literature, have buried the reform.[241] Those cases include: *Grosert*,[242] *John-ston*,[243] and *Henderson*.[244] In all of the cases there was a presence defect; the wills were not signed or attested by a proper amount of witnesses. It seemed that according to the position represented there, *substantial compli-ance* wasn't a mean of discerning testamentary intent. It was rather a new formal requirement that must be established independently of testamen-tary intent.[245] It was observed that the standard for this formality was es-

---

236 ibid.
237 ibid.
238 Queensland Succession Act (1981), § 9(a).
239 Langbein, 'Substantial Compliance with the Wills Act' (n 10).
240 WA Lee, 'Queensland Succession Act 1981' (1983) 3 Oxford Journal of Legal Studies 442, 442.
241 Langbein, 'Excusing Harmless Errors in the Execution of Wills: A Report on Australia's Tranquil Revolution in Probate Law' (n 42) 42.
242 Grosert, [1985] 1 QR 513.
243 Johnston, [1985] 1 QR 516.
244 Henderson, [1985] QSC 611.
245 Langbein, 'Excusing Harmless Errors in the Execution of Wills: A Report on Australia's Tranquil Revolution in Probate Law' (n 42) 44.

sentially quantitative, and the compliance cannot be discussed as substantial unless the defect was minimal. This can be read in the final judgement decided in the *Henderson* case by the High Court of Australia made after the appeal: there was no reason to doubt that the attestation by two witnesses is a substantial requirement, and that if the will is attested by one witness only there has been a failure of substantial compliance.[246] The same thought can be read in another case decided in Queensland in 1990, where a will was witnessed by two witnesses, but there was evidence that they were not present at the same time.[247] Such rulings have laid the foundations for another reform. It was signalized in the Queensland Law Reform Commission Report on wills prepared in 1997.[248] It can be read there that the former recommendation of Commission that there must be *"substantial compliance"* has proven to be such a great stumbling block, that the provision has had poor success, and that the cases that would almost certainly have been found to come within the dispensing power in other jurisdictions have failed in Queensland. To address the difficulties and uncertainties with respect to the concept of *"substantial compliance"* it was recommended to replace this with a testamentary intention test whereby the court would be able to admit a document to probate if it is satisfied the document incorporates the testamentary intentions of the deceased person, even though it does not comply with the formal requirements for executing a will. This was adopted only in 2005, when the new provision of the Queensland *Succession Act* (1981) has been enacted.[249] The new variation of the *"substantial compliance"* provision was placed in the § 18 of the Act. According to § 18 Subsection 2 of the Act, the document or the part forms a will, an alteration of a will, or a full or partial revocation of a will, of the deceased person if the court is satisfied that the person intended the document or part to form the person's will, an alteration to the person's will or a full or partial revocation of the person's will. In making a decision under this provision, the court may, in addition to the document or part, have regard to (a) any evidence relating to the way in which the document or part was executed; and (b) any evidence of the person's testamentary intentions, including evidence of statements made by the person (§ 18 Subsection 3 Queensland *Succession Act*).[250]

---

246 White v. Public Trustee & Blundell, [1986] Qld FC 28.
247 Will of Eagles, [1990] 2 QR 501.
248 Queensland Law Reform Commission, *The Law Of Wills. Report No. 52* (1997).
249 The Queensland Succession Amendment Bill 2005.
250 Purser and Cockburn (n 55) 47.

With these Australian examples in mind (both laws are still in force today), two different approaches to minimising formal requirements can be distinguished: *substantial compliance* and *dispensing power*. The first one is based on the assumption that the court may omit only minor defects, while the second one is based on the analysis of the existence in a given case of a prerequisite of the testator's intentions. The *dispensing power* idea does not refer to "*substantial compliance*" with the wills execution requirements, it rather gives a general power to the court to dispense with the formal requirements for execution of a will if the court is satisfied that the deceased person intended the instrument to constitute his will. The latter approach has gained more recognition in the doctrine. It has become the basis for the adoption of similar solutions in other Australian states[251] as well as in other countries. This was noted, among others, by John H. Langbein, who in his other article, published in 1987,[252] stressed the predominance of the *dispensing power* doctrine over its prototype - the doctrine of *substantial compliance*. Since then, one can basically speak of the *substantial compliance* doctrine and its variations. These variations have at least one more variety (or at least a one more name) - the doctrine of *harmless error* - which is basically a copy of the doctrine of the *dispensing power*. However typically this is also called the "*dispensing power*" because it allows the courts to dispense with the strict wills act formalities.[253]

---

251 For example, the Northern Territory has adopted this rule in the *Wills Act* (1990): "A document purporting to embody the testamentary intentions of a deceased person, notwithstanding that it has not been executed with the formalities required by this Act, is deemed to be a will of the deceased person where the Supreme Court, upon application for admission of the document to probate as the last will of the deceased person, is satisfied that there can be no reasonable doubt that the deceased person intended the document to constitute his will" (§ 12 Subsection 2 of the Northern Territory *Wills Act* (1990)); the State of Victoria has adopted similar provision in the Wills Act (1997): "The Supreme Court may admit to probate as the will of a deceased person a document which has not been executed in the manner in which a will is required to be executed by this Act; or a document, an alteration to which has not been executed in the manner in which an alteration to a will is required to be executed by this Act if the Court is satisfied that that person intended the document to be his or her will" (§ 9 Subsection 1 of the Victorian *Wills Act* (1997)).

252 Langbein, 'Excusing Harmless Errors in the Execution of Wills: A Report on Australia's Tranquil Revolution in Probate Law' (n 42).

253 Generally, the term "*dispensing power*" is mainly used in Canada and Australia, and the term "*harmless error*" is usually used in the United States of America. These terms are interchangeable. Both terminologies, as can be assumed, are useful and satisfactory. The "*harmless error*" terminology brings the scope and

When writing about the *substantial compliance* doctrine and its variations the already mentioned person of John H. Langbein should be brought up. As already explained, it was him that has extensively present in the doctrine of succession law the idea of *substantial compliance* with wills formalities and has started a broad discussion on this subject. In his well known article published in 1975 he argued that the law of wills is notorious for its harsh and relentless formalism and the most minute defect in formal compliance is held to void the will, no matter how abundant the evidence that the defect was inconsequential.[254] He advocated that the insistent formalism of the law of wills is mistaken and needles, the finding of a formal defect should not lead to automatic invalidity of a will, but to a further inquiry: "does the noncomplying document express the decedent's testamentary intent, and does its form sufficiently approximate formality to enable the court to conclude that it serves the purposes of the law".[255] At that time he was convinced that the courts should have developed a *substantial compliance* doctrine as a matter of judicial interpretation of the wills formalities law. Therefore no statutory changes were proposed. However, after twelve years, in 1987, he has published his another well known article, in which he evaluated the statutes of South Australia and Queensland that abrogated the traditional rule of *strict compliance* with the requirements of wills formalities and have noticed that the idea of *substantial compliance* already was a failure.[256] Observations of the two Australian examples led him to the recommendation that the *dispensing power* doctrine should be incorporated into the wills law because, among other things, the intent-serving goal of the wills act is achieved better without than with the rule of *strict compliance*.[257] He concluded that "the abiding lesson that emerges from the decade's experience with the *harmless error* rule in South Australia is that the rule works".[258] However, he has also noticed that "the *substantial compliance* doctrine will, however, remain available to do the work for which it was devised; it is the one means by which a court may

---

reason for the rule to mind every time it is used. The *"dispensing power"* terminology brings to mind the effect of the power. *Cf.* Alberta Law Reform Institute, 'Wills: Non-Compliance with Formalities' (2001) 20 Estates, Trusts & Pensions Journal 155.

254 Langbein, 'Substantial Compliance with the Wills Act' (n 10) 489.
255 ibid.
256 Langbein, 'Excusing Harmless Errors in the Execution of Wills: A Report on Australia's Tranquil Revolution in Probate Law' (n 42) 41–45.
257 ibid 53.
258 ibid 51.

relieve an execution error when legislation has not yet intervened to supply a statutory *harmless error* rule".[259]

This John H. Langbein's deliberations have had an impact on subsequent legislation. The following years have been a period of increased interest by legislators in some countries in legislative changes to reflect the testator's last will. His comments were often analysed and referred to.[260] The same has happened with the first legislative experiences. They have also led to the increased interest in the doctrine.[261] Individual works considered the legitimacy of changes in the law on succession,[262] the desired scope of the changes[263] or the optimal shape of the testamentary formalism.[264] This discussion has basically continued until today. John H. Langbein was also continuing it.[265]

The greatest legislative changes, following the pattern of *substantial compliance*, took place in Australia, New Zealand, Canada, the United States of America and South Africa. Basically, all these countries, to a greater or lesser extent, have adopted solutions based on the idea of reflecting the testamentary intent at the expense of formal requirements.

The first non-Australian solution based on Australian patterns appeared in the Canadian province of Manitoba. In 1980 a Report on the wills act and the doctrine of *substantial compliance* has appeared.[266] As it was described there, the testamentary formalities of Manitoba as for that time were similar to those in force in most *common law* jurisdictions, and since that a literal compliance with the formalities was mandatory. This formal-

---

259 ibid 53.
260 *Cf.*, e.g.: Miller, 'Reforming the Formal Requirements for the Execution of a Will' (n 90); Institute (n 253) 154; Lloyd Bonfield, 'Reforming the Requirements for Due Execution of Wills: Some Guidance from the Past' (1996) 70 Tulane Law Review 1893; Dorman (n 134); Gray (n 130).
261 *Cf.*, e.g.: du Toit (n 99) 160; George Holmes, 'Testamentary Formalism in Louisiana: Curing Notarial Will Defects Through a Likelihood-of-Fraud Analysis' (2014) 75 Louisiana Law Review 511; David Horton, 'Tomorrow's Inheritance: The Frontiers of Estate Planning Formalism' (2017) 58 Boston College Law Review 540; Brook (n 50).
262 *Cf.*, e.g.: J Rodney Johnson, 'Dispensing with Wills' Act Formalities for Substantively Valid Wills' (1992) 18 Virginia Bar Association Journal 10.
263 *Cf.*, e.g.: Lindgren (n 80).
264 *Cf.*, e.g.: John M Greabe, 'The Riddle of Harmless Error Revisited' (2016) 54 Houston Law Review 59.
265 Langbein, 'Absorbing South Australia's Wills Act Dispensing Power in the United States: Emulation, Resistance, Expansion' (n 94).
266 Manitoba Law Reform Commission, *Report on 'the Wills Act' and the Doctrine of Substantial Compliance* (1980).

istic approach has created a body of harsh and often inconsistent case law. This is why the results of law enforcement were called as unfortunate.[267] It was noticed however, that it is not the formalities which create the difficulties but rather the approach taken to them.[268] This is why, according to the Report, the need for remedial provisions was necessary.[269] The South Australian provision of Section 12(2) of the South Australia *Wills Act* was named as the "optimal approach for such a section",[270] however the standard of proof applied in the South Australian law was questioned. As it was stated, "the Manitoba provision should employ the normal civil standard of proof on the balance of probabilities".[271] As the result, the Report's recommendations were to introduce into the Manitoba's law a provision allowing the court to admit a document to probate despite a defect in form, if it is proved on the balance of probabilities, that the document embodies the testamentary intent of the deceased person (in 1983).[272] This gave grounds for the adoption of the Section 23 of Manitoba *Wills Act*: "Where, upon application, if the court is satisfied that a document or any writing on a document embodies (a) the testamentary intentions of a deceased; or (b) the intention of a deceased to revoke, alter or revise a will of the deceased or the testamentary intentions of the deceased embodied in a document other than a will; the court may, notwithstanding that the document or writing was not executed in compliance with all the formal requirements imposed by this act, order that the document or writing, as the case may be, be fully effective as though it had been executed in compliance with all the formal requirements imposed by this act as the will of the deceased or as the revocation, alteration or revival of the will of the deceased or of the testamentary intention embodied in that other document, as the case may be".[273] The provision was changed in 1995 and the wording "was not executed in compliance with all of the formal requirements" was substituted for "was not executed in compliance with any or all of the formal requirements" and since then it sounds as follows: "where, upon application, if the court is satisfied that a document or any writing on a document embodies (a) the testamentary intentions of a deceased; or (b) the intention of a deceased to revoke, alter or revive a will of the deceased

---

267 ibid 7.
268 ibid 17.
269 ibid.
270 ibid 27.
271 ibid.
272 ibid 30.
273 Manitoba Wills Act SM 1982-83-84, C. 31, Section 23.

or the testamentary intentions of the deceased embodied in a document other than a will; the court may, notwithstanding that the document or writing was not executed in compliance with any or all of the formal requirements imposed by this act, order that the document or writing, as the case may be, be fully effective as though it had been executed in compliance with all the formal requirements imposed by this act as the will of the deceased or as the revocation, alteration or revival of the will of the deceased or of the testamentary intention embodied in that other document, as the case may be" (Section 23 of Manitoba *Wills Act*).[274] Hence this meant that the courts could order that a testamentary document was effective "notwithstanding that the document or writing was not executed in compliance with any or all of the formal requirements..." so that, apart from the requirement of a document, proof of testamentary intention become the only prerequisite for the document to be regarded as the final will of the testator.[275]

As can be seen, there were two main changes in comparison to the South Australian statute. The Manitoba standard of proof is not the "beyond-reasonable-doubt" standard and refers to the balance of probabilities. The Manitoba version of the *substantial compliance* variation clearly relates not only to the preparation of a will, but also to the revocation and alteration of it, as in the new Queensland version. The only threshold requirement under this provision was testamentary intention in a documentary form and that neither substantial nor any compliance with other formalities was required. This proposal has also been and still is often analysed, both in the doctrine and during the legislative process considering the possibility of adapting a similar solution to one' own legal system.[276] Therefore, despite relying mainly on the South Australian model, Manitoba's proposal also played an important role in the development of law in this area.

Likewise, a proposal from another Canadian province, British Columbia, can be assessed since its adoption was a very interesting process. This proposal was widely consulted by the British Columbia Law Reform Commission with a number of correspondents in the early 1980s. After the

---

274 Manitoba Law Reform Commission, *Section 23 of the Wills Act Revisited*, Informal Report 22B (1992).

275 Tafadzwa Jairos Alfred Banda, *The Court's Power to Condone a Document in Terms of Section 2(3) and Section 2A of the Wills Act 7 of 1953: A Comparative Analysis and Recommendations* (University of Pretoria 2012) 64 ff.

276 JG Miller, 'Substantial Compliance and the Execution of Wills' (1987) 9 International and Comparative Law Quarterly 343, 574.

consultations, the Commission was convinced that a court should be given the power to admit a will to probate notwithstanding that no attempt has been made by the testator to comply with the wills act, as long as the court is satisfied that the deceased intended the document to constitute his will.[277] However, the Commission pointed out that no embodiment of testamentary intent should be admissible to probate unless it satisfies threshold requirements: the will is in writing, it is signed by the testator and there is a civil litigation standard of proof satisfied by the balance of probabilities that a document is a last will of a testator. What is also interesting is that the Commission has noticed that in then-recent years (1980s) modern technology has brought methods of storing data, undreamt of by the draftsman of the wills act and this is why, in the opinion of the Commission, the law should be open to the possibility that a will may be probated even though the "writing" consists of images mechanically or electronically reproduced.[278] In the light of the above, according to the Commission, the British Columbia *Wills Act* should have been amended by adding a section comparable to the following: "a document is valid as a will if (a) it is in writing, (b) it is signed by the testator, (c) the testator dies after this section comes into force, and the court is satisfied that the testator knew and approved of the contents of the will and intended it to have testamentary effect".[279] However, the amendments were not adopted then. Only after consultation on the new law proposal and observation of practice, about 25 years later, the changes were recommended again. In the 2006 Succession Law Report, the British Columbia Law Institute recommended that a *dispensing power* to relieve against formal invalidity of a will in proper cases shall be included in British Columbia's wills legislation.[280] This recommendation was enacted in 2009, and can be found now in the section 58 subsection 3 of the *Wills, Estates and Succession Act* (which came into force in 2014): even though the making, revocation, alteration or revival of a will does not comply with this act, the court may, as the circumstances require, order that a record or document or writing or marking on a will or document be fully effective as though it had been made (a) as the will or part of the will of the deceased person, (b) as a revocation, alteration or revival of a will of the deceased person, or (c) as the testamentary intention

---

277 Law Reform Commission of British Columbia, *Report on the Making and Revocation of Wills (LRC 52)* (1981).
278 ibid 54 ff.
279 ibid.
280 British Columbia Law Institute (n 15).

of the deceased person. The court may make an order under this subsection if the court determines that a record, document or writing or marking on a will or document represents (a) the testamentary intentions of a deceased person, (b) the intention of a deceased person to revoke, alter or revive a will or testamentary disposition of the deceased person, or (c) the intention of a deceased person to revoke, alter or revive a testamentary disposition contained in a document other than a will (section 58 subsection 2 of the *Wills, Estates and Succession Act*. This variety of the "*dispensing power*" doctrine is usually called the "curative" *dispensing power*.[281] It allows the court the discretion to admit a document to probate despite formal defects if the court is satisfied the document embodies the deceased's final testamentary wishes. As can be judged, it's a very interesting formula, mainly restricted to the examination of testamentary intent. As it was explained in the first reported decision based on the new law, two principal issues for consideration emerge: is the document authentic, and if so, whether the non-compliant document represents the deceased's testamentary intentions.[282]

When analysing Canadian law, another aspect of it should be mentioned: the solution known from the legislation of the province of Quebec. It may be interesting for civil law states since this is one of the few Anglo-American examples where civil law is based on a civil code.[283] As early as 1982, a bill proposed a new provision, which was to become Article 714 of the *Civil Code of Québec*.[284] According to its content, a will that would be invalid due to failure to observe mandatory formalities may be valid as a will if the court makes sure, after hearing the parties concerned, that the document contains, in an unquestionable and unequivocal manner, the last wishes of the deceased. In a subsequent version of the 1994 draft,[285]

---

281 du Toit, 'Remedying Formal Irregularities in Wills: A Comparative Analysis of Testamentary Rescue in Canada and South Africa' (n 7).

282 Estate of Young, [2015] BCSC 182.

283 Didier Frechette, Frank Zylberberg and Martin Raymond, 'Canada - Quebec' in Louis Garb and John Wood (eds), *International Succession* (Oxford University Press 2010).

284 Loi portant réforme au Code civil du Québec du droit des successions, Projet de loi 107, art. 759.

285 Loi portant réforme au Code civil du Québec du droit des personnes, des successions et des biens, Projet de loi 20, art. 765.

this provision was almost literally repeated, while the 1995 draft[286] made it clear that a will that would be invalid because of a failure to observe the formalities may be valid as a will before the witnesses or as a holograph will, if it essentially meets the required conditions, and the court, after hearing the persons concerned, will make sure that the document contains, unquestionably and unequivocally, the last wishes of the deceased. This new version therefore laid down the formal requirements for the validity of a will and required that a written document should fulfil the essential conditions required for its validity in its original form or another form. Subsequently, in 1990 draft,[287] in accordance with the first version of the act, this section was substantially amended by deleting the expression "after hearing the persons concerned". The last version of the act was adopted in 1991,[288] and was to create the *Civil Code of Québec*, that came into force in 1994. The final draft did not change the provision created in 1990, and gave Article 714 of this Code. According to its wording: a holograph will or a will made in the presence of witnesses that does not meet all the requirements of that form is valid nevertheless if it meets the essential requirements thereof and if it unquestionably and unequivocally contains the last wishes of the deceased.[289] Justifying the introduction of this provision, the Minister of Justice therein indicated that the court may thus recognise the validity of a will on the grounds of failure to comply with compulsory formalities if it is satisfied, after hearing the parties concerned, that the document contains, in an unquestionable and unequivocal manner, the last wishes of the deceased. In his view, this provision is intended to respect the freedom and intent of citizens and to give them priority over formal requirements where there is no doubt as to the scope of the document prepared.[290] However, the act does not apply to all defects in the drafting of wills, but only to those which are not essential to the formal validity of the will.[291] The legislator does not specify which elements are to

---

286 Étude détaillée du Projet de loi 20 – Loi portant réforme au Code civil du Québec du droit des personnes, des successions et des biens, Journal des débats de la Sous-commission des institutions,5e session, 32e législature, 26 juin 1985, S-CI-619.

287 Code civil du Québec, Projet de loi 125, art. 713.

288 Projet de loi 125, art. 714.

289 *Civil Code of Québec*, art. 714.

290 Ministre de la Justice du Québec, *Commentaires du ministre de la Justice* (Les Publications du Québec 1993) 426.

291 Lefebvre (n 80) 424 ff.

be regarded as essential and which may be regarded as non-essential.[292] It also has to be noticed that the Quebec provision does not apply to notarial wills, and is somewhat different than other Canadian variations of the *substantial compliance* doctrine: it applies to a "will" rather than to a "document".[293]

The concept of *substantial compliance* has found supporters also in South Africa. In 1991, the South African Law Commission after observing the practice of the courts recommended that the court should be vested in the power to accept a document notwithstanding non-compliance with wills formalities as a person's last will.[294] In 1992 the South African legislature enacted its version of the *substantial compliance* variation by importing section 2(3) – the so-called "condonation" provision – into the South African *Wills Act* (1953). According to the Section 2(3) of the *Wills Act*, if a court is satisfied that a document or the amendment of a document drafted or executed by a person who has died since the drafting or execution thereof, was intended to be his will or an amendment of his will, the court shall order the Master[295] to accept that document, or that document as amended, for the purposes of the *Administration of Estates Act* (1965), as a will, although it does not comply with all the formalities for the execution or amendment of wills.[296] According to this provision, there must be a document, it has to be drafted or executed by a person who has died and it has to be done with the intention that the document was this person's will.[297] A court is empowered to issue the condonation order only if the require-

---

292 Martin (n 55) 437.

293 Jacques Beaulne, *La liquidation des successions* (Wilson & Lafleur 2002) 41 ff.

294 South African Law Commission, *Review of the Law of Succession* (1991).

295 To fully comprehend this provision it is necessary to understand the significance of the Master of the High Court in South Africa. As explained in the doctrine, the Master is a functionary charged with the administration of deceased estates. The *Administration of Estates Act* assigns various functions to the Master regarding testators' wills, including the inspection of wills to ascertain whether these comply with the formalities prescribed by the law. If the Master is satisfied that a particular will is formally compliant, the Master will accept such a will for the purposes of winding-up the testator's estate in terms of the *Administration of Estates Act*. If, however, the Master is of the opinion that the will does not comply with one or more formalities, the Master will reject the will. If someone wishes to contest the Master's decision to reject the will, that person must do so before the High Court. *Cf.* du Toit (n 99) 165.

296 Wills Act (1953), section 2(3).

297 Banda (n 275) 2 ff.

ments stipulated in section 2(3) of the *Wills Act* have been met *prima facie*.[298]

In the light of the above, the process of adopting amendments to the succession law on the basis of recommendations of various committees responsible for the shape of legal regulations in a given jurisdiction can be observed. This is why an interesting way for the adoption of new law seems to be the one chosen by the USA, where – as it is known – the succession law is a domain of state law. Meanwhile, changes in the local state law resulted from the work of two national-level institutions, the Uniform Law Commission and the American Law Institute. In the late 1980s the Uniform Law Commission was engaged in preparing a comprehensive revision of the *Uniform Probate Code*, which is a model act that governs, in the states that have decided to enact it, both probate procedure and the substantive succession law. The drafters of the revised Code, officially promulgated in 1990, determined to add into the Code a version of the *dispensing power*, which became new provision of the Code - § 2-503.[299] According to this provision, although a document or writing added upon a document was not executed in compliance with the formalities, the document or writing is treated as if it had been executed in compliance with the formalities if the proponent of the document or writing establishes by clear and convincing evidence that the decedent intended the document or writing to constitute: (1) the decedent's will, (2) a partial or complete revocation of the will, (3) an addition to or an alteration of the will, or (4) a partial or complete revival of his [or her] formerly revoked will or of a formerly revoked portion of the will.[300] Also, the American Law Institute in 1995 when revising its *Restatement of Property: Wills and Other Donative Transfers*, a set of treatises on legal subjects that seek to inform judges and lawyers about general principles of common law, took the occasion to approve as a principle of American law[301] that "a *harmless error* in executing a will may be excused if the proponent establishes by clear and convincing evidence that the decedent adopted the document as his or her will".[302]

---

298 du Toit (n 99) 166.

299 Langbein, 'Absorbing South Australia's Wills Act Dispensing Power in the United States: Emulation, Resistance, Expansion' (n 94) 5.

300 Uniform Probate Code (1969), § 2-503.

301 Langbein, 'Absorbing South Australia's Wills Act Dispensing Power in the United States: Emulation, Resistance, Expansion' (n 94) 6.

302 American Law Institute, *Restatement (Third) of Property: Wills and Other Donative Transfers* (1999) vol 1, § 3.3, 217.

It can be seen that this provision, so-called the *harmless error* rule,[303] was drafted on the basis of the South Australian statute, however the American drafters made two significant changes.[304] They have extended the *dispensing power* to defects in compliance with revocation formalities as well as execution formalities, and also, they have decided that the standard of proof should be "a clear and convincing evidence" instead of a "beyond-reasonable-doubt" standard. This provision was adopted, not without a resistance, only in some US states,[305] sometimes with modifications.[306] The latest adoption of this provision was enacted by the state of Minnesota in 2020. Under the new rule, Minnesota courts are empowered to recognize a will or will modification as valid as long as there is "clear and convincing" evidence that the testator intended the document to be controlling, even if it fails to meet one of the traditional requirements (§ 524.2.503 of the *Minnesota Statutes*). What is interesting about this solution, however, is that it was introduced as a temporary solution in response to the COVID-19 pandemic, and it applies only to documents and writings executed on or after March 13, 2020, but before February 15, 2021 (§ 524.2.503(b) of the *Minnesota Statutes*).[307] However, the sunset for a harmless error provision was removed by a bill enacted in February 2021 (S.F. No. 258).

As can be seen, the *harmless error* rule in its American variation is a mechanism that reworks the conclusive presumption of invalidity for an imperfect execution into a rebuttable presumption that can be overcome

---

303 This is the name of this section in the Uniform Probate Code. As it can be noticed, the terminology comes from the criminal law, and is connected with the obligation imposed on appellate courts to vacate or reverse criminal judgements marred by constitutional error unless the government demonstrates that the *error* was *harmless* beyond a reasonable doubt. *Cf.* Roger J Traynor, *The Riddle of Harmless Error* (Ohio University Press 1970) 16 ff.

304 Crawford (n 36) 269 ff.

305 As for 2020 only twelve states have codified some form of the *harmless error* rule. See: California Probate Code § 6110(c)(2); Colorado Revised Statutes § 15-11-503; Hawaii Revised Statutes Annotated § 560:2-503; Michigan Compiled Laws § 700.2503; Minnesota Statutes § 524.2.503; Montana Code Annotated § 72-2-523; New Jersey Statutes Annotated § 3B:3-3; Ohio Revised Code Annotated § 2107.24; Oregon Revised Statutes § 112.238; South Dakota Codified Laws § 29A-2-503; Utah Code Annotated § 75-2-503; Virginia Code Annotated § 64.2-404.

306 Langbein, 'Absorbing South Australia's Wills Act Dispensing Power in the United States: Emulation, Resistance, Expansion' (n 94) 6.

307 Matthew J Frerichs and Ena Kovacevic, 'What Could Be the Harm? Minnesota's Harmless Error Statute' (*Lexology*, 2020) 2020/06/23 <https://www.lexology.com/library/detail.aspx?g=74e38c22-0717-4e2d-bc0f-3412e1ecd60f>.

with clear and convincing evidence that the decedent intended the instrument to be his or her will.[308] Although sometimes it is indicated that "the larger the departure from the formalities, the harder it will be to satisfy the court that the instrument reflects the testator's intent",[309] the practice shows a broad spectrum of flawed wills that were admitted to probate.[310] American solutions are often the subject of foreign doctrine research and constitute a model that is indicated as a one that could serve as a basis for introducing its own version of *substantial compliance* provision into a particular legal system.

In order to complement the world's picture of searches for models that allow to reflect the last intent of the testator at the cost of formal requirements, it is still necessary to mention at least the solution functioning in New Zealand. It is a system with a *strict compliance* background,[311] where a provision based on the Australian pattern was adopted in 2007.[312] As indicated in the doctrine,[313] the Australian experience and the benefits of saving wills from invalidity on purely technical grounds persuaded the New Zealand Law Commission to recommend the adoption of a similar power in its Report from 1997.[314] That recommendation was implemented with the adoption of the new New Zealand's *Wills Act* enacted in 2007. The so-called "validation power" is implemented in the section 14 of the *Wills Act* (2007). According to the subsection 2 of this section, the High Court may make an order declaring the document valid, if it is satisfied that the document expresses the deceased person's testamentary intentions.[315] This subsection applies to a document that: (a) appears to be a will; and (b) does not comply with the formalities and (c) came into existence in or out of New Zealand (section 14(1) of the *Wills Act*).[316] This provision enables the power to be used in respect of all non-compliant wills, when the four

---

308 Robert H Sitkoff, 'Freedom of Disposition in American Succession Law' in Antoni Vaquer Aloy, María Paz Sánchez González, Esteve Bosch Capdevila (eds), *La libertad de testar y sus límites* (Marcial Pons 2018) 501 ff.

309 Crawford (n 36) 283.

310 ibid 284 ff.

311 *Cf.* Joseph Dainow, 'Restricted Testation in New Zealand, Australia and Canada' (1938) 36 Michigan Law Review 1107, 1107 ff.

312 Peart (n 98) 27 ff.

313 Peart and Kelly (n 98) 74.

314 New Zealand Law Commission, *Succession Law. A Succession (Wills) Act* (1997) 19.

315 Nicola Robbins, *New Zealand and the Holographic Will* (Victoria University of Wellington 2016) 25 ff.

316 Wills Act (2007), section 14.

abovementioned requirements are met (1. there must be a document; 2. it must appear to be a will; 3. it must not comply with the formalities; 4. it must have been made in or outside New Zealand).[317] Its literal wording suggest that there is a potential to give good effect to the testamentary intentions. As in many other countries, this potential depend upon the courts and their willingness to use the power provided by the law.

Certainly it is not possible to mention all the regulations that are made to validate flawed wills, but it is necessary to highlight at least two more examples met in the world's legislations. The first one is the already mentioned Dutch *Burgerlijk Wetboek*, a regulation that is often pointed out in the literature as very strict, due to the construction providing only for the notarial form of wills (Article 4:94 of the *Burgerlijk Wetboek*). The second one, is the Polish *Kodeks cywilny*, with the regulation validating certain defect of informal holographic wills (Article 949 § 2 of the *Kodeks cywilny*). In the context of the transformation of the law of succession in the world, the Dutch proposal, in force since 1 January 2003, may come as a bit of a surprise, although it is precisely here that the rigour of the form is strongly mitigated. A manifestation of such mitigation is a rule provides for the nullity of wills created in breach of statutory requirements, but this applies only to certain requirements (lack of the testator's or notary's signature), and in the case of other requirements, failure to comply with the rules on the form of the will does not automatically result in the nullity of the will, it is only voidable (Article 4:109(4) of the *Burgerlijk Wetboek*) – "the non-observance of other formal requirements set by law for the validity of a last will makes the last will voidable").[318] On the other hand, the Polish provision of the *Kodeks cywilny* says that "a lack of a date shall not result in the invalidity of a hand-written testament if it does not raise doubts as to the testator's capacity to draw up a testament, contents of the testament and the mutual relationships among several testaments".[319] These are also examples of the recognition by legislators of the need to protect the testator's last intentions and to reflect it, the sources of which lie in the same ideals as the doctrine of *substantial compliance* and its variations. These are certainly also another examples that show that the law in this area can be further developed.

---

317 Peart and Kelly (n 98) 81 ff.
318 Du Mongh (n 170).
319 Michał Krawczyk, 'Testament własnoręczny w świetle regulacji kodeksowej , poglądów doktryny i orzecznictwa Sądu Najwyższego' (2009) 7 Zeszyty Naukowe 123, 123 ff.

The practice of succession law also knows a number of attempts to keep the testator's last will in force despite the lack of an explicit statutory instrument for such action by the court. This kind of action is based on the well-known and commonly accepted in the succession law principle of *favor testamenti*, which begins to gain meaning not only in terms of interpretation of the testator's last will expressed in the will, but also in terms of interpretation of the applicable law in a manner favourable to the testator.[320] This practice can be found especially in continental European countries, including the mentioned Germany, and also some other countries, e.g. Spain or Poland.[321] Traditionally, the principle of *favor testamenti* is considered as an interpretative rule, according to which the will must be translated in such a way as to preserve the testator's will as much as possible. For some time now, however, the application of this rule has become more widespread, and social, economic and legal practice indicates situations in which the *favor testamenti* principle allows the legally invalid form of will to be considered valid.[322] As a consequence, the *favor testamenti* principle, which applies to the interpretation of civil law, also applies to the very form of testamentary acts which, despite its *ius cogens* nature, may be relaxed in specific cases.

In this light, at least the following types of mechanisms to reflect the testator's last will at the expense of formal requirements can be distinguished: genuine *substantial compliance* (possibility to cure defects if the will substantially complies with the formalities, e.g.: Israel, Queensland until 2005, South Africa [at least to some extent], Germany or Poland with the provisions on the holographic will), *dispensing power* (possibility to cure defects if testamentary intent is present, e.g.: South Australia, other Australian states, New Zealand, Canadian provinces), *harmless error* (a variety of the *dispensing power* specific for the US legislation), *favor testamenti* (possibility to cure defects by generous interpretation, e.g.: Germany, Poland, Spain). It seems that the requirements of modern societies are precisely such that they seek to reflect the bequeather's last will, rather than strictly adhering to the formal requirements that destroy that will. The flawed wills might not be as flawed as it sometimes seems.

---

320 Aloy (n 17) 10 ff.

321 This is analogous to the proposal to apply the doctrine of substantial compliance mentioned by John H. Langbein in 1987. *Cf.* Langbein, 'Excusing Harmless Errors in the Execution of Wills: A Report on Australia's Tranquil Revolution in Probate Law' (n 42) 53.

322 Milena Perka, 'Zasada favor testamenti w prawie spadkowym' [2017] Palestra 57.

It is also necessary to mention the period of development of regulations on the form of wills related to the COVID-19 pandemic, because this is also a period during which some legislators have decided to introduce mechanisms to mitigate formal requirements or to simplify the use of dispositions of property upon death. The reason for this type of change was the increased interest in drawing up wills in society and the barriers which existed for this purpose in the traditional methods of drawing up wills, which were related, among other things, to the participation of other people, which, during a period of social isolation, often proved difficult or even impossible. [323] The statutory changes to this area of law was an option chosen, for example, by New Zealand. The government there has made a law change to modify the requirements for signing and witnessing wills under the New Zealand's *Wills Act* of 2007. *Epidemic Preparedness (Wills Act 2007—Signing and Witnessing of Wills) Immediate Modification Order 2020* introduced the principle that during the pandemic wills could have been signed and witnessed using audiovisual links (modification of Section 11(3)-11(6) of *Wills Act* of 2007). The change allowed wills to be done by Zoom, Skype, Facetime, Google Meet etc. The same has happened, for instance, in Australia.[324] For example in Queensland, as of 15 May 2020, according to *COVID-19 Emergency Response – Wills and Enduring Documents Regulation 2020*, video conferencing technology was admitted to be used for having important end of life legal documents witnessed (Section 7 of the Regulation). Also, some Canadian provinces have taken some steps to allow individuals to witness a will through videoconferencing technology. The changes have also affected notarial wills. According, for example, to the new Quebec's pandemic regulation (*Order 2020-010 of the Minister of Health and Social Services*), as of 1 April 2020, notarial wills were admitted to be signed remotely. Similar solutions have also been introduced in other legal systems. The pandemic has therefore caused amendments of formal requirements for wills, and to some extent, these solutions complemented regulations based on the doctrine of *substantial compliance* and its variations. However, many legislators have only adopted the new regula-

---

323 Jemma Slingo, 'Coronavirus: Demand for Wills Jumps by 76%' *The Law Society Gazette* (31 March 2020).

324 Julia Newbould, 'Demand for Wills on the Rise as Coronavirus Fears Set in for Australians' *Money Magazine* (8 April 2020).

tions temporarily - until the end of the COVID-19 pandemic. After this period, everything is to return to the state it was before the pandemic.[325]

When exploring the instruments used for the validation of flawed wills and thinking about the further development of this area it has to be stated that there are also jurisdictions where the idea of introduction into the law of one of the variations of the *substantial compliance* doctrine was rejected. An English law can serve as an example. In a consultative document released in 1977 the English Law Reform Committee solicited a comment on the possibility of introducing a "general *dispensing power*" into the *Wills Act* (1837). However, in their Report on making and revocation of wills, issued in 1980,[326] that option was rejected: "While the idea of a dispensing power has attractions, most of us were more impressed by the argument against it, namely that by making it less certain whether or not an informally executed will is capable of being admitted to probate, it could lead to litigation, expense and day, often in cases where it could least be afforded, for it is the homemade wills which most often go wrong".[327] Another attempt has been made in 2017.[328] The Law Commission in its 2017 consultation on reform of the law on wills recommended that a *dispensing power* should be introduced in English law.[329] The recommendation was supported by the doctrine.[330] So far as the statutory amendment has not yet been passed,[331] it should be noted that while there is no *dispensing power* in the law of England and Wales, there is a statutory power to rectify wills, which in some cases may produce results similar to those of the *dispensing power* doctrine.[332] According to the Section 20(1) of the *Administration of Justice Act* (1982), if a court is satisfied that a will is so expressed that it fails to carry out the testator's intentions, in consequence - (a)of a clerical error; or (b)of a failure to understand his instructions, it may order that the

---

325 *Cf.* Załucki, 'Preparation of Wills in Times of COVID-19 Pandemic - Selected Observations' (n 52).
326 Law Reform Committee, *Making and Revocation of Wills* (1980).
327 ibid 4.
328 Law Commission, *'Making a Will' Consultation Paper 231* (2017).
329 ibid 97–98.
330 Hedlund (n 46).
331 In July 2020, as a response to the COVID-19 pandemic, the British Government has proposed to relax the formalities of witnessing the wills, allowing for the remote witnessing of wills. *Cf.* https://www.gov.uk/government/news/video-witnessed-wills-to-be-made-legal-during-coronavirus-pandemic
332 Lately it was used with the problem of "switched" wills, where two testators making mirror wills has signed in each other's will in error. See: Marley v. Rawlings, [2014] UKSC 2.

will shall be rectified so as to carry out his intentions. Hence, there is a degree of overlap between *dispensing powers* and a power to rectify wills, but certainly this overlap is not complete. In addition, it should be pointed out that some changes to the law there have recently taken place in this area, which was linked to the COVID-19 pandemic. Section 9 of the *Wills Act* (1837) was amended on 4 September 2020 by *The Wills Act 1837 (Electronic Communications)(Amendment) (Coronavirus) Order* and the remote witnessing of wills via the use of video-conferencing technology was introduced, with retrospective effect, applying to wills made on or after 31 January 2020, when the first confirmed case of COVID-19 was recorded in the UK, and unless extended, it has a sunset clause providing for it cease to apply after 31 January 2022.

Certainly, English law is not the only example of rejection of the doctrine of *substantial compliance* and its variations, therefore before analysing the functionality of solutions that reflect the testator's last will at the expense of formal requirements, it is necessary to look at the opinions evaluating these solutions in a negative way. Despite a certain area of potential changes in legislation that have been noticed, it is not at all clear whether the possible arguments of opponents of such changes should not be relevant to the assessment of the issues identified at the beginning of this book. This is why, at this point, it is worthwhile to look at the views proclaimed against the doctrine of *substantial compliance* and its variations, which emphasize the legitimacy of continuing the rules of *strict compliance* with the wills formalities.

3. The views against the ideas for the validation of flawed wills

Solutions based on the primacy of the testator's last will at the expense of the formal requirements of *mortis causa* dispositions are relatively often criticised. It is stressed, *inter alia*, that succession law is an area of law where there is no room for much freedom and discretion, especially since a will, if made, has an *erga omnes* formative effect, and what is fair and just should be assessed only in relation to the parties concerned and not to society as a whole.[333] There are also voices that any relaxation of formal requirements is contrary to the law and its purpose, as formal requirements

---

333 Beinke (n 194) 39.

are not used to subsequently introduce mechanisms to relax them.[334] The formal requirements in the case of wills are intended to achieve a certain effect in the future, where the main focus is on the reliable recreation of the testator's last will (intent). The purpose of their presence in the law is to control the subsequent fact of acting with the intention and awareness of testation, which is difficult, if not impossible, when withdraw from formalism.[335] It is, after all, the characteristic of succession law that the testator, when his will is subject to examination, is no longer able to explain it and determine his real last will. While the freedom of testation is common, it is stressed that it must be linked to formal requirements. It cannot be arbitrary.

In this light, a broad and liberal interpretation of the formal rules in force (to which come down some mentioned concepts of reflecting the testator's last will), applying the principles of equity or fairness cannot be, according to some, an acceptable solution. While in some cases such a solution might prove to be justified, it is noted that in the long run this limits legal certainty and uniformity of application of the law. This is particularly mentioned in *civil law* systems,[336] where a judicial precedent is known not to be a source of law. It is claimed that too much discretionary power of the court may give rise to legal uncertainty in this respect, and it is the formal rigour rather than the assessment of the court that is supposed to give the highest probability that the will contains the real intention of the testator.[337]

In the opinion of some, the strict formal requirements must be extensive and detailed, as it serves, among other things, to persuade the testator to maturely consider the legal significance of the act being performed and its content. It also ensures consistency between the content that was determined by the testator at the time of drafting the will and the content that will be reproduced and have legal effects. Therefore, it's been said that the formal requirements must be strictly applied and should be subject to strict grammatical interpretation. According to this opinion, this is necessary in the light of the objectives to be achieved through their application and any attempt to liberalise formal requirements should be considered inadvisable. If an attempt is already made to liberalise formal requirements,

---

334 Joachim Gernhuber, 'Formnichtigkeit und Treu und Glauben', *Festschrift zum 70. Geburtstag von Walter Schmidt-Rimpler* (C F Müller 1956) 158 ff.
335 Häsemeyer (n 193) 203 ff.
336 Solzbach (n 60) 192 ff.
337 Elżbieta Skowrońska-Bocian, *Testament w prawie polskim* (Lexis Nexis 2004) 18.

it is observed that this should be done with extreme caution. According to the views sometimes expressed, the mere fact that the application of the provisions on the form of wills may lead to the invalidity of the dispositions made, is not a sufficient argument against a strict interpretation of those provisions.[338]

Criticism of judicial discretion, even in systems where appropriate solutions to liberalise the law of succession have been in place for some time, is widespread. It is noted, among other things, that solutions based on the doctrine of *substantial compliance* actually introduce another form of a will[339] - a judicial will.[340] In this respect, it is argued that the requirement to meet formal requirements was in fact introduced in order to limit the discretion of the court.[341] The authors criticise the uncertainty and ambiguity of the criteria for the exercise of a judge's powers, or the lack of guidelines that could shape discretionary judicial powers.[342] It is raised that allowing the courts to assess whether the formality imposed by the legislator is necessary, on the basis of a specific case, contradicts the need to approach the formal requirements *in abstracto*, and leads to "throwing testamentary formalism into the trash".[343] As it is believed, this should not be the aim of the mechanisms mitigating formalities, if at all.

Some other voices argue that it is not the role of the courts to create new forms of dispositions of property upon death (as sometimes the rules based on the doctrine of *substantial compliance* are evaluated), as the judge should not look for an act of testation in any action taken by the testator, but only in that which results from the applicable law. If similar mechanisms are already in place, which many people find doubtful anyway, they should encourage the overly severe consequences of sanctions against wills to be mitigated with a minor defect rather than practising, as is sometimes called, the art of divination.[344]

---

338 ibid 62.
339 Nicholas Kasirer, 'The "Judicial Will" Architecturally Considered' (1996) 99 Revue du notariat 3.
340 Lefebvre (n 80) 420.
341 *Cf.* Germain Brière, *Traité de droit civil - Les successions* (Éditions Yvon Blais 1994) 551.
342 Lefebvre (n 80) 422.
343 Pierre Ciotola, 'La vérification d'un testament sur disquette ou l'art de vers le formalisme testamentaire à la corbeille informatique' (1997) 4 Entracte 10.
344 Jacques Beaulne, 'Bilan d'une première décennie en droit des successions' (2003) 105 Revue du notariat 271, 271 ff.

Sometimes when criticizing the liberal approach to the problems of testamentary formalities, it is assumed that to use the form of a will actually means to use the freedom of testation. Formalism is not seen as its limitation, that is why the formal rules do not need any relaxation.[345] The purpose of the strict form of a will is to ensure the free expression of a declaration of last will and its future preservation, including the possibility of later restoration.[346]

According to this group of views, the formal regime is intended to be a natural complement to the effectiveness of the freedom to dispose of property upon death, and is intended to protect or guarantee that the disposer's declaration of last will is consistent with the disposer's real will.[347] According to some other views expressed on many occasions, the need for *strict compliance* with formal requirements is also related, among other things, to the protection of the testator, who, often in his old age, no longer understands the importance of his dispositions, and therefore the relaxation of formalism could result in taking into account a will that has not in fact been freely and consciously expressed.[348] Therefore, a lenient approach to formal matters may in fact distort the will of the testator, even though it may seem different. For this reason, the importance of formalism is stressed,[349] which is at the same time supposed to be a counterbalance to the views pointing to the need to move away from it.

The doctrine considering the legitimacy of the concept of *strict compliance* also emphasises that it does not have to be harsh and relentless, as it is sometimes indicated. It also argues that judicial decisions applying the doctrine of *substantial compliance* are often inconsistent.[350] It is emphasised that the formalities may provide sufficient protection against witnesses who would misrepresent the wishes of those who are dead and unable to give direct evidence of their testamentary wishes and acts.[351] For this rea-

---

345 *Cf.* Alfonso Cossío, 'Dolo y captación en las disposiciones testamentarias' (1962) 1962 Anuario de Derecho Civil 277.
346 *Cf.* Aloy (n 17) 10.
347 ibid.
348 Olga de Lamo Merlini, 'Los vicios de la voluntad testamentaria: Apuntes para una interpretación del articulo 673 del Código Civil' (2007) 2007 Revista General de Legislación y Jurisprudencia 50, 50 ff.
349 Aloy (n 85).
350 Wendel, 'Wills Act Compliance and the Harmless Error Approach: Flawed Narrative Equals Flawed Analysis?' (n 122) 361.
351 William F Ormiston, 'Formalities and Wills: A Plea for Caution' (1980) 54 Australian Law Journal 451.

son, in those forms of will where witnesses are required to attend the testation act, the doctrine recommends that courts should be hesitant to admit testimony concerning the testator's direct expressions of intent because the testator, who is no longer alive to testify at probate, may not have made such expressions sincerely.[352] Therefore, while there is public dissatisfaction with the rigor of formal *mortis causa* dispositions, the doctrine also suggests that the legislatures should not give courts discretion to excuse all formal defects in wills but the legislatures should instead reconsider which required formalities are truly necessary and reform their statutes.[353]

Opponents of the doctrine of *substantial compliance* also raise that courts applying *dispensing power* statute must examine intent of the testator and state that determining intent after the testator has died is difficult and leads to unclear results.[354] It is argued that this theory therefore does not serve the purpose of the will form at all,[355] and the results achieved by the *dispensing power* are unpredictable.[356] The testator's interests would be better served if the law from the beginning only laid down formal requirements and if these requirements were strictly observed.[357] In the application of this doctrine, it is difficult, according to some, to assess whether the functions of the will form regulations are fully preserved.[358]

It is criticised that a system of succession law based on equitable justice may be fraudulently used by persons who belong to the circle of heirs interested in a specific court decision favourable to them.[359] It is pointed out that the court's powers in such cases are too far-reaching,[360] as successions should not be assessed from an individual perspective, but only from an objective perspective.[361] It is also stressed that society can only be motivat-

---

352 ibid 455.
353 ibid 457.
354 Lydia Clougherty, 'An Analysis of the National Advisory Committee on Uniform State Laws' Recommendation to Modify the Wills Act Formalities' (1991) 10 Probate Law Journal 283.
355 Gail B Bird, 'Sleight of Handwriting: The Holographic Will in California' (1981) 32 Hastings Law Journal 605, 630 ff.
356 Charles Nelson and Jeanne Stark, 'Formalities and Formalism: A Critical Look at the Execution of Wills' (1978) 6 Pepperdine Law Review 331, 356.
357 ibid.
358 C Douglas Miller, 'Will Formality, Judicial Formalism, and Legislative Reform: An Examination of the New Uniform Probate Code "Harmless Error" Rule and the Movement Toward Amorphism' (1991) 43 Florida Law Review 167.
359 Clougherty (n 354) 283.
360 Bonfield (n 163).
361 Orth (n 163) 81.

ed to comply with formal requirements with leniency[362] and that the principle of *harmless error* consequently leads to an increase in the number of court disputes, their duration and costs.[363] In practice, the collection of evidence confirming the intention to draw up a will may turn out to be a lengthy process, which will have a negative impact on the speed with which succession cases are dealt with.[364]

Another trend that calls into question solutions based on the doctrine of *substantial compliance* emphasises that as a result of compliance with formalism, the negative freedom of testation is also protected. The fact whether the testator intended to draw up a will or only, for example, a draft, can be assessed best when formal requirements are observed. In other words, according to this opinion, a deviation from the strict formal requirements is constantly leading to the neglect of the function of the law on testamentary inheritance.[365] This leads to an uncertainty in legal transactions, since, according to the critics, it is not possible to fully reconstruct the testator's real last will after his death. It has been highlighted that the criticised doctrine belief that the healing of formal defects may occur after the testator's death, without his participation, meanwhile, the testator's participation in such an action, done to reconstruct his last will, seems important and desirable, but is impossible. This is why only strict formal requirements can work properly, rather than a lenient *ex post* evaluation of clear and convincing evidence.[366]

It is also raised that while for the *dispensing power* or the *harmless error* rule there are normative grounds in the law, for the application of the doctrine of *substantial compliance* it is not sufficient merely to provide a generous orientation of the interpreter, since he should also have a legal basis for such orientation, however the assumptions of the doctrine of *substantial compliance* do not provide for this. This is why it cannot be argued that a will does not have the effect of invalidity if there is no effective legal basis for such a claim. In other words, the principles of generous interpretation cannot be applied to formal rigours if the law provides that a failure to comply with the form leads to invalidity of a given legal act. A legal mech-

---

362 Adam J Hirsch, 'Inheritance and Inconsistency' (1996) 57 Ohio State Law Journal 1057, 1067.
363 Miller, 'Substantial Compliance and the Execution of Wills' (n 276) 581.
364 Emily Sherwin, 'Clear and Convincing Evidence of Testamentary Intent: The Search for a Compromise Between Formality and Adjudicative Justice' (2002) 34 Connecticut Law Review 453, 471.
365 Solzbach (n 60) 170.
366 ibid 171.

anism should have a legal basis, and due to this view, the *substantial compliance* idea understood as an interpretation tool does not have it.[367]

All such arguments discrediting the application of the doctrine of *substantial compliance* and its variations seem to be important in assessing whether and how to modify the rules of testamentary succession in a given legal system. Undoubtedly, the certainty of succession law and its predictability are extremely important features. Reflecting the testator's will as the most important value of succession law has in fact proved impossible more than once. This was and still is the case, after all, the testator is already dead when the carrier of his alleged declaration of last will is assessed. He cannot therefore explain his last will clearly, even though he may have tried to do so before his death. In this light, it is necessary to look at the practice of applying these solutions before making any assessment of the legitimacy of the individual solutions aimed at reflecting the testator's last will at the expense of formal requirements. Only the analysis of the issues that have actually happened will allow for proper observations as to the legitimacy of applying specific solutions, as well as possibly for distinguishing a proper theoretical model of a tool allowing for reflecting the testator's last will in the maze of surrounding formalism. This will be the subject of further consideration.

---

367 ibid 182.

(3) Practice of the wills formalities regulations in the context of mechanisms to relax its rigour

1. Introductory remarks

The models of solutions used in the selected legal systems, presented so far, aimed at deviating from formal requirements to reflect the testator's last will, are solutions which, in the opinion of many, are a route to follow for the legislators who would like to adapt the succession law to contemporary standards.[368] The possibility to reflect the testator's last will seems to prevail over the formal requirements and the legislators are beginning to notice that it is not the formal rigour that is the most important value of the law of succession.[369] Finally the whole mechanism of the testamentary succession is ultimately about taking into account the testator's last will and not the legislator's hypothetical assumptions.[370] For this reason, often despite criticism, ever new legal systems decide to adopt solutions that lead to the relaxation of the formal requirements of *mortis causa* dispositions.[371] More and more jurisdictions that issue decisions criticized within the society[372] consider this possibility[373] and look for a mechanism to restore the law of succession to its functionality.[374]

Due to the mentioned facts it seems like the law in this area continues to develop and the practice of applying this law presents further chal-

---

368 *Cf.*, e.g., most recently: Maciej Rzewuski, 'Wykładnia testamentu a okoliczności zewnętrzne towarzyszące testowaniu' (2015) 2015 Przegląd Sądowy 106; Aloy (n 17); Dubravka Klasiček, '21 St Century Wills' (2019) 35 Pravni vjesnik 29; Crawford (n 36).

369 This could have been observed for example in connection with the appearance of the COVID-19 pandemic, considering social distancing measures and the reaction of some legislators to facilitate the execution of wills. *Cf.* Załucki, 'Preparation of Wills in Times of COVID-19 Pandemic - Selected Observations' (n 52).

370 Eccher (n 57) 47 ff.

371 *Cf.* Horton, 'Tomorrow's Inheritance: The Frontiers of Estate Planning Formalism' (n 261) 597.

372 *Cf.* Tucker (n 94).

373 *Cf.* Langbein, 'Absorbing South Australia's Wills Act Dispensing Power in the United States: Emulation, Resistance, Expansion' (n 94); Hedlund (n 46).

374 *Cf.* Załucki, 'About the Need to Adjust the Regulations Regarding the Form of Will to the Modern Requirements' (n 14).

lenges.[375] In the end, it is in practice, and not at the desks of scientists or legislators, that needs arise to which it is possible and sometimes necessary to react. The area of testamentary succession, as it seems, is precisely such an area where, in countries where this has not yet been done, the time for change has come. The solutions well known from the past are not necessarily still adequately functional in a modern society benefiting from the advantages of new technologies and not considering the formalism of their actions.

The practice of inheritance law knows numerous cases of *mortis causa* actions, which at first sight do not comply with the statutory pattern for such actions. In this respect, an important dilemma often arises for authorities applying the law: to seek to reflect the testator's last will or to rely on formal requirements.[376] The first way is to try to keep the disposition in case of death in force at the expense of formal requirements. The latter means the invalidity of the disposition of the last will, not taking into account the bequeather's wishes. Therefore, after the presentation of possible statutory solutions in this respect so far, it is worthwhile to look at how the chosen mechanisms for maintaining the testator's last will are applied in practice, to determine what problems the courts faced and how they dealt with them. This will allow to consider whether the chosen mechanisms actually serve to reflect the testator's last will and whether, on their basis, it is possible to recommend a solution that could constitute a contemporary model system of taking into account the testator's wishes expressed informally.

2. Selected case-law based on the substantial compliance approach

The jurisprudence of succession law is faced with various dysfunctions of bequeathers on a daily basis.[377] However, the existing mechanisms are often not sufficient to achieve a satisfactory result. While for many, the effect of reflecting formal requirements is acceptable, the pursuit of such a result at all costs is no longer supported. In other words, the application of a favourable interpretation must have a legal basis for it to take place in prac-

---

375 Horton and Weisbord (n 52).
376 *Cf.* Brook (n 50).
377 Milos Vukotic, 'Importance of Will Execution Formalities in Serbian Law' in Bojan Milisavljevic, Tatjana Jevremovic Petrovic and Milos Zivkovic (eds), *Law and Transition* (University of Belgrade 2017) 473 ff.

tice. Modification of the sanction of invalidity should be based on the applicable law. This was the basis for the solution that emerged in Israel in 1965, which can be treated as the first *substantial compliance* source in action. It should be recalled that according to the Section 25 of the *Israeli Succession Law (חוק הירושה)*[378], valid until 2004, where the court had no doubt as to the genuineness of a will, it could have granted probate thereof notwithstanding any defect with regard to the signature of the testator or of the witnesses, the date of the will, the procedure of preparation of a will, or the capacity of the witnesses.

One of the widely commented cases examined under the this law was the case of *Koenig* v. *Cohen* decided in 1982.[379] This ruling was made against the background of the following facts. A woman who had been abused by her husband checked into a hotel room with her three year old daughter. She decided to jump out of the window with her daughter, and the fall killed them both. A series of unsigned and undated notes in the woman's handwriting were found in the hotel room, which instructed her husband not to attend her funeral, and that her estate should go to her brothers rather than to her husband.[380] Analysing the case, the court held that the statute could cure defective formalities, but not the complete omission of a will formality, as the court assessed the facts of the case. According to the court, complete lack of a signature or a date was not a kind of defect that could have been cured. Because the section 25 of the *Israeli Succession Law (חוק הירושה)* solely allowed – according to the court - only to cure a formality that was attempted but improperly executed, lack of a date and signature could have not been assessed as an attempted formality but should be treated as omitted formality. The omission, according to the court, could not have been cured, and this was why the husband inherited his wife's estate.[381]

On the background of this decision, that was evaluated in the doctrine as a wrong one,[382] it was suggested that in the Israeli law there is an important difference between defects and omissions that should be derived from the legislative history. According to this point of view, the drafters of the section 25 the *Israeli Succession Law (חוק הירושה)* intended to allow the dis-

---

378 Israeli Succession Law 5725-1965.
379 Koenig v. Cohen, [1982] 36(3) Israeli Supreme Court 701.
380 Flaks (n 203) 40.
381 Koenig v. Cohen, [1982] 36(3) Israeli Supreme Court 701.
382 Langbein, 'Excusing Harmless Errors in the Execution of Wills: A Report on Australia's Tranquil Revolution in Probate Law' (n 42) 49.

pensation of technical faults in the signature of the testator or of the witnesses but they did not intend to permit the probating of a will that completely lacked such elements.[383] This is why, according to the court in this case, the court cannot cure a document that lacks an "essential component" of a will.[384] According to this concept, not all the formal requirements of a will, despite the obvious intention of the testator, could be dispensed with in practice. The court found that there is a group of formalities that cannot be rescued. This was, as one might think, the inspiration for the subsequent statutory changes, which in Israel since 2004 have referred to the concept of "fundamental parts of a will". However, it can be assumed that this ruling was also initially assessed as inappropriate there, because before the changes in 2004, a change was made in 1985, and indicated that the courts may dispense with an "omission of a signature or date" in a holographic will.[385] Interestingly enough, omissions in formalities for attested and notarial wills were still fatal for such wills.[386]

In this regard, it was noted, that the enacted in 1965 solution did not meet the expectations, however, it did not lead the legislator to more liberal approach to formal requirements, but instead gave the impression of accepting section 25 of the *Israeli Succession Law* (חוק הירושה) as it stands now, distinguishing between significant and insignificant defects.[387]

The unsuccessful stage with a solution based on *substantial compliance* with wills formalities is also behind the Australian state of Queensland. It should be recalled that in its original form, the section 9(a) of the Queensland Succession Act (1981) was formulated as follows: the court may admit to probate a testamentary instrument executed in substantial compliance with the formalities prescribed [by the law] if the court is satisfied that the instrument expresses the testamentary intention of the testator. This provision was the basis for the decision in the three cases noticed all around the world (all decided in 1985). The first of the cases, *Grosert*, was made against the background of the following facts. The preparation of the will by the testator was followed by witnesses' signatures, however there was evidence that one of the witnesses attested the deceased's signature and then signed her own, but on an occasion when the other witness (who later signed) was not present. The court stated, that it had no doubt that the instru-

---

383 Flaks (n 203) 41.
384 Koenig v. Cohen, [1982] 36(3) Israeli Supreme Court 701, 708.
385 Succession Law (Amendment No. 7) 1985, (1985) SH 1140.
386 Flaks (n 203) 43.
387 Menashe (n 54).

ment expressed the testamentary intention of the testator, but held there was no "substantial compliance" because the signature of the testator was not subscribed in the presence of two or more witnesses and because it was unclear as to whether the signature of the testator was placed in the presence of either one of the witnesses.[388] This is why the court found that there had been insufficient compliance with the Succession Act formalities. The second case's facts, *Johnston*,[389] were similar. The court reached the same conclusion when the document had not been signed by the testator in the presence of any witness. The conclusion of the court is though interesting, since before the final verdict, the court said that "the alteration to the law effected by section 9 [of the Succession Act] was obviously to enable the rigid attitudes, that had been developed by the courts, to be departed from. It would be unfortunate if courts, by a series of decisions, returned to the old rigid attitudes, and I would expect a liberal approach be taken in applying the 'substantial compliance' provisions"[390].

The presence problem was also the issue in the third of the cases, *Henderson*.[391]The court declared that it was satisfied that the instrument express the testamentary intention of the testator, however it did not apply the *substantial compliance* doctrine since the will was executed with only one witness present and *substantial compliance* was "cumulative to the requirements of testamentary intent".[392] This view was repeated in the second instance court, where it was argued that the attestation by two witnesses is a *substantial* requirement.[393]

As it was commented in the doctrine, the Queensland's *substantial compliance* approach was no longer a means of discerning testamentary intent, but it was rather a new formal requirement that must be established independently of testamentary intent.[394] The standard of this formality was estimated as essentially quantitative, so the *compliance* was not able to be *substantial* unless the defect was minimal.[395]

This is why, as can be seen, the first applications of regulations based on the doctrine of *substantial compliance*, at least in the above cases, have not

---

388 Grosert, [1985] 1 QR 513.
389 Johnston, [1985] 1 QR 516.
390 Johnston, [1985] 1 QR 516.
391 Henderson, [1985] QSC 611.
392 Henderson, [1985] QSC 611.
393 White v. Public Trustee & Blundell, [1986] 17 Leg. Rep. S.L. 4.
394 Langbein, 'Excusing Harmless Errors in the Execution of Wills: A Report on Australia's Tranquil Revolution in Probate Law' (n 42) 44.
395 ibid.

brought the expected result. However, this does not mean that the idea of this doctrine is completely inappropriate. An example is the ruling of a probate court in the US state of Pennsylvania.[396] This court, in 1981, examined the case of a will drawn up by a blind person who had signed a will contrary to the law in force there at the time. The attorney who prepared the will had the testator's name typed on the will in advance of the execution rather than during its preparation by the testator as the statute required. The court upheld the will, reasoning that the purposes of the particular formality had been achieved despite the formal breach.[397] The court said that "the intent of the testator was plain", and "no useful purpose can be served by destroying the will he created by a technical adherence to the law, the principal purpose of which is to make certain that the intent of a testator is effectuated".[398]

Similar effect was achieved in other Queensland case, decided in 1984. The facts of the case disclosed that there was a difference of opinion between the witnesses as to whether or not the testatrix signed the will in their joint presence.[399] The court said that it was unnecessary to resolve this dispute, since even assuming that only one witness had been present at the time of signature, the formal requirements of the law had been *substantially complied* with.[400]

Also, some South African cases with the court's condonation power as a tool similar in practice to the genuine *substantial compliance* mechanism can serve as a successful examples of the use of the *substantial compliance* doctrine. In *Macdonald*, a case decided in 2002, the deceased indicated in a note written shortly before he committed suicide that his will was to be found on his office computer.[401] The High Court, satisfied that the security measures with regard to the computer file were not breached and, therefore, that the unexecuted hard-copy version of the electronic document reflected the deceased's authentic testamentary dispositions, issued a condo-

---

396 It has to be stated, that the state of Pennsylvania did not adopt the *substantial compliance* doctrine into its legislation.

397 Langbein, 'Excusing Harmless Errors in the Execution of Wills: A Report on Australia's Tranquil Revolution in Probate Law' (n 42) 8.

398 Kajut, [1981] 2 Pa. Fiduc. 2d 197, 204.

399 Langbein, 'Excusing Harmless Errors in the Execution of Wills: A Report on Australia's Tranquil Revolution in Probate Law' (n 42) 42.

400 McIlroy, [1984] QSC 375.

401 MacDonald v. The Master, [2002] South African Law Reports 64.

nation order.[402] Also, in the judgment of the *Van der Merwe* case decided in 2010[403] an unexecuted will, sent as an electronic document by email, was granted a condonation order (after the appeal).[404] The court said that the very object of the *substantial compliance* section in the wills act is to ameliorate the situation where the formalities have not been complied with but where the true intention of the drafter of a document is self-evident.[405] Both courts, before admitting the wills to probate, considered that the formal requirements are sufficiently fulfilled. Without meeting some of the requirements, such rulings would be impossible.

In the aforementioned circumstances, the interesting case resolved in South Africa is the case *Ex Parte Maurice* decided in 1985,[406] that explains the South African approach. In this case, the deceased forwarded a draft of his will in his own handwriting to a building society, along with a letter asking them to "knock this document into shape and finalise it in legal jargon." The question before the court was whether it should exercise its discretion to declare the will valid, even though it had not been signed by any witnesses. The court held that there are three requirements which must be fulfilled before condonation is given: 1) the document must be drafted or executed by a person; 2) who has since died; 3) and who intended the document to be his will. The court held that the document was merely a draft, not the final will of the deceased and did not declared it as a valid will. This standard (threshold requirements) is applied in the latter court decisions.

In the light of the above, the genuine *substantial compliance* seems to be a model solution that differs only little from the solutions that are based on the *favor testamenti* doctrine in continental European countries.[407] Wherever a generous approach to maintaining the testator's last will is possible, that is where it happens. However, if there is a doubt about one of the key requirements of a given form of a will, there, despite the lack of

---

402 Michael Cameron Wood-Bodley, 'MacDonald v. the Master: Computer Files and the Rescue Provision of the Wills Act' (2004) 121 South African Law Journal 34.

403 Van der Merwe v. Master of the High Court & Another, [2010] ZASCA 99.

404 Van der Merwe v. Master of the High Court & Another, [2010] ZASCA 99.

405 *Cf.* Sylvia Papadopoulos, 'Electronic Wills with an Aura of Authenticity: Van Der Merwe v Master of the High Court and Another' (2012) 24 South African Mercantile Law Journal 93.

406 Ex Parte Maurice, [1985] 2 SA 713.

407 Aloy (n 17) 9 ff.

doubt about the testator's intention, the will has no legal effect.[408] Against the background of the above experience, it can be noted that despite the concept of a softened approach to the formal requirements of wills, the doctrine of *substantial compliance* in its original version requires the emergence in practice of some essential positive formal requirements that cannot be dispensed with.[409] According to the practice that has occurred, not all the formal requirements can therefore be dispensed with. The threshold requirements are usually set in this concept. They are set at a lower level than the standard requirements for execution of a will, and often, as a minimum, a writing act is required. The court can evaluate then whether the essential requirements are met, or whether the testator had attempted to comply with those requirements. The assessment of which requirement should be regarded as essential is certainly another issue that requires broad discussion. Nevertheless, this model of relaxation of formal requirements is still a model where some requirements must be strictly observed and only some can be dispensed with.

This does not mean that the model has to be completely rejected. This model can be used primarily as an interpretative guideline for courts, in systems where there is no clear legal basis for maintaining a will that is not prepared according to formal requirements. The *favor testamenti* rule, in this sense, may find a different application than traditional ones. It should not only serve to make a generous interpretation of the content of the will and the intent expressed by the testator, but can also be applied to a generous interpretation of the binding law.[410] Wherever possible, a lenient and functional approach to the formal requirements for wills seems necessary, especially when there is no doubt about the testator's intention expressed in case of death. Examples of such benevolent interpretation can be multiplied: the bequeather's signature logically linked to the contents of his declaration does not necessarily have to be under this disposition; the date of drafting the will does not have to be indicated unless there are doubts as to the order of the will (if several wills have been drawn up); signatures do not have to be made simultaneously; signatures do not have to be made in the same place; the carrier of the declaration of last will does not have to

---

408 Maciej Rzewuski, 'Wykładnia słusznościowa testamentu' [2014] Białostockie Studia Prawnicze 227.

409 Miller, 'Reforming the Formal Requirements for the Execution of a Will' (n 90) 86.

410 Rzewuski, 'Formalisation of the Testament in the Light of the Favor Testamenti Principle' (n 48).

be traditional; the contents of the declaration of last will do not have to be expressed in a conventional manner; it is possible to use means of distance communication; the requirement of the presence of witnesses can be met remotely, etc. With such an interpretation, a generous approach to the testator, will functionally be, within the limits of the applicable law.

The invalidity of a *mortis causa* disposition made contrary to the provisions of the law as a result of the testator acting with the testamentary intention, resulting directly from the law, cannot and does not mean that the provisions of the law must be read in a literal manner.[411] Not every action of the testator, but only the one that is irreconcilable with the formal requirement formulated, should lead to the invalidity of this disposition. Therefore, as a result of interpretation, wherever it seems possible to keep the will in force, this should happen. For example, a handwritten will prepared electronically on a tablet should not be considered automatically null and void simply because it has been drawn up on a non-traditional medium that does not allow the character of the testator's handwriting to be reflected unequivocally. On the other hand, one should look at, for example, an attempt to make a holographic will through a video recording. A video testament itself, without an attempt to make it with one's own hand, would not contain the necessary elements of a holographic will, which means that it could not be considered a valid holographic will, because in fact, it would be a different form of a will (which does not mean that it could not be the basis for the inheritance if the legislator knew such a form of will or modified the prerequisites for making a will with one's own hand in such a way that it would be sufficient). This is, as one might suppose, the tenor of the *substantial compliance* doctrine, and so - in the light of the applicable law, even if it is strict - it is possible to restore functionality to the law of succession, although of course this is not the answer to all the legal challenges in this area.

The application of this kind of thinking took place at least in one of the cases recognized in Poland (decided in 1982).[412] The will was drawn up in such a way that the testator, in the presence of two witnesses, declared her last will orally to the village leader (*sołtys*), what, in the opinion of the first instance court, made the will null and void, since it contains a declaration of the testator's last will made to an unauthorized person, not mentioned in the article 951 of the *Kodeks cywilny*. According to this provision, the be-

---

411 Załucki, 'Współczesne tendencje rozwoju ustawodawstwa testamentowego' (n 22).
412 III CZP 5/82, [1982] Legalis 23044.

queather may declare his last will orally only to the *voit* (mayor, president of a city), a *staroste*, a marshal of a voivodeship, a secretary of a *poviat* or *gmina* or a head of a civil register office. The village leader is not mentioned there. Meanwhile, the Supreme Court, while recognizing the legal issues that raised doubts presented to it by the court of second instance, came to the conclusion that the invalidity of the will provided for in article 951 of the *Kodeks cywilny*, due to the failure to observe the applicable law, may be considered a special circumstance within the meaning of article 952 § 1 of the *Kodeks cywilny*,[413] justifying the treatment of the testator's declaration of his last will as an oral will. Based on the instrument of conversion and the principle of *favor testamenti*, it has rendered the testamentary inheritance valid. This kind of tendency is known wider.

3. Selected case-law based on the dispensing power approach

A variant of the doctrine of *substantial compliance*, known primarily from the Australian state of South Australia, subsequently propagated in several other jurisdictions, is the *dispensing power* doctrine. More than forty years of applying the rules based on this doctrine in practice has led to interesting decisions many times. Therefore, it is worthwhile to trace the most important of them here. This will allow to evaluate this solution in comparison with other methods resulting in taking into account the intention of the testator at the expense of formal requirements.

The first examples of using the *dispensing power* mechanism are obviously coming from South Australia. The first case decided upon the South Australian *dispensing power* provision was the so-called case of *Graham* (in 1978).[414] In the facts of the case there was no attempt to comply with the formalities, since the will was not signed by the witnesses in the joint presence of them and the testatrix. The court has rejected a narrow interpretation of *dispensing power* provision and the argument that there had to be at least some attempted compliance with the formalities before section 12(2) of the South Australian *Wills Act* could be successfully invoked.[415] Thus, al-

---

413 Article 951 § 1 of the *Kodeks cywilny*: "If there is a probability of imminent death of the testator or if, due to extraordinary circumstances, the observance of the ordinary form of the testament is impossible or very difficult, the testator may declare his last will orally in the simultaneous presence of at least three witnesses."

414 Re Estate of Graham, [1978] 20 S.A. State Reports 198.

415 Miller, 'Substantial Compliance and the Execution of Wills' (n 276) 568.

ready in the first ruling of the *dispensing power* doctrine the difference between the idea of *substantial compliance* and the idea of *dispensing power* can
be seen. The latter idea seems to be interpreted more flexibly, it is the testator's intention that plays the most important role. This can also be seen in
other rulings from South Australia and other jurisdictions that have adopted this doctrine.

In the case *Estate of Clayton*,[416] the case decided in 1982, the deceased
had written out his will on a will form and signed and dated it, but the
printed attestation clause had not been completed and the will was not
witnessed. There was evidence of statements by the testator indicating that
he considered he had made a valid will. It appears that he intended, having
signed the will, to have his signature witnessed, but was unaware of the requirements that the testator should make or acknowledge his signature in
the joint presence of the witnesses, and that the witnesses should sign in
the presence of the testator. The court said, that it was satisfied on the facts
that there could be no reasonable doubt that the deceased intended the
document to constitute his will and admitted it to probate.[417] In the case
Estate of Smith (decided in 1985),[418] the testatrix made her will in her own
handwriting on a printed will form, and signed and dated it. However, it
was never witnessed, although the testatrix had some years earlier made a
will which was executed in accordance with the formal requirements. After executing the later document, the testatrix told her relatives she had
made her will. She kept the document with her important papers and took
it to hospital with her. The court held that there was no reasonable doubt
that the testatrix intended the document to be her will, and admitted it to
probate.[419] In the case *Estate of Kelly* (decided in 1983),[420] a medical practitioner signed a will which also bore the signature of two witnesses. However, it subsequently appeared that the will had not been duly executed as
the testator had not signed or acknowledged his signature in the joint presence of the witnesses. Between the date of that will and the practitioner's
death he prepared several further testamentary documents none of which
were duly executed. Shortly before his death he handed a notebook to a
woman employed by him for office work, telling her to use the book for
notes. The notebook remained in her possession until after his death when

---

416 Re Estate of Clayton, [1982] 31 S.A. State Reports 153.
417 ibid.
418 Re Estate of Smith, [1985] 38 S.A. State Reports 30.
419 ibid.
420 Re Estate of Kelly, [1983] 32 S.A. State Reports 413.

it was found to contain two sheets in the practitioner's handwriting, beginning: "MY LAST WILL AND TESTAMENT", and signed and dated by the practitioner with the words added: "WRITTEN AS I HAVE CONSIDERABLE CARDIAC
PAIN AND IRREGULARITY AT TIME", but the signature was not witnessed.[421] In
the abovementioned facts, the court stated that there was no reasonable
doubt that the testator intended the two sheets of paper in the notebook to
constitute his will and accordingly ordered that the sheets be admitted to
probate.[422] Similar thought can be met also in the recent South Australian
case law. For example, in the case *Re Estate of Wilden*,[423] decided in 2015,
the deceased left two items of a testamentary nature, a DVD containing a
video recording of the deceased and a typed document signed by the deceased but not witnessed. The applicant's solicitors prepared a transcript of
the words spoken by the deceased as recorded on the DVD. The transcript, *inter alia*, provides:

> "...THIS IS AH SOMEWHAT OF AN OFFICIAL LAST WILL AND TESTAMENT AS I
> DON'T HAVE A WRITTEN DOCUMENT ANYWHERE AT THIS STAGE. THIS IS JUST
> UM A FAIL SAFE UNTIL SUCH TIME AS I DO GET SOMETHING LIKE THAT
> DONE. UM. UM. MY WILL IS THAT EVERYTHING THAT I OWN GOES TO MY
> YOUNGER SISTER SANDRA CARPENTER AND HER HUSBAND MICHAEL CAR-
> PENTER AND MY TWO NEPHEWS LACHLAN AND JACOB. UM I DON'T HAVE A
> WIFE OR ANY CHILDREN OR ANYTHING LIKE THAT AT THIS STAGE SO IF ANY-
> THING SHOULD HAPPEN TO ME NOW OR IN THE NEXT FEW YEARS OR WHAT-
> EVER UM THIS IS JUST SO THERE IS SOME KIND OF AN OFFICIAL RECORD OF
> HOW THINGS SHOULD BE DISTRIBUTED. I DON'T WANT THE REST OF MY
> FAMILY IE MY OTHER BROTHERS AND SISTERS TO GET ANYTHING... SO UM
> SELL ALL MY STUFF, UM UM THOUSANDS OF DOLLARS WORTH OF AUDIO
> EQUIPMENT UM THAT SHOULD EASILY BE SOLD OFF TO GO SEE MY EMPLOY-
> ER, HE WILL PROBABLY BUY IT ALL OFF YOU...UM YEH KEEP WHAT YOU
> WANT SANDRA, SELL WHAT YOU WANT, ENJOY, KEEP THE MONEY...".[424]

The second left document, in typed form, was signed by the deceased and
provided:

---

421 The facts of the case are fully presented in the Report on the adoption of the
     substantial compliance doctrine, *cf.*: The Law Reform Commission of Western
     Australia, *Report on Wills: Substantial Compliance* (1985) 26.
422 Re Estate of Kelly, [1983] 32 S.A. State Reports 413.
423 Re Estate of Wilden, [2015] 121 S.A. State Reports 516.
424 ibid.

"LAST WILL AND TESTEMENT [sic] WAYNE GREGORY WILDEN.

THIS IS AN OFFICIAL LAST WILL AND TESTEMENT [sic] FOR MYSELF, WAYNE WILDEN. THIS IS TO ADD TO MY VIDEO OF MY LAST WILL AND TESTEMENT [sic] RECORDED ON 11.5.05.

I WOULD LIKE TO OFFICIALY RECORD THAT MY WILL IS THAT EVERYTHING I OWN GOES TO MY YOUNGER SISTER SANDRA CARPENDER AND HER HUSBAND MICHAEL CARPENDER AND MY TWO NEPHEWS [J] and [S].

THIS INCLUDES MY PROPERTY AT [address], ALL POSSESSIONS, ALL MY MONEY IN BANK ACCOUNTS AND ALL SUPERANNUATION PAYMENTS AS MY NEXT OF KIN.

I DO NOT WANT MY OTHER BROTHERS AND SISTERS OR THEIR FAMILIES TO RECEIVE ANYTHING".

The court has admitted the abovementioned documents to probate, stating that testamentary intentions are an expression of what a person intends to happen to his or her property upon death, and evaluating that both documents expressed testamentary intentions.[425] According to the court, their content makes it clear that the deceased intended that both documents were to constitute his will and together govern the disposition of his estate after his death. In the opinion of the court, it was possible to "take a more liberal approach" and extend the range of possible documents constituting wills to wills made in non-traditional forms or using non-traditional media, including by a recording in the form of a DVD, because it is consistent with the liberal construction that is to be accorded to remedial legislation, such as the section 12(2) of the South Australian *Wills Act*.[426]

This approach to the *dispensing power* in the circumstances of new technologies is nothing surprising. It has happened many times that a will was made not in accordance with the formalities, but in a manner that is reflecting the use of technology, and the court using the *dispensing power* has kept the will in force at the expense of formal requirements. For example, such an order was made in Queensland in 2013 (after the state has adopted the *dispensing power* instead of the genuine *substantial compliance*). In the case *Mellino v Wnuk*,[427] the court stated that it is satisfied that the document (the DVD) embodies or was meant to embody the testamentary intentions of the deceased, what was "clear from the fact that he has written

---

425 ibid.
426 ibid.
427 Mellino v Wnuk [2013] QSC 336.

'my will' on the DVD itself and also from the substance of what he says in the video recording on the DVD".[428] It has also appeared in New South Wales, in 2015 (*Re Estate of Wai Fun Chan*), where a dying woman sat in her kitchen and was delivering her last will to a video camera, and that will was, *inter alia*, to alter a written will signed two days earlier. The court said that the woman made a "series of short, and apparently well-considered, disciplined statement of intent (coupled with motherly exhortations in passing) that stand nearly with the will as an alteration of the primary document" and there was "no room for doubt" the will was voluntarily made, and because of this, has admitted the will to probate being satisfied with the requirements stated in the section 8 of the New South Wales *Succession Act*.[429] It is also an idea known in different jurisdictions. The use of new technologies in inheritance law is relatively frequent, hence such judgments cannot be surprising, and what is more, it is to be expected that in the future such cases will be much more significant. According to the above, it seems that the *dispensing power* doctrine is already prepared for this future. The informal nature of a will does not exclude it from being sufficient to represent the deceased's testamentary intentions.[430]

A similar situation, concerning new technologies, appeared in 1996 in one of the succession cases that took place in Canada (Quebec province). There, the testator left an envelope with a diskette inside on which he has written and signed that it was his will. The diskette consisted of an electronic file that contained *mortis causa* dispositions, reflecting the will of the testator. Although the disposition did not meet the formal requirements of the law, since *Civil Code of Quebec* required a notarized, holographic or witnessed form (Art. 712), the court considered the disposition to be valid by applying the rule based on the *dispensing power* doctrine contained in Art. 714 of the *Civil Code of Quebec*.[431] Already at that time, it was signalled in the doctrine, that in modern times, the will should not be regarded as a strict formal act, especially since technological developments force us to view the provisions of the will form as *ad probationem* rather than *ad solemnitatem*.[432] According to this view, the preservation of the form is to be the proof of the last will and not a constructional element of it.[433] It has also

---

428 ibid.
429 Re Estate of Wai Fun Chan, [2015] NSWSC 1107.
430 Re Estate of Nichol, [2017] QSC 220.
431 Rioux v. Coloumbe, [1998] 19 Estates and Trust Reports (2d) 201.
432 Nicholas Kasirer, 'From Written Record to Memory in the Law of Wills' (1998) 29 Ottawa Law Review 43.
433 ibid.

been noted that the times of electronic communication can bring about intensive changes in the law in this area, enabling the recording of human
intent in a computer memory.[434] This assumptions came true quickly; it
was only a matter of time when the technological need for the legislators,
in the area of testamentary formalities, had arisen.[435]

The application of the *dispensing power* in practice often depends on one
condition - that the testamentary intent can be identified. That is the case,
for example, of the Manitoban law, where only a single requirement has to
be satisfied in order for a court to exercise the dispensation power: the document in question must embody the deceased's testamentary intentions.[436]
In one of the cases decided in 1997,[437] it was said that the *dispensing power*
provision demands of a court to establish on a balance of probabilities that
the document at issue contains the deceased's testamentary intentions, and
the latter in this context mean that the deceased must have evinced his or
her *animus testandi* as a "deliberate or fixed and final expression of intention as to the disposal of his/her property on death".[438] This was also emphasized in the case *Timm* v. *Rudolph*, decided in 2016,[439] where the court
has stated that the deceased must have contemplated the document at issue
as a testamentary document to be admitted to probate when the time
came, and that the deceased must thus not have regarded it simply as a
document that disclosed his or her distributive wishes at the time. If the
court is satisfied that the document indeed embodies the deceased's testamentary intentions and the application that it be given full legal effect is
unopposed, no practical hindrance precludes a judge from exercising the
dispensation power.[440] According to the judiciary there, the testamentary
intentions requirement can thus be treated as the core requirement of the
dispensing power mechanism. However, the impact is also placed on the authenticity requirement, since the reasoning of judges suggest that the judicial exercise of the dispensation power is also dependent on a court being
satisfied regarding the authenticity of the document at issue. Such an approach is consistent with, e.g., the case law of British Columbia, where the
core requirement for the judicial exercise of the curative power is similar

---

434 ibid.
435 *Cf.* Hirsch, 'Technology Adrift: In Search of a Role for Electronic Wills' (n 83).
436 du Toit, 'Remedying Formal Irregularities in Wills: A Comparative Analysis of
     Testamentary Rescue in Canada and South Africa' (n 7).
437 George v Daily, [1997] 115 Manitoba Reports (2d) 27.
438 ibid.
439 Timm v Rudolph 2016 MBQB 123
440 ibid.

to the Manitoban one. It can be noticed, e.g., in the court's argumentation form the case decided in 2015, *Estate of Young*.[441]. The court has stated that it must be satisfied that a document represents the testamentary intentions of the deceased before granting an order that it is fully effective as a will, and before analysing that, it has to determine whether the document is authentic.[442]

The recent *dispensing power* judgement that was widely commented around the world, and explains the abovementioned standard, is the case decided in 2019 in British Columbia, *Re Hubschi Estate*.[443] In the facts of the case it was found that the notation left on a computer by the deceased does not meet the formal requirements of the *Wills Estates and Succession Act*. The court has stated that the deceased's testamentary intention was present and since there is no minimum level of execution or other formality for a testamentary document to be found fully effective, it has found the will to be sufficient to be ordered as valid electronic will. The ruling is all the more important because the court stressed what the *dispensing power* doctrine standard looks like. According to the court, that testamentary intention means much more than the expression of how a person would like his or her property to be disposed of after death. It has explained that the burden of proof that a non-compliant document embodies the deceased's testamentary intentions is a balance of probabilities. A wide range of factors may be relevant to establishing their existence in a particular case. Although context specific, these factors may include the presence of the deceased's signature, the deceased's handwriting, witness signatures, revocation of previous wills, funeral arrangements, specific bequests and the title of the document. It has also reminded that while imperfect or even non-compliance with formal testamentary requirements may be overcome by application of a sufficiently broad curative provision, the further a document departs from the formal requirements the harder it may be for the court to find it embodies the deceased's testamentary intention.[444]

Interesting in the abovementioned model are also some cases decided in New Zealand. For example, in the case *Re Feron*,[445] decided in 2012, the deceased gave her instructions to the solicitor by the phone. The solicitor took detailed notes and confirmed the instructions in an email exchange

---

441 Re Estate of Young, [2015] BCSC 182.
442 ibid.
443 Re Hubschi Estate, [2019] BCSC 2040.
444 ibid.
445 Re Estate of Feron, [2012] 2 NZLR 551.

with the client. Due to the Christchurch earthquake, the solicitor was unable to prepare the will before testator's death. Then, the solicitor prepared a draft will based on the client's instructions and submitted the draft, the notes, and the emails to the court in support of an application for probate. The court rejected the draft, since it did not exist before the testator's death, but the court was satisfied that the solicitor's notes and the emails reflected the deceased's testamentary intentions and therefore granted probate. The court stated that it prefers "to approach the interpretation of the *Wills Act* 2007 in a manner that gives full vent to the ostensible purpose of section 14, namely to validate documents that plainly express the testamentary wishes of a deceased person".[446] According to the opinion expressed there, the New Zealand's succession law "confers a discretionary power to make a declaration on satisfaction that the document expresses the deceased person's intention".[447] In line with this position there was an observation that this law "is concerned with substance not form".[448] The court has also stressed that this provision is applicable "where the clear testamentary intentions of the deceased are deemed to outweigh any defects in form" and in contradistinction, the court has indicated that "where the courts have not been satisfied of testamentary intentions, the courts have refused to accept the notes or draft will".[449]

Similar approach was made in another New Zealand's case, decided in 2013, *McVicar*.[450] The court has dealt with a hand amended draft will signed by the will-maker and a single witness, lacking a signature of a second witness. The court said that is satisfied that the will meets the requirements for a will, since it truly represents the testamentary intention of the deceased and, in this case, this clearly outweighs the defect in form by the absence of a second witness. The court therefore concluded that the existence of the testamentary intent has a curative power for a defective will and evaluated such circumstances as a "robust consideration" to validate a will.[451] In this light, another and more recent decision from there is also interesting. A court in 2018 gave effect to an audio-will on the ground that a *post mortem* transcript of the audio recording qualified as a writing subject to the *dispensing power*.[452] According to the court, an audio recording

---

446 ibid. 553.
447 ibid.
448 ibid.
449 ibid.
450 Estate of McVicar, [2013] NZHC 2201.
451 ibid.
452 Pfaender v. Gregory [2018] NZHC 161.

of the deceased's will instructions did not qualify as a "document" (what is necessary in accordance to the law binding there), however, the written notes taken of his oral instructions were a document which the court could, and did, validate. The court also said that in the modern world, with "widespread use of smartphones and other personal devices", it is increasingly likely that people having important conversations will record their oral instructions. It was also suggested that while a recording itself might not qualify as a "document" which could be validated as a will, a transcript of such a recording might be validated.[453]

As it seems, the courts under the *dispensing power* do their best to keep the last will valid. The flexibility of this mechanism and the relatively broad framework of discretionary power of the courts allow for a benevolent approach, often resulting in the maintenance of a will that is blatantly contrary to formal requirements, often without even containing elements that could be described as "essential elements". This kind of approach seems to be appropriate, putting the testator's intention in the first place, without taking into account formal requirements, treating it as a mere indication, which is not obligatory. In assessing this approach, however, one must not forget the negative overtones of mild or minor formalities, which may be conducive to falsifying the testator's last will. It should be noted, however, that in practice it is not so that all cases analysed by the courts through the prism of the *dispensing power* mechanism end up with the recognition of an informal will as valid.

For example, in another New Zealand's case, *Fitzgibbons v Fitzmaurice*,[454] a suicide note addressed to the deceased's executor removing the deceased's only sister and leaving all his assets to the Salvation Army was not admitted to probate. The court was not satisfied that the evidence established that the deceased had testamentary capacity when the note was written. Because of that, the court was not satisfied that document expresses testator's testamentary intentions.[455]

The problem in assessing whether there is a will against the *dispensing power* doctrine may also be the issue of infinite wills or their drafts. Where a will is drafted but never signed, the court must be satisfied the will represents the final testator's intentions and that the testator did not delay signing because of rethinking the dispositions or changing his mind. These were, for example, the facts in the case *Re Estate of Bishop*, decided in 2014,

---

453 ibid.
454 *Fitzgibbons v Fitzmaurice, [2014] NZHC 710.*
455 ibid.

where a different reason for the delay was found,[456] or the facts in the case *Re Estate of Uruamo*, decided in 2017, where the court has found that the testatrix simply did not realise that the will required her signature.[457] By applying the *dispensing power* doctrine, the courts have thus dealt with a problem that can often be expected in practice.[458] The same has happened in one of the Australian cases, where the court was dealing with two informal wills and their changes in suspicious circumstances. In the case *Re Hobbs*,[459] decided in 2017, the court refused to probate two documents that contained very different provisions for the distribution of the estate (both with annotated changes), stating that there was significant doubt as to what really took place when the first and second documents were prepared and signed. According to the court, there was a significant risk that the testatrix was under exerted pressure or influence in order to obtain her writing and signature on the first and second documents and it was inherently unlikely that she conceived, wrote and signed additions and changes to the will on two separate occasions without assistance from someone else, and then held the two signed documents for over six years without telling anyone. The court was not persuaded to the requisite standard that either the first document or the second document should be admitted to probate. In the court's opinion, there were "simply too many factors and uncertainties which excite suspicion or mitigate against the admission to probate of either document".[460] It was "not satisfied that either the first document or the second document expresses or records the testamentary intentions"[461]of the testatrix, or "that either document was intended by her to be her last will".[462] Similar considerations were present, e.g., in the case decided in 2020, *Estate of Violet Filomena Cox*.[463] In this case, the testatrix made frequent changes to her expressed testamentary disposition, and the court considering her testamentary capacity has stated that it is not satisfied that her notes represent her final testamentary intention. Deciding the case, the court made a distinction between "musings" and testamentary dispositions. The changes in the documents were seen as her thoughts as to

---

456 Re Estate of Bishop, [2014] NZHC 3355.
457 Re Estate of Uruamo, [2017] NZHC 931.
458 McKenzie Rogers, 'If It Looks like a Will, There's a Way' (2017) 43 Lawtalk 32.
459 Re Estate of Hobbs, [2017] VSC 424.
460 ibid.
461 ibid.
462 ibid.
463 Re *Estate of Violet Filomena Cox, [2020] NZHC 1310.*

possible changes she might confirm rather than her actual testamentary intention.[464]

In the practice of the *dispensing power*, therefore, there is no desire to maintain the informal will at all costs, but only when it seems obvious to the court that there is an unquestionable last intention of the testator present in a given case. The practice, when confronted with different circumstances, seems to rationally assess different inclinations as to a possible falsification of the last will, or attempts to acquire an inheritance in a manner inconsistent with what seems fair. The basic factor determining whether a given will is considered valid is to convince the court of the existence of the testator's intent. This, of course, does not always work. However, it can be imagined that on this basis, for example, a will that is drawn up in the following circumstances can be considered as valid: unsigned drafts, a series of notes, an unsigned will prepared on a will kit form, a will in electronic format in the computer. Despite the lack of compliance with formal requirements, such *mortis causa* dispositions could be considered, according to the *dispensing power* standard, as valid if they contained the testator's final intention.

4. Selected case-law based on the harmless error approach

The doctrine of *harmless error*, a mirror image of the *dispensing power* doctrine, which in the common opinion differs primarily by the name used to describe it,[465] is a commodity known under US law.[466] As it is known, so far only some states have decided to adopt it, although the number is still growing.[467] Nevertheless, American case law is important in order to clarify the essence of the mechanism based on the primacy of the testamentary intent. This is primarily because in this country, solutions based on the concept discussed here were widely commented on. These comments continue to appear. This is particularly interesting because the individual states present the *harmless error* rule sometimes from a slightly different perspective.

---

464 ibid.
465 *Cf.* Miller, 'Will Formality, Judicial Formalism, and Legislative Reform: An Examination of the New Uniform Probate Code "Harmless Error" Rule and the Movement Toward Amorphism' (n 358) 187 ff.
466 Wendel, *Wills, Trusts, and Estates* (n 26) 150 ff.
467 *Cf.* Frerichs and Kovacevic (n 307).

This remarks can start with an observation that the first legislative adoptions of the *Uniform Probate Code*'s provision on the *harmless error* has happened in the early 1990s. For example, Montana's *harmless error* statute was enacted in 1993. The enacted § 72-2-523 of the *Montana Code Annotated* follows directly the *Uniform Probate Code*. In the case *Re Estate of Kuralt*,[468] decided in 2000, this provision was used to remedy a nonconforming codicil and alter an original will. The deceased who prepared a formal will earlier, has became suddenly ill and wrote a letter to his mistress that said:

"I'LL HAVE THE LAWYER VISIT THE HOSPITAL TO BE SURE YOU INHERIT THE REST OF THE PLACE IN MT. IF IT COMES TO THAT."

He died two weeks later. She sought to probate the letter as a holographic codicil to the original will. The court found that the letter represented a valid holographic codicil. The court focused on the deceased testamentary intent and made specific reference to the word "inherit" in his letter and that he was very close to death when he wrote the letter. The court upheld the deceased testamentary wishes by looking at his intent.[469] This demonstrates how the *harmless error* provision function in Montana, where the courts are rather guided by the bedrock principle of honoring the intent of the testator.[470]

Similar thoughts can be found in some different US states that has adopted this doctrine, even if their approach to this doctrine is different. This is the case, for example, of the state of Colorado, where the *harmless error* statute was adopted in 1994. It expressly states that for *harmless error* to apply a testator's signature must be present, with an exception for swapped wills of spouses. According to the § 15-11-503 of the *Colorado Revised Statutes*:

"(1) Although a document, or writing added upon a document, was not executed in compliance with [the law] the document or writing is treated as if it had been executed in compliance with [the law] if the proponent of the document or writing establishes by clear and convincing evidence that the decedent intended the document or writing to constitute:
(a) The decedent's will;
(b) A partial or complete revocation of the will;

---

468 Re Estate of Kuralt, [2000] MT 359.
469 ibid.
470 Sitkoff and Dukeminier (n 37) 213 ff.

(c) An addition to or an alteration of the will; or

(d) A partial or complete revival of the decedent's formerly revoked will or a formerly revoked portion of the will.

(2) Subsection (1) of this section shall apply only if the document is signed or acknowledged by the decedent as his or her will or if it is established by clear and convincing evidence that the decedent erroneously signed a document intended to be the will of the decedent's spouse".[471]

According to the doctrine, the application of the *harmless error* in Colorado has been very limited. It applies only when there are minor execution errors.[472] However, the main focus is placed on the testamentary intent, as shown in the case decided in 2000, *Fisher* v. *Barnes*[473] (the court found that because the will was not signed by the testatrix or represented to others that this was her will, there was not enough clear and convincing evidence of her intent),[474] or in the case *Re Estate of Wiltfong*,[475] decided in 2006 (the court found that there was not clear and convincing evidence that the letter was intended to be the deceased's will).[476]

Slightly different, more relaxed approach, can be observed, for example, in Michigan. The state of Michigan has enacted its version of the *Uniform Probate Code*'s *harmless error* provision in 2000 (§ 700.2503 of *Michigan Compiled Laws*):

"Although a document or writing added upon a document was not executed in compliance with [the law], the document or writing is treated as if it had been executed in compliance with [the law] if the proponent of the document or writing establishes by clear and convincing evidence that the decedent intended the document or writing to constitute any of the following:

(a) The decedent's will.

(b) A partial or complete revocation of the decedent's will.

(c) An addition to or an alteration of the decedent's will.

---

471 § 15-11-503 of the *Colorado Revised Statutes*.

472 Daniel Miller, 'How Harmless Is Harmless? An In-Depth Look Into the Harmless Error Rule' [2013] ACTEC Foundation: Mary Moers Wenig Writing Competition Winners 1, 12.

473 Fisher v. Barnes, [2000] 13 P.3d 1231.

474 ibid.

475 Re Estate of Wiltfong, [2006] 148 P.3d 465.

476 ibid.

(d) A partial or complete revival of the decedent's formerly revoked will or of a formerly revoked portion of the decedent's will".[477]

One of the published cases was decided by two instances in 2002 (*Re Estate of Smith*).[478] The deceased one day after executing her will met with her church pastor and executed a document, in the Korean language, which the parties has agreed is translated as follows:

"I WANT TO DONATE $150,000 TO GOD IN ORDER TO BUILD A CHURCH".

Following the testatrix' death, the church claimed this document was a codicil to her original will, while her family said that the document expressed her present intent to give the church money. The probate court identified the central issue as whether to admit the document into probate, rather than the construction of the document, and determined that for a document to be considered a will or codicil, testamentary intent must be apparent from the writing itself. The probate court concluded that, on its face, the document at issue was not a testamentary instrument because it made no reference to death, a prior will, its effective date, or the intent of the deceased that it became effective upon her death, nor was it physically attached to a will. Concluding that the document was not a testamentary instrument, the probate court denied its admission and granted summary disposition in favour of respondents. On appeal, petitioner argued, in essence, that the probate court erred in granting respondents' motion for summary disposition on the basis of its conclusion that extrinsic evidence is not permitted to establish the testamentary intent of a document.[479] The second-instance court has stated that intent that a document constitutes a testator's will can be established by extrinsic evidence, including, for a holographic will, portions of the document that are not in the testator's handwriting. According to this court, the burden of proof that the document constitutes a valid disposition upon death is to be shown by clear and convincing evidence that the decedent intended the document to constitute his will or codicil. In this case, by failing to allow for the admission of extrinsic evidence, the first-instance court deprived petitioner of the opportunity to make such a showing. This is why in sum, the first-instance court erred in granting summary disposition on the basis that the docu-

---

477 § 700.2503 of *Michigan Compiled Laws*.
478 Re Estate of Smith, [2002] 252 Michigan Appeals Reports 120.
479 ibid.

ment at issue failed to reflect testamentary intent. Thus, summary disposition, according to the second-instance court, was improper.[480]

Interesting were also the facts of the *Re Estate of Smoke* case, decided there (Michigan) in 2007.[481] The testator has created a will in 1977. The will left only $1,000 to the respondent, who was a young child when the will was made, and it left the remainder of deceased estate to his siblings. Respondent objected to the admission of the will to probate because he claimed to possess letters, written by the deceased, that purportedly expressed the deceased testamentary intent that, after his death, respondent should receive all property of the deceased. In one of the letters written in 2002, the deceased has written:

> "I MENTION THIS TO YOU, AS YOU ARE MY ONLY OFFSPRING (NEXT OF KIN), SHOULD I DIE, OR BECOME UNABLE TO CONDUCT MY OWN AFFAIRS. AT LEAST YOU WILL HAVE SOME IDEA OF WHAT ASSETS ARE INVOLVED IN COURT LITIGATION, AND CAN REPRESENT MY LEGAL INTERESTS, AS MY AGENT; IF THIS SHOULD BECOME NECESSARY. YOU CAN PRESENT THIS LETTER TO MY LAWYER(S) AS PROOF OF MY INTENT THAT YOU SHOULD ACT AS MY AGENT IN THE ABOVE MATTERS. OKAY? SO FAR, I AM IN GOOD HEALTH, AND ABLE TO CONDUCT MY OWN AFFAIRS."
>
> "SO, IF THE LAND PASSES TO YOU UPON MY DEATH BE SMART, AND DON'T CAVE INTO PRESSURE TO UNLOAD THE LAND FOR PEANUTS."[482]

In another letter, directed to his sister and brother, he has written:

> "I FEEL THAT THE PROPERTY SHOULD BE PARTITIONED IN 3 EQUAL PARCELS OF APPROXIMATELY 50± ACRES TO RESOLVE THE ISSUE OF 'WHO OWNS WHAT' AND TO RESOLVE THIS LEGAL IMPASSE ONCE AND FOR ALL. I AM GETTING OLDER AND I WANT TO AVOID ANY PROBLEMS OF BEING ABLE TO DEVISE MY SHARE OF THE 152 ACRES TO MY SON, TIM SMOKE, IF I SHOULD EXPIRE UNEXPECTEDLY. TIM SHOULD NOT HAVE TO BE CONCERNED ABOUT GETTING INVOLVED IN LEGAL SQUABBLES ABOUT WHO OWNS WHAT PART OF THE 152 ACRES WHEN HE IS ON ACTIVE DUTY IN THE ARMY. I BELIEVE I WOULD BE REMISS IN MY OBLIGATIONS AS HIS FATHER TO LEAVE HIM AN EXPENSIVE LEGAL HEADACHE THAT CAN BE AVOIDED."[483]

---

480   ibid.
481   Re Estate of Smoke, [2007] Michigan Court of Appeals 273114.
482   ibid.
483   IBID.

The first-instance court rejected the letters as wills that has modified the 1977 will, finding that the letters do not meet the requirements of a formal will under the Michigan law, because they were not witnessed. The court has also noticed that it could have been treated as if it had been executed in compliance with the *harmless error* rule if the proponent of the document or writing established by clear and convincing evidence that the deceased intended the document or writing to constitute his will. The court determined that the purpose of the statute is to permit a probate court to overlook technical deficiencies in what clearly stands as a clear, accurate, written statement of the deceased's testamentary intent. However, to invoke the Michigan *harmless error* provision, the proponent of a document must demonstrate, by clear and convincing evidence, that the deceased intended the document to state the deceased's testamentary intent, whether through "a more recent will, or a partial or complete revocation, or an addition or alteration of the decedent's will, or a partial or complete revival of a formerly revoked will or a formerly revoked portion of a will." It has stated, that it is important to note that the proponent of the document must demonstrate that the document itself represents a valid and more recent testamentary instrument. In other words, it is not enough that a document reflects the deceased's intent to someday make changes to his will, or that it hints that the deceased has long abandoned the intent embodied and formalized in the will, or even that it expresses the deceased's regret about ever making the will in the first place. Here, the court placed substantial emphasis on the fact that the two letters with purported testamentary effect did not contain deceased's signature, so it was highly unlikely that either of them were intended to carry out the deceased's testamentary wishes. The court found that the lack of signature fatally undermined respondent's reliance on them as testamentary instruments, because the Michigan's *harmless error* provision was not intended to remedy such a glaring void in a will's formation.[484] This view was also accepted by the second-instance court.[485]

Widely commented was also the case decided in Michigan in 2018 (*Estate of Horton*)[486]. According to the facts of the case, the testator left behind a suicide note that included testamentary instructions which he typed, ending with a typed signature, on his cell phone. The court observed that an electronic note, which was unwitnessed and undated contrary to the re-

---

484 ibid.
485 ibid.
486 Re Estate of Horton, [2018] 925 N.W.2d 207.

quirements for holographic wills in Michigan, does not meet the formal requirements for a will. However, the will was admitted to probate by invoking the *harmless error* provision, assuming, *inter alia*, that a digital image can qualify as a writing, what is necessary in the Michigan's law for a will to be valid.[487]

These examples show a very interesting approach to the *harmless error* doctrine, finding the primacy of intent, and not searching for the faults of the will. This is an important guideline on how to reflect the testator's last wishes, and seems to be recognized somewhat differently from many other jurisdictions that apply the principle of *harmless error*.

Another US state that has adopted the *harmless error* rule is the state of New Jersey. It has happened in 2005 when the § 3B:3-3 of the *New Jersey Revised Statutes* came into force. According to this provision:

> "Although a document or writing added upon a document was not executed in compliance with [the law], the document or writing is treated as if it had been executed in compliance with [the law] if the proponent of the document or writing establishes by clear and convincing evidence that the decedent intended the document or writing to constitute:
> (1) the decedent's will;
> (2) a partial or complete revocation of the will;
> (3) an addition to or an alteration of the will; or
> (4) a partial or complete revival of his formerly revoked will or of a formerly revoked portion of the will".[488]

The first case published since the passage of the *harmless error* statute was the case *Re Probate of Will and Codicil of Macool*.[489] The deceased executed a will in 1995 through her attorney and named her husband as the sole beneficiary and his children, grandchildren and great-grandchildren as contingent beneficiaries. After her husband has died, she went to her attorney to change her will and brought a handwritten note that reflected her wish to add as a beneficiary her niece, and that her home be left in her family. After she left the attorney's office, he prepared a draft will based on their conversations, but before reviewing it, she has died. Her niece attempted to admit the draft will to probate despite there being no signature of the tes-

---

487 Hirsch, 'Technology Adrift: In Search of a Role for Electronic Wills' (n 83) 854 ff.
488 § 3B:3-3 of the *New Jersey Revised Statutes*.
489 Re Probate of Will and Codicil of Macool, [2010] 416 N.J. Superior Court 298.

tatrix or witnesses. She relied on the *harmless error* rule and argued that the deceased intended for the draft will to be her will. The first-instance court found that the will does not meet the statutory formalities, the deceased intended her niece to be included in her testamentary plan, however, the deceased did not intend the draft will to be her will and therefore the will could not be probated due to the *harmless error* rule. The court also held that a signature by a testator is necessary for the *harmless error* rule to apply. The second-instance court found that there was not clear and convincing evidence, that the deceased would have intended the draft will to be her will. The second-instance court ruled that for *harmless error* to be applied in this case, the proponent must have proved by "clear and convincing evidence that (1) the decedent actually reviewed the document in question and (2) thereafter gave her final assent on it". This was not met in the case. The second item the second-instance court focused on was the court's ruling that in order for *harmless error* to apply there needed to be a signature by the testator. The court has stated that the *harmless error* statute is to fix execution errors and that an execution error in signature should not prevent the *harmless error* rule from applying. Therefore, the second-instance court found that a will could be admitted to probate without the testator's signature through the *harmless error* rule as long as there is clear and convincing evidence of the testator's intent.[490] What's more interesting is that in the doctrine it was commented that since the court has established a broad understanding of the *harmless error* rule, the notes of the testatrix should have been approved as a holographic codicil through the *harmless error* rule, since it has reflected her intent.[491] However, this has not happened.

A very interesting example of the New Jersey's use of the provision on *harmless error* is also the case decided in 2012.[492] In this case, the deceased, a trust and estates attorney with fifty years of experience, passed away in 2009. His only next of kin were his deceased brother's three children, of whom he had a relationship only with one and told his friends that he was leaving the estate to him. Two month's after he died, a fourteen page will was found with no signatures by the decedent and no witnesses. On the cover page it was written:

"ORIGINAL MAILED TO H.W. VAN SCIVER, 5/20/2000".

---

490 ibid.
491 Miller, 'How Harmless Is Harmless? An In-Depth Look Into the Harmless Error Rule' (n 472) 21.
492 Re Estate of Ehrlich, [2012] 427 N.J. Superior Court 64.

The will has named Sciver as the executor and one of his brother's children as a beneficiary of 75% of the estate. The original document was never found. The first-instance court found that the deceased created the will and although it was not executed correctly his writing on the first page demonstrated clear and convincing evidence that it was "final assent" that the document was his will and admitted it to probate. The second-instance court upheld the ruling. The court looked into the fact that the beneficiary was the only relative the deceased had a relationship with and that the will was prepared in a professional manner. It has looked into the final assent of the unexecuted will, and found that the deceased telling others that he made a will that would leave the majority of his estate to his relative was clear and convincing evidence of his final assent.[493] As commented in the doctrine, this case seems to be the broadest reading of the *harmless error* statute.[494]

Another example of the *harmless error* doctrine is the one from the state of California which has adopted the rule in 2009 (§ 6110 subsection 2 of *California Probate Code*). However, the California's *harmless error* statute does not follow the section 2-503 of the *Uniform Probate Code* word for word but allows errors to be fixed if the "proponent of the will establishes by clear and convincing evidence that, at the time the testator signed the will, the testator intended the will to constitute the testator's will".[495]

The first widely reported case in California regarding *harmless error* was decided in 2011 (*Estate of Stoker*)[496]. In 1997, the decedent executed a will naming beneficiaries of his personal property and leaving the residue of his estate to the trustee of a trust he created that same day. In 2005, decedent executed a handwritten document that expressly revoked the 1997 trust. The will was not signed by any witnesses. The major issue in this case was that the 2005 will did not follow attestation rules because it was never signed by the two witnesses. It could not be considered a holographic will because it was not in the deceased's handwriting. The second-instance court found that the deceased had intent to revoke the 1997 will and that the 2005 will was to be probated because it was intended to be the deceased will, even though it was executed incorrectly. The court found that it was the legislative intent to not invalidate wills due to improper execu-

---

493 ibid.

494 Miller, 'How Harmless Is Harmless? An In-Depth Look Into the Harmless Error Rule' (n 472) 22.

495 § 6110(2) of *California Probate Code*.

496 Re Estate of Stoker, [2011] 122 California Reporter 3d 529.

tion and found that applying the *harmless error* rule would be following the legislative intent.[497]

Another interesting case decided in California, was the case *Re Estate of Richards*, that was filed in 2008, and finally decided in 2011.[498] There were two wills in question, the first had supposedly testator's signature but no witness signatures and the second will had two witness' signatures but not the signature of the testator. The court did not admit the documents into probate and highlighted that the *harmless error* rule should not apply due to lack of clear and convincing evidence of testator's intent. As noticed in the doctrine, the court looked at many different factors to determine that *harmless error* rule shouldn't apply to the case.[499] These factors were, *inter alia*, the age of the testator, the mistakes found in the drafting of the will, the pages not being stapled together, the witnesses not knowing who prepared the will, the expert testimony declaring that they were unable to tell who signed the will, and the improper execution.[500]

As estimated in the doctrine, the Californian solution can be named as a "partial" *harmless error* since a statute can only cure some deviations from the law, not all of them.[501] The language of the *harmless error* provision reveals that the rule only applies to instruments that do not comply with attestation defects.[502] California's version of the doctrine might salvage a would-be will that has one witness or that was signed by two people who were not "present at the same time", but it cannot cure problems related to the testator's signature.[503]

Other US states that has adopted the doctrine of *harmless error* has followed the section 2-503 of the *Uniform Probate Code*, certainly sometimes with changes. For example, the state of Ohio has not adopted the *Uniform Probate Code*'s *harmless error* doctrine in its entirety. Ohio's version of *harmless error* (*Ohio Revised Code* section 2107.24), provides as follows:

---

497 ibid.
498 Re Estate of Richards, [2011] B226261.
499 Miller, 'How Harmless Is Harmless? An In-Depth Look Into the Harmless Error Rule' (n 472) 9.
500 ibid.
501 David Horton, 'Partial Harmless Error For Wills: Evidence From California' (2018) 103 Iowa Law Review 2027.
502 Gökalp Y Güre, 'No Paper? No Problem: Ushering in Electronic Wills Through California's "Harmless Error" Provision' (2016) 49 University of California Davis Law Review 1955, 1957 ff.
503 Horton, 'Partial Harmless Error For Wills: Evidence From California' (n 501) 2048.

"(A) If a document that is executed that purports to be a will is not exe-cuted in compliance with the requirements of [the law], that docu-ment shall be treated as if it had been executed as a will in compliance with the requirements of that section if a probate court, after holding a hearing, finds that the proponent of the document as a purported will has established, by clear and convincing evidence, all of the following:
(1) The decedent prepared the document or caused the document to be prepared.
(2) The decedent signed the document and intended the document to constitute the decedent's will.
(3) The decedent signed the document under division (A)(2) of this section in the conscious presence of two or more witnesses. As used in division (A)(3) of this section, 'conscious presence' means within the range of any of the witnesses' senses, excluding the sense of sight or sound that is sensed by telephonic, electronic, or other distant commu-nication".[504]

This section was applied, for example, to validate an electronic will drafted on a tablet in 2013 (*Estate of Castro*).[505] In that case, the deceased was ad-mitted to a hospital and advised that he would die without a blood transfu-sion. He declined the transfusion for religious reasons, and then began talking with his two brothers about his will. Neither of his brothers had a paper, pen or pencil, so one brother took notes on a tablet. The decedent dictated the will while his brother handwrote it after discussing it. The three and decedent's nephew all signed the will on the tablet. Decedent then died, and his brother held onto the tablet continuously and had a password to it since then. The court has admitted it to probate finding, by clear and convincing evidence that the deceased signed the will, that he in-tended the document to be his last will and that the will was signed in the presence of two or more witnesses.[506] It seems like the approach to the *harmless error* in Ohio is liberal, however, it is noted that the case was an uncontested proceeding, so there was no one arguing that it should not be admitted to probate.[507]

In light of the above, the American version of the *dispensing power* doc-trine differs from the source not only in name but also in scope. The use of

---

504 § 2107.24 of *Ohio Revised Code*.
505 Re Estate of Castro, [2014] 27 Quinnipiac Probate Law Journal 412.
506 ibid.
507 *Cf.* Jessica Uzcategui, 'Application of the Harmless Error Doctrine in California and Beyond' (2015) 21 California Trusts & Estates Quarterly 1, 3.

the so-called *harmless error* in individual states varies, it is not uniform. In general, the impression is given that not all defects in wills can be cured this way, but the basic indicator of this process is the clear and convincing evidence of testamentary intent.[508] In the American approach usually there is a search for some elements of the will that can be considered as the "essential elements". This is not, of course, the practice of each American state, but it is also possible to observe this kind of tendencies there. Of course, there are also systems such as New Jersey or Michigan, where the significance of formal defects is diminished by the testator's intent proven by means of clear and convincing evidence. This is an interesting model, because in individual states the functions performed by some wills formalities are viewed differently and their significance is also different.

5. Selected case-law based on the favor testamenti approach

When analysing solutions based on taking into account the testator's intent at the expense of formal requirements, it is still necessary to pay attention to those legal systems which, despite the existing regulations based on the *strict compliance* regulations, take a generous approach to the issue of the lack of wills formal requirements by applying the *favor testamenti* rule, commonly known worldwide as the rule of interpretation of the testator's will. As already suggested, this rule therefore begins to take on a second meaning at times, and serves to interpret not only the will, but also the rules that are to reflect that will.

According to the above, Spanish law can be presented as one of the examples of judicial tenets to mitigate formal requirements using the principle of *favor testamenti*. It has to be mentioned that the case law of that jurisdiction defines the formal requirements of the will as fundamental requirements for the protection of the testation process,[509] but this does not mean that their observance is rigorous in every case. Outside the area in which the exhaustion of formal rigorism is used as a guarantee of freedom of testation, a tendency to relax compliance with testamentary formalities can be affirmed when their strict observance would lead to the nullity of

---

508 *Cf.* Dorman (n 134); Horton, 'Tomorrow's Inheritance: The Frontiers of Estate Planning Formalism' (n 261); Langbein, 'Absorbing South Australia's Wills Act Dispensing Power in the United States: Emulation, Resistance, Expansion' (n 94); Crawford (n 36).

509 STSJC Cataluña, 30.05.2016, [2016] STSJC 3774. *Cf.* Cossío (n 345).

the will, despite the fact that there is no doubt about the intent of the testator when drafting the last will provisions. In the recent case law, an inspiring thought can be found: "the nullity of a will cannot be exaggeratedly formalistic, so as not to damage the principle of the supreme sovereignty of the will of the testator".[510]

This seems to be a ground for the interpretation of wills formalities law[511] since, as the doctrine underlines, the requirement for a declaration of last will to comply with the testamentary formalities, present in Spanish law, has often been modulated by the courts in order to respect the freedom of testation.[512] The idea presented by the courts was best reflected in one of the judgements: "what cannot be admitted is that the trees of an extreme formalism prevent the forest of the testator's last will from being seen, or in other words, that the rigorous and reverential fulfilment of the testamentary forms, beyond what is strictly indispensable, hides the very essence of this type of *mortis causa* legal transactions, which is none other than the exercise of the right of a person to dispose of his estate after his death".[513] In this light, there is no doubt, therefore, that the Spanish case-law is trying to mitigate its excessive rigour of testamentary formalities by opening up an anti-formalistic interpretation line, as it is sometimes indicated, especially in those cases where the formality omitted is merely incidental and irrelevant.[514]

The abovementioned standard can be seen, for example, in the following cases. In the case decided in 2014, an 82-year-old illiterate testator prepared a will in such a way that he agreed on his last will with his daughter, who passed it on to a notary, and a notary after preparing a will has read it, after which the testator, accepting will provisions, nodded his head that he agreed. The court considered that "in this case, it is credited that the will was read in its entirety and aloud by the notary after the testator had waived the right to do so, and that it was also signed", this is why it was decided that "it meets the necessary requirements for validity".[515] All this has happened despite the fact that the law there (Article 697(2) of the *Código Civil*) provides for two witnesses to be present when the testator does not or cannot read the will himself, and the witnesses were not present. In

---

510 STS, 20.03.2013, [2013] STS 4755.
511 *Cf.* Sergio Cámara Lapuente, 'New Developments in the Spanish Law of Succession' (2007) 2007 InDret 2, 20 ff.
512 Aloy (n 17) 12 ff.
513 SAP Girona, 17.03.2003, [2003] AC 756.
514 Aloy (n 17) 13.
515 SAP Valencia, 15.12.2004, [2014] SAP 1202.

another case, decided in 2004, where the validity of the holographic will was concerned, a will that was partially typed was treated as meeting the formal requirements, even though the law requires for its validity to be handwritten. The court stated that it took into consideration that "the nucleus device was written autographically, with the date also handwritten, while the typed words act as a template with suspension points on which the testator writes, basically her personal data, so that correctly the essential solemnities were considered to have been fulfilled".[516] A very interesting reasoning was also the base for the case decided in Spain in 2011,[517] concerning the significance of the testator's signature. According to the facts of the case, the testator being at the age of 96 has prepared his eighteenth will and signed it differently than the previous wills. When deciding on the matter, it was pointed out that it is not so much the use of a particular style or modality that identifies the author that is important, but rather the existence of the intention to create a particular act. The decisive factor is that the signature is intended to emphasise the unquestionable will of the signatory, whether he does so using his traditional form of signature or otherwise.[518]

There are many other examples of case law there where the formal requirements were not looked at very strictly. As the doctrine there indicates, all this is the result of the fact that the principle of *favor testamenti*[519] has been taken into account in interpreting the rules in force, reducing the formalistic approach to a minimum.[520] However, according to the doctrine there, this does not mean that all the formalities for drawing up a will can be waived.[521] According to this opinion, the relaxation of formalism must be based on the functions carried out by the rules on the form of wills,[522] which – as it has been said - are primarily intended to guarantee the testator's freedom to express and preserve his will.[523] This means that the formalities relating to the authenticity of the will are necessary and formal relaxation is only possible if there is no doubt as to the intent of the testator.

---

516 AP Baleares, 17.10.2004, [2005] JUR 21892.
517 STS, 5.5.2011, [2012] STS 1101.
518 Aloy (n 17) 22 ff.
519 Lidia Arnau Raventos, 'The Formal Validity Of The Mortis Causa Provisions In The Regulations 650/2012 (EU): An Article on Spanish Law' (2016) 22 ILSA Journal of International & Comparative Law 515, 525.
520 Aloy (n 17) 28 ff.
521 ibid 29.
522 Merlini (n 348).
523 Aloy (n 17) 29.

To this effect, the changes to the form of the will, regardless of the current wording of the form rules, are to be aimed at, as this is the spirit of the times in this area.[524] This is why it is emphasised that the law should take into account and follow technological and social requirements of the wills law.[525]

The mechanism based on the principle of respect for the testator's last will is also known, for example, in Polish law. The most characteristic feature of this is its use within the framework of the so-called conversion of wills, which is the result of the courts' judicial activity. The basis for providing judgements in this respect has always been the need to reflect the testator's actual intentions, hence in specific cases the testator's *animus testandi* has been referred to as a premise leading to the maintenance of the will decision, albeit in a different form than that originally chosen by the testator.[526]

One of the most frequently quoted rulings based on this mechanism in the Polish literature is the ruling of the Supreme Court decided in 1981,[527] where it was definitively acknowledged that from the point of view of a will conversion, it is possible to maintain the testator's declaration of last will, regardless of whether the will's invalidity is the result of the testator's failure to comply with the formal rigours provided for in this type of disposition, or for other reasons (e.g. participation of a person not authorised to withdraw the declaration of will), if only the testator's *mortis causa* declaration as a legal action achieves the intended effect in another legal form provided for. The content of this ruling, moreover, emphasises that "there is no doubt that social considerations play a significant role, namely the desire to respect the testator's last will",[528] which prompted the court to seek the possibility of keeping the defective will in force. This view was recalled, for example, in the judgement of second-instance court from 2017.[529] The court has stated, that it is assumed in the judicature that the invalidity of the will referred to in Article 951 of the *Kodeks cywilny* (will made before an official) due to the testator's mistaken idea that he declares

---

524 Cobas Cobiella and de Joz Latorre (n 92) 62 ff.
525 Marta Otero Crespo, 'La sucesión en los «bienes digitales». La respuesta plurileg-islativa española' (2019) 6 Revista de Derecho Civil 89, 89 ff.
526 Maciej Rzewuski, 'Konwersja testamentu' in Piotr Stec and Mariusz Załucki (eds), *50 lat kodeksu cywilnego. Perspektywy rekodyfikacji* (Wolters Kluwer 2015) 412 ff.
527 III CZP 68/80, [1981] OSNCP 6.
528 ibid.
529 III Ca 645/16, [2017] Legalis 2053415.

his last will towards a person entitled to accept such declarations in accordance with Article 951 § 1 of the *Kodeks cywilny* may be considered - in a specific case - as a special circumstance within the meaning of Article 952 § 1 of the *Kodeks cywilny* (oral will), as a result of which it is impossible or very difficult to maintain the ordinary form of the will, and due to this, such a will under conversion can be accepted as a valid extraordinary will (as an oral will). In this regard, it should be made clear that the Polish law provides for the content of Article 952 of the *Kodeks cywilny* that, if there is a probability of imminent death of the testator or if, due to extraordinary circumstances, the observance of the ordinary form of the testament is impossible or very difficult, the testator may declare his last will orally in the simultaneous presence of at least three witnesses.[530] This is why, flawed ordinary will, in the mentioned circumstances, can be converted into the extraordinary will (oral will), certainly only if the requirements for such a will are met.

The use of the *'favor testamenti'* rule can also be seen in Polish law in another example, not related to the institution of conversion. This was the case, to mention just one example, in the situation of an oral will, where the protocol for making it up was incorrectly prepared. The question was whether it was possible to re-draw up such a protocol when the first one is faulty. The court deciding this case has stated that taking into account the trend represented in the case law based on the principle of *favor testamenti*, "which requires that the testator's intent be kept as much as possible", has stated that the possibility of re-drafting the protocol referred to in Article 952(2) of the *Kodeks cywilny* should also be allowed in the case of a formal defect of the original document if the time limit indicated in that provision has not yet expired.[531] As the court has evaluated, it is a consequence of "the theory of the will and the resulting principle of *'favor testamenti'*, which applies not only to the interpretation of wills, but also to the interpretation of the rules on the form of wills".[532]

Polish jurisprudence has repeatedly pointed out the demand for such an interpretation of the provisions on the form of wills,[533] which provides the furthest possible guarantees that the order of succession will be shaped in

---

530 Jan Gwiazdomorski and Andrzej Mączyński, *Prawo spadkowe w zarysie* (Państwowe Wydawnictwo Naukowe 1985) 100 ff.

531 V CSK 254/17, [2018] OSNC 3.

532 ibid.

533 *Cf.*, e.g.: Jacek Wierciński, 'Uwagi o zamiarze testowania (animus testandi)' (2012) 2012 Przegląd Sądowy 132.

accordance with the testator's real will.[534] It has been stressed that an equitable interpretation is extremely important, and the purpose it serves - to reflect the testator's last will as closely as possible - is very important from the point of view of the function of succession law.[535] The courts have set an example of this on many occasions when applying the law. It can therefore be assumed that, despite the relatively strict wording of the regulations in force in Poland (Art. 958 of the *Kodeks cywilny*: A testament made with the infringement of the provisions of [the law] shall be null and void), the practice finds the need to mitigate the effects of formal rigour, although Polish law in this area does not provide for any mechanism allowing this in the substantive law. The easing of formalism is therefore part of a generous interpretation of the law.

It should be added that Polish law also knows the statutory mechanism, the application of which is similar to that of genuine *substantial compliance*, however – due to the binding law - it concerns only holographic wills. In this light it has to be reminded that according to the Art. 949(1) of the *Kodeks cywilny*, a holographic will must be, *inter alia*, dated by the testator. However, according to the Art. 949(2) of the *Kodeks cywilny*, lack of a date shall not result in the invalidity of a hand-written testament if it does not raise doubts as to the testator's capacity to draw up a testament, contents of the testament and the mutual relationships among several testaments. Based on that, a flawed holographic will can be treated as valid. This was the case, for example, in the judgement decided in 1992, where the court has stated that the law entails wills' invalidity only if the court proceedings do not lead to the removal of the doubts referred to in Art. 949(2) of the *Kodeks cywilny*.[536] What is more interesting is that, despite the wording of the law, courts are trying to use this mechanism to different forms of wills. This was, for example, the background of the case decided in 1977,[537] where it was stated that an undated will made before an official may be valid despite the fact that the provision of Art. 951(2) of the *Kodeks cywilny* does not contain a mechanism similar to the one included in the Art. 949(2) of the *Kodeks cywilny*. According to the court, the legislator generally regulates typical situations, and such a situation may be

---

534 *Cf.* Rzewuski, 'Wykładnia testamentu a okoliczności zewnętrzne towarzyszące testowaniu' (n 368) 231 ff.

535 Grzegorz Wolak, 'Animus testandi na tle orzecznictwa Sądu Najwyższego' (2015) 2015 Rejent 1, 1 ff.

536 III CZP 90/92, [1993] OSNCP 1-2.

537 IV CR 494/77, [1978] OSNCP 11.

the omission of a date in a will drawn up by a citizen who is not always aware of the criteria for the validity of his legal acts. On the other hand, the omission of a date by an official (notary, commune head and other appointed persons), who has the required knowledge of these criteria, constitutes a pathological phenomenon - as evidenced by the uniqueness of this case - which does not need to be regulated directly in the act. In the opinion of this court, a correct interpretation of the binding law cannot justify the conclusion that the consequences of the lack of a date are to be more detrimental to the effectiveness of the testator's last will if, in an attempt to ensure such effectiveness, he chose the form of an official will rather than if he had only made use of his handwritten will.[538]

There is no doubt, therefore, that Polish case-law, using in practice the principle of a generous interpretation of the existing legal regulations, has often sought to maintain the testator's last intent, even when it appeared *prima facie* to be in conflict with the regulations in force.[539] Despite the lack of a clear legal basis for such an action, the *favor testamenti* principle expressed in Polish law as a standard for the interpretation of the content of wills (Art. 948 of the *Kodeks cywilny*: A testament must be interpreted so as to ensure the possibly fullest compliance with the testator's will) has on many occasions been a rescue for defective wills (drawn up against the regulations on form). Some of the flaws in such wills, certainly those of little importance, can therefore be cured in such way. It is, however, quite widely accepted in the doctrine that the current regulation on the form of wills is unsatisfactory, which for some commentators is just the beginning of a reflection on changes to this state of affairs,[540] including the introduction of a rule based on the doctrine of *substantial compliance* or its variations.

An example of a legal system where a generous interpretation of the law applies alongside a generous interpretation of a testator's last will is the German law. The doctrine there assumes, among other things, that the purpose of an interpretation of a will is to reveal a testator's intent and the form of a will is a condition for its effectiveness, hence sometimes a distinction is made between the construction of a will and the form of a will. The problem of interpretation of a last will and the problem of the form is therefore dealt with in two separate stages. The first step is to determine the testator's intent, while only later - as it is indicated - should it be clari-

---

538 ibid.
539 *Cf.* Wójcik (n 40) 190 ff.
540 Konrad Osajda, 'Wpływ rozwoju techniki na uregulowanie formy testamentu - rozważania de lege ferenda' (2010) 2010 Rejent 50, 51 ff.

fied whether the testator's intent has been declared in a proper form.[541] In this respect, it is believed, among other things, that private wills in particular, including holographic wills, are an instrument where there is plenty of room for interpretation, as the testator's intent is usually expressed there in an incomplete or unclear manner. Extrinsic evidence to the content of the will can also be used for interpretation.[542] This also applies to the completion of the will. However, the doctrine sometimes raises the contradiction of such reasoning with the purpose of the provisions on the form of wills.[543]

In this regard a very interesting is the judgement done there already in the 1935. One of the cases described in the literature was an attempt to validate a will recorded on a gramophone[544]. It is worth mentioning since it was considered there that although the authenticity of the will declared in that way raises no doubts, in accordance with the binding *Bürgerliches Gesetzbuch* provisions the will may not be declared with the use of other media except for one's own handwriting, and only the legislator could decide otherwise. Despite the attempt to qualify such will as a holographic one, declared finally as invalid (what was further slightly criticised by the doctrine), interesting reasoning is worth mentioning, namely the indication that the requirement of one's own handwriting should not be treated literally, and a voice recording may be practically treated as a one fulfilling the requirement of handwriting.[545] This reasoning shows that the need to reflect the intent of the testator was already being considered at the time, although it has not yet been successful. This was not the case a few decades later, in a judgment of the German Supreme Court that is, according to many, significant for the interpretation of the German law.[546] According to the facts of this case, the testatrix drew up her will in such a way that on the top and first inside of the folded sheet of paper she made her declaration of her last will, which she signed at the end of it (on the first inside of the folded sheet). She then observed that she had forgotten one disposition, which she had placed on the unsigned pages, as the previous pages no longer contained any space. She did not sign that disposition. The court pointed out that it is not the position of the signature that should decide

---

541 Solzbach (n 60) 183 ff.
542 ibid.
543 Knut Werner Lange, *Erbrecht* (C H Beck 2017) 79 ff.
544 Reichsgericht judgement of 18 July 1935, Deutsche Juristenzeitung 1935, p. 78.
545 See G. *Ponath, Die Beschränkungen der Testierfreiheit durch das Testamentsrecht*, Frankfurt-Mannheim 2006, s. 251.
546 *Cf.* Grundmann (n 61) 434 ff.

here, but the intent of the testator, and in its opinion, by adding something to the will, the testator usually has the intent to change the disposition, and such additions include *animus testandi*.[547] Another ruling of this court refers to the question of the will's hand-writing, which remained only as a tracing paper (a carbon copy) of a declaration of last will, the original of which was never found. In this case, too, the court, guided by the rule to keep the last will in force, recognised the admissibility of such a will.[548]According to the court, a carbon copy disclosed the individual characteristics of the testator's handwriting sufficiently and accurately to warrant the conclusion that it had been the testator himself who had wanted to make a disposition *mortis causa*.[549] Both decisions were widely commented and accepted in the German doctrine.[550] Of course, there are also other court decisions that follow the same approach. In general, even if there are voices in Germany to reform the binding law on testamentary formalities, there are also opinions that dispensation with some formalities may occur by the generous interpretation of the binding rules.[551]

The *favor testamenti* approach is a usual approach for continental European countries. In general, continental European countries are to be marked as strict compliance systems, where strict observance of the binding law shall apply. However, because of the social expectations and some other factors, the courts consider generous approach to testamentary intent as an important mean to solve succession cases. This could be seen, for example, in the Swedish law, in a case decided in 2012.[552] In this case a last will was transmitted to one of the beneficiaries by the text message sent on a smart phone. The first-instance court, analysing if the will can constitute a valid holographic will, has stated that since the introduction of the Swedish law on testamentary formalities (1958) society has undergone technological development that is unprecedented and that, in the facts of the case, the deceased wanted the text message to constitute his last will. Due to the unprecedented technological development and the impact of this development on the way people communicate, it should, in the opinion of the first-instance court, be possible in this way to declare one's will. In the light of the *favor testamenti* approach, which was never highlighted

---

547   BGH, 20.3.1974, [1974] NJW 1083.
548   BGH, 3.2.1967, [1967] BGHZ 47.
549   ibid.
550   *Cf.*, instead of many, Reinhard Zimmemann *in* Reid, De Waal and Zimmermann (n 31) 199.
551   Grundmann (n 61) 475 ff.
552   Tingsrätt, 16.11.2012, [2012] T5746-11

by the court, the text message shall be deemed to meet the requirements of a self-written and signed act. This is why, according to the first-instance court, the will was declared valid. However, the second-instance court has reversed this decision in 2013, declaring an obligation to strict interpretation of the Swedish law.[553] According to the court, the law permits no exception from the requirements of wills formalities.[554] But what is interesting about this case, is that the second-instance court was widely criticized by the doctrine.[555] There were voices that the legal formalities are "old-fashioned" and should be modernized.[556] It seems like more lenient approach to the formalities is postulated there.[557] Such approach can be seen, for example, in France, where courts are sometimes more flexible with the statutory requirements,[558] or in Hungary, where formal defects are not automatically void (only an interested party can object an informal will) and the courts emphasize the principle of *favor testamenti* to discover and fully implement the true intentions of the testator.[559]

In order to complete the picture of such an approach to formal requirements, it is also necessary to mention the *constructive trust* construction found in the case law of the American State of Florida.[560] It is an equitable device with dual objectives: to restore property to the rightful owner and to prevent unjust enrichment. This measure was first applied to informal wills in 1993. In the case of the *Estate of Tolin*,[561] the testator drew up an effective will. After a few years, he established an effective codicil, appointing another person as his heir, thereby changing his will. Later on, the testator wanted to withdraw the codicil and thus bring about the original

---

553 Hovrätt, 13.06.2013, [2013] T11306-12.

554 ibid.

555 See, for example, the statement of Margareta Brattström, who indicated the law to be "ancient". (in "SMS not a valid last will and testament" (2014) The Local of 24.02.2014, https://www.thelocal.se/20140224/sms-not-valid-last-will-and-testament-court.

556 *Cf.* Britta Olsson, *Handläggning av testamente - från upprättande till skifte* (Stockholms Universitet 2014) 15 ff.

557 *Cf.*, w.g.: Tatjana Westman, *Tolking av testamente* (Stockholms Universitet 2013) 41 ff.

558 For example the courts are accepting undated wills even though a date is a legal obligatory requirement. *Cf.* Cour de Cassation, 10.05.2007, [2007] Répertoire du Notariat Defrénois 1432.

559 *Cf.* Lajos Vékás *in* Reid, De Waal and Zimmermann (n 31) 269.

560 Elena Marty-Nelson and others, *Florida Wills, Trusts, and Estates. Cases and Materials* (Carolina Academic Press 2016) 815 ff.

561 Re Estate of Tolin, [1993] 622 So. 2d 988.

regulation of the will. He showed the codicil to his friend's lawyer and tore it up on his advice. The testator assumed that he had torn the original. After the testator's death, however, it turned out that he only destroyed the photocopy of the codicil. The Supreme Court of Florida stated that, in order to invalidate the codicil under the Florida Statute, the testator would have to break the original document, therefore in this case the codicil remained in force. However, there was to be *constructive trust* in the original will. The court found that the testator had the intent to annul the codicil and was only exposed to an error as to the originality of the deed during its execution. Without *constructive trust*, the codicil heir would have benefited from the testator's mistake at the expense of the person originally intended.[562] This construction was applied certainly also in different cases.[563]

In this light, there is little doubt that the quest to reflect the last will is not just the domain of the doctrine of *substantial compliance* and its variations. It is a much broader approach, taking into account modern technological solutions and the needs of society. Despite some criticism, there are many signs (in principle, all over the world) that a formalistic approach to succession law is no longer necessary. Rational, functional, subdued consideration of the testator's last intent, without prejudice to legal transactions, is a thought that is increasingly emerging in the systems of succession law, including those that think about the wills formalities in terms of the need for a *strict compliance*. For this reason, it is precisely in these countries, and therefore specifically in Continental Europe, that there is room for a tool that could, to a greater extent than before, reflect the testator's last will in the case of wills drawn up informally. However, the scope of the formalities that could be involved here requires some discussion. In the light of the solutions presented above, it is worth considering how far such a mechanism could reach and whether it would allow the objectives of the provisions on the form of wills to be fulfilled in the various systems. This requires further considerations, which, in order to determine whether some or all of the formalities for making wills should be dispensed with, are to consider the functions which those formalities may be performing.

---

562 ibid.

563 John CP Goldberg and Robert H Sitkoff, 'Torts and Estates: Remedying Wrongful Interference with Inheritance' (2013) 65 Stanford Law Review 335, 349 ff.

(4) Functions of the wills formalities regulations in the light of mechanisms to relax its rigour

1. *Introductory remarks*

The reality of applying the provisions of the law of succession, mistakes made by testators caused by an erroneous interpretation of the applicable legal norms as well as a lack of awareness of the requirements imposed on wills by legal regulations, have often led in practice to the declaration of invalidity of the will[564] and, as a consequence, to a statutory succession, incompatible with the intent of the testator.[565] In many cases, this has also led to the dissatisfaction of the public, whose legal awareness of the succession law is not, as may be assumed, high.[566] The conflict between the automatism of succession law formalism and flexible legal circulation needs is growing. It is for this reason, among others, that some legislators have decided to introduce into their legal systems solutions to keep the defective wills in force (as valid wills).

The practice of applying individual solutions in this area shows that in the vast majority of cases the testator's intention takes precedence over formalism.[567] However, the problem of unsatisfactory legislative solutions in the area of regulations on the form of wills still exists, as one might think. This can be seen especially in the context of the legal regulations of European countries where the principle of *strict compliance* continues to be respected.[568]

In this regard, and following the latest trends, it is important to mention the voices emphasizing that, wherever it is possible, there should be a complete abandonment of formalism, *inter alia*, in order to encourage people

---

564 *Cf.* Harry T Edwards, 'To Err Is Human, But Not Always Harmless: When Should Legal Error Be Tolerated?' (1995) 70 New York University Law Review 1167.

565 *Cf.* Miller, 'How Harmless Is Harmless? An In-Depth Look Into the Harmless Error Rule' (n 472) 1 ff.

566 Załucki, 'About the Need to Adjust the Regulations Regarding the Form of Will to the Modern Requirements' (n 14).

567 Horton, 'Tomorrow's Inheritance: The Frontiers of Estate Planning Formalism' (n 261).

568 *Cf.* Vukotic (n 377) 473 ff; Aloy (n 17).

to make use of legal instruments that fall under the scope of the law of succession. In this sense, the transition away from formalities is a right vehicle to achieve the goal of wider access to succession planning tools.[569] This is why it can be asked whether the application of a solution based on the doctrine of *substantial compliance* or its variations distorts the meaning of the provisions on the form of wills, and whether the provisions on the form of wills are still necessary and play an important role in the succession law. As it is sometimes suggested, the only reason for these provisions to be introduced in the modern legislation is the need to authenticate the testator.[570] Therefore, it is important to answer the question whether it is really so, or does wills formalities perform other essential functions in this area of law. Therefore, before the analysis to identify a proper theoretical model of a tool allowing for reflecting the testator's last will in the maze of surrounding formalism, consideration should be given to determining what functions are currently performed by the provisions on the form of wills and whether these functions should continue to be performed by the provisions on wills formalities in the future. While the assessment of the current practice in the systems that allow for the mitigation of formal requirements seems, in principle, positive, it is necessary to consider whether formalism in general still has any real functions in succession law and what should be taken into account when shaping the theoretical model to reflect the testator's last will.

In this respect, it has to be reminded that the requirement to comply with a specific form for a legal transaction is not, of course, traditionally typical only of wills or other *mortis causa* acts. It is, however, particularly characteristic of continental Europe legislation.[571] German law, for example, points out that the purpose of coercion at the level of the form of legal acts is to protect legal transactions, since in some cases, the person making the declaration of intent should be protected against ill-considered or too hasty obligations because of the risks involved in the act.[572] The form of a legal transaction may also have an informative function, for example by providing reliable information about the rights and obligations obtained.[573] In exceptional cases, the provisions providing for the obligation to comply with the form may aim to ensure that the activity can be effec-

---

569 Crawford (n 36) 269 ff.
570 ibid 293.
571 Załucki, *Videotestament. Prawo spadkowe wobec nowych technologii* (n 33) 167 ff.
572 Solzbach (n 60) 10 ff.
573 Zerres (n 200) 72 ff.

tively controlled by the authorities.[574] The same applies in other legal systems.[575] Dutch law states, for example, that the determination by the legislator of the form of a legal transaction may prevent uncertainty as to its validity.[576] French law indicates that such a provision is, for example, about proof of a given act.[577] In Poland, on the other hand, it is argued that the establishment of a specific form by the legislator serves to remove doubts as to whether a statement has been made, to facilitate evidence, to protect parties against ill-considered decisions, to make actions open to third parties, and to facilitate state control over the performance of legal actions.[578]

It has to be reminded that, as it is believed in the traditional view presented in the law of succession, where – as can be judged - the formalism of legal transactions has grown over the years to the fullest possible extent,[579] the functions of the provisions concerning the form of will are not only to authenticate the testator (as it has been suggested lately in the doctrine),[580] but also to provide reliable proof that the testator's action was intentional (testamentary intention),[581] that it was done without pressure from third parties,[582] and that the testator understood the seriousness of the action performed.[583] As it was already explained, this position gave grounds for distinguishing in the doctrine of succession law the four functions: 1) the evidentiary function, 2) the channelling function, 3) the cautionary function and 4) the protective function.[584] The importance of each

---

574 Jurgen Ellenberger, in *Palandt Bürgerliches Gesetzbuch Kommentar* (74th edn, CH Beck 2015) 109.

575 *Cf.* Samuel Fulli-Lemaire, 'Le formalisme en droit patrimonial de la famille: regard comparatiste' (2016) 17 Max Planck Private Law Research Paper 10 ff.

576 *Cf.* PHM Gerver, 'Het nieuwe erfrecht ingevoerd' [2003] Nederlands Juristenblad 72.

577 Henri Mazeaud, Leon Mazeaud and Jean Mazeaud, *Leçons de Droit Civil* (Editions Montchrestien 1999) 271.

578 Zbigniew Radwański (ed), *System prawa prywatnego, vol. 2, Prawo cywilne - część ogólna* (C H Beck 2008) 116.

579 *Cf.* Horton, 'Tomorrow's Inheritance: The Frontiers of Estate Planning Formalism' (n 261).

580 Crawford (n 36) 293.

581 *Cf.* Beinke (n 194) passim.

582 *Cf.* Ronald J JR Scalise, 'Undue Influence and the Law of Wills. A Comparative Analysis' (2008) 19 Duke Journal of Comparative and Intenational Law 41, 1 ff.

583 *Cf.* Pietro Rescigno, 'Il testatore anziano e la forma del testamento' [2017] Jus civile 382, 382 ff.

584 Langbein, 'Substantial Compliance with the Wills Act' (n 10) 492 ff.

of these functions is different in specific legislations on succession law, as well as their perception in the legal doctrine.[585]

This is all the more important because any consideration of the formal requirements for any disposition of property upon death, as it is traditionally believed, should first answer the question of whether the specific solutions meet the standard of form for a legal transaction such as a will set by the doctrine and individual legislators. Therefore, below I will consider whether these functions are still (and shall be) of any importance in the modern succession law, is there a standard that should be applicable in this regard and whether this standard will be complied with when using mechanisms to relax the rigour of wills formalities.

2. *The evidentiary function of the wills formalities regulations*

The risk of failure to preserve the testator's intentions, and therefore the impossibility of reconstructing it after his death, seems to support the need to construct legal norms to provide reliable evidence of the testator's intentions.[586] The reality in which the testator creates a will many years before his death is not unusual.[587] The passage of time does not serve to preserve certain events in human memory, therefore, in the vast majority of solutions found in the world, individual legislators decide to preserve the testator's will within a document, both private and public. The analysis of the existing variants in this respect *prima facie* indicates the necessity of existence of some kind of physical evidence of testation, which can be done

---

585 Some reflections on these functions have already been included in my recent book written in Polish: Załucki, *Videotestament. Prawo spadkowe wobec nowych technologii* (n 33) 169–195.

586 The broad analysis of this problem was already done by me in a different paper. *Cf.* Załucki, 'Evidentiary Function of the Provisions on the Form of Wills in the Contemporary Succession Law. Is the Complete Abandonment of Formalism Possible?' (n 45).

587 As an example, the results of research conducted in Poland on the files of inheritance cases can be shown, where the issues of making holographic wills were analysed. It was found that about 86% of wills were made by people over 60 years of age, and about 14% of wills were made by young adults. More than 7% of wills were made more than 3 years before the testator's death. See Liżyńska (n 59). Also, in the United States of America, a study conducted in the State of California found that, on average, wills were made about a decade before the testator's death. See Horton, 'Wills Law on the Ground' (n 59) 1129.

both during its execution and some time after.[588] As I have already observed, the legislators have noticed that any circumstance which, in the form prescribed by law, confirms facts related to an individual's *mortis causa* disposition may play an essential role in the sphere of cognition and establishment of facts relevant to the settlement of a given succession case.[589] For this reason, specific legal systems require a specific document to prove that the testation has occurred.[590] This requirement has different forms, ranging from the bequeather's handwriting of his last will in full, the bequeather's obligation to sign his last will or the public authority's obligation to draw up an appropriate protocol.[591] In principle, each of the forms of perpetuating the last will is primarily pursuing this - evidential - objective. Examples include the following data: French wills: holographic, official or mystical require a writing (Article 969 of the French *Code civil*).[592] The Dutch *Burgerlijk Wetboek* provides for the possibility of drawing up a will in the form of a notarial will or a holographic will deposited with a notary, and therefore also requires the existence of a written document (Article 4:94 of the *Burgerlijk Wetboek*).[593] The German *Bürgerliches Gesetzbuch* as part of the ordinary forms of will also lists notarial and holographic wills which obviously require a written document (§ 2232 and § 2247 of the *Bürgerliches Gesetzbuch*).[594] The English *Wills Act* 1837 provides for the existence of a writing for the validity of a will (Section 9 *Wills Act* 1837).[595] Similarly, under the *Probate Code* of the U.S. State of California, a will shall be in writing and signed (§ 6110 of the California Probate Code).[596] Even in the case of a special forms of will - an oral will - an appropriate

---

588 Załucki, 'Evidentiary Function of the Provisions on the Form of Wills in the Contemporary Succession Law. Is the Complete Abandonment of Formalism Possible?' (n 45).

589 *Cf.* Rosalind F Croucher and Prue Vines, *Succession: Families, Property and Death* (Lexis Nexis 2018).

590 Mathias Schmoeckel and Gerhard Otte (eds), *Europäische Testamentsformen* (Nomos 2011) passim.

591 Lucia Ruggeri, Ivana Kunda and Sandra Winkler (eds), *Family Property and Succession in EU Member States. National Reports on the Collected Data* (Sveučilište u Rijeci 2019).

592 *Cf.* Georges Wiederkehr and others, *Code Civil* (Dalloz 2014) 1225 ff.

593 *Cf.* Alain-Laurent Verbeke, 'Het nieuwe erfrecht international gestitueerd' [2003] Weekblad voor Privaatrecht, Notariat en Registratie 20, 20 ff.

594 *Cf.* Dieter Leipold, *Erbrecht* (Mohr Siebeck 2014) 89 ff.

595 *Cf.* John G Ross Martyn and others, *Theobald on Wills* (Thomson Reuters 2010) 3 ff.

596 *Cf.* Horton, 'Partial Harmless Error For Wills: Evidence From California' (n 501).

protocol is required (e.g. Article 952 § 2 of the Polish *Kodeks cywilny*,[597] § 2250(3) of the *Bürgerliches Gesetzbuch*,[598] § 2107.60 of *Ohio Revised Code*).[599] Similar solutions are provided for in most other legal systems, therefore, regardless of the specific statutory solutions, the existing rule is that the testation activity is immortalized in writing. A document is created from the testation activity. In principle, such solutions cannot be surprising. As I have already suggested, after all, the contemporary use of a document is the basis for the functioning of all institutions, including those that have any competence in the area of succession law.[600] The need to make various types of statements on a document in writing, although today it can be considered as anachronistic, accompanies citizens in everyday life.[601] Therefore, it also accompanies the law of succession, enjoying the greatest preference among all means of evidence encountered in court proceedings. In principle, it is impossible to find a legal system in which a document is not used to register testamentary intention.[602] This is done for the possibility to recreate this intention, as well as the opportunity to confirm testator's identity. The use of a document makes it also possible to state that the testator had the testamentary intention and that the behaviour undertaken by the testator constituted the creation of the will and not a different legal action.[603]

It should be noted that a similar position should be taken in the context of the mechanisms to relax the rigour of wills formalities met in some jurisdictions. The Israeli solution should be indicated here, for example, where, as fundamental part of a handwritten will or an oral will the writ-

---

597 *Cf.* Konrad Osajda, 'Sposoby stwierdzenia treści testamentu ustnego' [2013] Monitor Prawniczy 463.

598 *Cf.* Hubert Bartsch and Malte B Bartsch, *Das aktuelle Erbrecht* (Walhalla Fachverlag 2013).

599 Załucki, 'Evidentiary Function of the Provisions on the Form of Wills in the Contemporary Succession Law. Is the Complete Abandonment of Formalism Possible?' (n 45).

600 ibid.

601 Łukasz Dyląg, 'Dokument a dokument a dokument elektroniczny w prawie cywilnym - pojęcie i istota desygnatu' [2011] Prawo Mediów Elektronicznych 8; Dariusz Szostek, *Nowe ujęcie dokumentu w polskim prawie prywatnym ze szczególnym uwzględnieniem dokumentu w postaci elektronicznej* (C H Beck 2012) passim.

602 *Cf.* Reid, De Waal and Zimmermann (n 31) passim.

603 Załucki, 'Evidentiary Function of the Provisions on the Form of Wills in the Contemporary Succession Law. Is the Complete Abandonment of Formalism Possible?' (n 45).

ing is indicated (Section 25 of *Israeli Succession Law* חוק הירושה), and is included into the elements that are intended to reflect the content of the last will (referred to as *static formalities*).[604] Also the law of South Australia, where the Section 12(2) of *Wills Act* clearly states the need for a document to be in existence in order for the informal last will to be considered valid,[605] or the solution adopted in the Canadian province of Manitoba, in which Section 23 of *Manitoba Wills Act* requires the existence of a document or any writing on a document to be fully effective as thought it had been executed in compliance with all the formal requirements imposed by the law.[606] The same is true of other solutions of this kind. This can be also seen in the wills formalities case law. American case of *Estate of Castro* or Polish case dealing with the incorrect preparation of a protocol stating the existence of will can serve as examples. In the first one, the court has emphasized that a will shall be in writing, and one of the questions that it had to answer was whether testamentary intentions stored in an electronic document can constitute a writing.[607] In the latter, the protocol needed to be re-drawn up, and the court has considered its new version as the one that can cure a formal defect of the original document.[608] In each case, the existence of the document was investigated and only its existence entailed further actions in the pending proceedings in order to keep the will in force (as a valid will). There is no doubt, therefore, that regardless of whether the law of succession is formed in a world of *strict compliance* or in a world of *substantial compliance*, the requirement to preserve the last will appears to be necessary, and the medium used for this purpose is usually the document.

In the light of the above, as I have already explained,[609] the importance of a document in the area of testamentary formalities is vital. The legal science indicates that the term document comes from the Latin *documentum* and has been used in many languages for several hundred years.[610] As it

---

604 Menashe (n 54).
605 Ken Mackie, *Principles of Australian Succession Law* (3rd edn, Lexis Nexis 2017) 131 ff.
606 Lefebvre (n 80) 420 ff.
607 Re Estate of Castro, [2014] 27 Quinnipiac Probate Law Journal 412.
608 V CSK 254/17, [2018] OSNC 3.
609 Załucki, 'Evidentiary Function of the Provisions on the Form of Wills in the Contemporary Succession Law. Is the Complete Abandonment of Formalism Possible?' (n 45).
610 *Cf.* Szostek (n 601).

can be judged today, it has many meanings and functions.[611] In the legal literature there are at least three concepts of a document mentioned. It can be understood as a material medium, as an expression of human thoughts recorded on a material medium, or, as a medium of evidence. In this sense, the meaning of a term "document" is not uniformed and unambiguous. The modern concepts of it include any object that expresses a certain thought to be a document, and it does not necessarily have to be a writing, what in the context of a contemporary view of private law, seems very attractive.[612] This view is accepted in many legal systems, therefore, as can be evaluated, today there is a much broader concept of the term "document" in the world than the one traditionally understood. This term no longer refers only to the paper form. Australian solutions can serve as an example. The provision of Section 38 of *Victoria's Interpretation of Legislation Act 1984* defines this concept broadly: the word document includes, in addition to a document in writing: (a) any book, map, plan, graph or drawing; (b) any photograph; (c) any label, marking or other writing which identifies or describes anything of which it forms part, or to which it is attached by any means whatsoever; (d) any disc, tape, sound track or other device in which sounds or other data (not being visual images) are embodied so as to be capable (with or without the aid of some other equipment) of being reproduced therefrom; (e) any film (including microfilm), negative, tape or other device in which one or more visual images are embodied so as to be capable (with or without the aid of some other equipment) of being reproduced therefrom; and (f) anything whatsoever on which is marked any words, figures, letters or symbols which are capable of carrying a definite meaning to persons conversant with them. Similarly broad concept can also be seen in the EU law. For example, the Directive 2003/98/EC of the European Parliament and of the Council of 17 November 2003 on the reuse of public sector information[613] in the content of Article 2 paragraph 3(a) provides that the term "document" means any content regardless of the medium used (written on paper or stored in electronic form or as a sound, visual or audiovisual recording). As indicated in the preamble, the Directive lays down a generic definition of the term "document", in line

---

611 GA Dvoenosova, 'The Functions of a Document' (2013) 40 Scientific and Technical Information Processing 17.

612 Załucki, 'Evidentiary Function of the Provisions on the Form of Wills in the Contemporary Succession Law. Is the Complete Abandonment of Formalism Possible?' (n 45).

613 OJ L 345 of 31.12.2003.

with developments in the information society. It covers any representation of acts, facts or information - and any compilation of such acts, facts or information - whatever its medium (written on paper, or stored in electronic form or as a sound, visual or audiovisual recording), held by public sector bodies[614]. Therefore, as can be seen, the concept of a document is very broad today and includes, *inter alia*, also those documents which in the doctrine of continental Europe are traditionally called electronic documents.[615] As it can be judged, the traditional understanding of a term "document" is already redefined. Today a "document" is a mean for the appropriate preservation of any information, what is to be achieved by any medium enabling its restoration.[616] The form of this medium is indifferent, thus allowing for both paper document and other instruments, including electronic or cloud-based recording. Although documents, as it is believed, have many functions[617], the basic feature and at the same time the function of each document is to maintain the information, the disclosure of statement, long enough for it to be exposed, reproduced, duplicated or transferred to another medium in an unchanged state.[618] A document is intended to store the information so that it can be preserved in a way that is reproducible and possible to access.[619] Differences can relate to the way in which the information is stored, the medium, the way in which the author is identified or finally, the evidential value.[620] The latter is often crucial for resolving cases, what is associated with granting documents a special preference among all means of evidence in court proceedings. Documents usually have a certain stabilizing and limiting value, which limits misunderstandings about the content of legal actions. They are generally characterised by their durability and the possibility to reproduce their content, which is not characteristic of other means of evidence. This is why legislators generally recognise that a document is a method of effective and

---

614 See recital 11 of the preamble to Directive 2003/98/EC, OJ L 345, 31.12.2003.
615 *Cf.* Maja Maciejewska-Szałas, *Forma pisemna i elektroniczna czynności prawnych. Studium prawnoporównawcze* (CH Beck 2014) passim.
616 Ross Harvey, *Preserving Digital Materials* (Walter de Gruyter 2012).
617 Dvoenosova (n 611).
618 *Cf.* Wojciech Kocot, *Wpływ Internetu na prawo umów* (Lexis Nexis 2004) 334.
619 Ross Harvey (n 616).
620 Szostek (n 601) 23 ff.

durable storage of a specific content that is suitable for reproduction and reuse.[621]

These attributes of a document are commonly known in the various systems of succession law, what was highlighted above, and show that a document plays an important role being used as a medium preserving a disposition of property upon death, creating the embodiment of the testator's last will.[622] This makes it possible to assume that, in principle, for the evidentiary function of the provisions on the form of wills, the existence of a document is necessary. The regulations on the form of wills that have evolved over the years, including the provisions on the doctrine of *substantial compliance* and its variations or other mechanisms to relax the rigour of wills formalities, use the document as a medium of testamentary intent.

Regardless of the different wording of the regulations, the different forms of wills, or the different provisions concerning the "cure" of wills drawn up defectively, reference is usually made to some form of document in the applicable legislation.[623] The following can serve as examples: Art. 970 of the French *Code civil* provides that a holographic will is not valid unless "it is entirely handwritten, dated and signed by the testator",[624] while § 2247(1) of the *Bürgerliches Gesetzbuch* states this type of will to be "a declaration written and signed",[625] both obviously requiring the testamentary intent to be preserved by a document that allows to reflect testator's handwriting; Art. 952 § 2 of the Polish *Kodeks cywilny* says that "the content of an oral will may be established in such a way that one of the witnesses or a third party writes down the testator's declaration within a year of it being made, giving the place and date of the declaration and the place and date of the written instrument, and the instrument is then signed by the testator and two witnesses or all the witnesses",[626] while § 2107.60 of *Ohio Revised Code* states that a will "shall be valid in respect to

---

621 Załucki, 'Evidentiary Function of the Provisions on the Form of Wills in the Contemporary Succession Law. Is the Complete Abandonment of Formalism Possible?' (n 45).

622 *Cf* Virgil M Harris, 'The Importance of the Last Will and Testament' (1908) 25 Banking Law Journal 377; Albery (n 64); Michał Niedospiał, *Testament jako dokument prawny (zagadnienia dowodowe i procesowe testamentu)* (Biblioteka Jagiellońska 2019).

623 Karen J Sneddon, 'Not Your Mother's Will: Gender, Language, and Wills' (2015) 98 Marquette Law Review 1537.

624 Malaurie and Brenner (n 21) 293 ff.

625 Röthel (n 113).

626 Witold Borysiak, *Funkcjonowanie w praktyce testamentu sporządzanego w formie ustnej (art. 952 k.c.)* (Instytut Wymiaru Sprawiedliwości 2014) 72 ff.

personal property if reduced to writing and subscribed by two competent disinterested witnesses within ten days after the speaking of the testamentary words",[627] both requiring of drawing up a document in order for an oral will to be valid; § 14-2518 *Arizona Revised Statutes* mandates an electronic will to "be created and maintained in an electronic record",[628] while Section 9(1)-(2) of the English *Wills Act* (1837) states that no will shall be valid "unless it is in writing and signed by the testator, or by some other person in his presence and by his direction",[629] and the presence "includes presence by means of videoconference or other visual transmission", what obviously comes down to the need for a document, although not necessarily a paper one; section 2(3) of the South African *Wills Act* provides that "if a court is satisfied that a document or the amendment of a document drafted or executed by a person who has died since the drafting or execution thereof, was intended to be his will or an amendment of his will, the court shall order the Master to accept that document, or that document as amended (...) as a will, although it does not comply with all the formalities for the execution or amendment of wills",[630] while section 14(2) of New Zealand's *Wills Act* says that a court may validate a will, if "it is satisfied that the document expresses the deceased person's testamentary intentions",[631] both requiring the existence of a document to cure a flawed will. Regardless of the type and purpose of a given legal regulation, its scope or consequences for the succession, the legislators require the existence of a document whose role in today's succession law is unquestionable. Therefore, in the law of succession, it is possible to outline the principle according to which the existence of a document is a precondition for the effective making up of a declaration of last will, and the absence of such a document means that it is impossible to inherit under the will. Even where it is permitted to prepare wills orally, the consequence of making a declaration in this way is to draw up a document whose task is at least to archive the oral declaration of last will. As can be judged, these solution perform the

---

627 Joseph Mentrek, 'Estate Planning in a Digital World' [2009] Ohio Probate Law Journal 195.

628 Hirsch, 'Technology Adrift: In Search of a Role for Electronic Wills' (n 83).

629 Mariusz Załucki, 'Testament w prawie angielskim' in Piotr Kostański, Paweł Podrecki and Tomasz Targosz (eds), *Experientia docet. Księga jubileuszowa ofiarowana Pani Profesor Elżbiecie Traple* (Wolters Kluwer 2017).

630 Francois du Toit, 'Testamentary Rescue: An Analysis of the Intention Requirement in Australia and South Africa' [2014] Australian Property Law Journal 56.

631 Peart and Kelly (n 98).

evidentiary function of form regulations, as it allows to identify the testator and his testamentary intentions after his death.[632]

In the light of the above, it may be considered that the evidentiary function that was traditionally recognized in the area of succession law still performs its role and still means the possibility and necessity of preserving the testator's intentions. It is essential that there is a possibility to reconstruct the testator's intentions as well as an opportunity to confirm his identity. The authority recognizing a given succession case should be able to state that the testator had the testamentary intention and that the behaviour undertaken by the testator constituted the creation of the will. The form of the will should therefore provide an opportunity to determine the bequeather's *animus testandi.*[633] The existence of the testamentary intention is, after all, an essential prerequisite for creating a will. The form of a will is therefore one of the possible instruments to assess that a given declaration of intent is the testator's final declaration. It is intended to provide evidence of the testator's intentions,[634] and this is sufficient argument to consider that such solutions in succession law are necessary. There is no other way today to achieve such a goal. The formalities are necessary to give evidence that a will was actually made, what is needed in order to protect the freedom of testation and reflect testamentary intentions. In the law of testamentary succession evidence of the testator's credible intentions plays the most important role. Without such evidence, it is difficult to assume that one is dealing with a last will, not to mention the absence of any *mortis causa* consequences.

What is important referring to the subject of this book, this can also be seen in those legal systems which allow for the effectiveness of the so-called informal wills, based on the doctrine of *substantial compliance* and its variations in the appearance of *harmless error* or *dispensing power.*[635] Generally, regardless of the content of specific legal norms on succession, the ba-

---

632 *Cf.* Wendel, 'Wills Act Compliance and the Harmless Error Approach: Flawed Narrative Equals Flawed Analysis?' (n 122).

633 Wolak (n 535) 1 ff.

634 Załucki, 'Evidentiary Function of the Provisions on the Form of Wills in the Contemporary Succession Law. Is the Complete Abandonment of Formalism Possible?' (n 45).

635 *Cf.* Miller, 'Substantial Compliance and the Execution of Wills' (n 276) 343–344; Johnson (n 262) 10–15; White (n 7) 56–60; Sherwin (n 364) 453–476; Leipold, 'Ist unser Erbrecht noch zeitgemäß?' (n 85) 802–811; Joan Marsal Guillamet, 'La Ineficàcia dels actes i disposicions d'última voluntat', *El Nou Dret successori del Codi Civil de Catalunya* (Documenta Universitaria 2012); du Toit, 'Tes-

sis for solutions reflecting the testator's intention is some kind of form of declaration of last will preserved by means of a document. Thus, even in those legal systems where the doctrine of *substantial compliance* or its variations is applied, the provisions of succession law provide for a certain minimum of formalities, primarily for evidentiary purposes carried out after the testator's death.[636] Demonstrating that the testator had the *animus testandi* and actually made a will is exactly a necessary minimum, the accomplishment of which may depend on the degree of formalities.[637] If the formalism of the regulation on the form of wills allows not only to identify the testator, but also to preserve his will and to reconstruct it after his death, the regulation on the form of wills is sufficient to achieve the objectives of the law of succession.[638] Consequently, the form of will should reflect the current needs and concepts prevailing in a given legal system, and the prerogatives of the evidentiary function of the wills form regulations. In other words, the accomplishment of evidential purposes by a given form of will should be a starting point for its possible design by the legislator. As I have indicated before,[639] this can be seen, *inter alia*, in recent legislative achievements in the field of wills formalities law in the world, including latest civil codes of Russia, Romania, or Hungary, the provisions enacted in some US states (Florida, Arizona) or the US Uniform Electronic Wills Act.[640] These laws, in the field of testamentary succession, are primarily aimed at the evidentiary function.[641] Even during the COVID-19 pandemic, when public expectations aimed at facilitating the drafting of

---

tamentary Rescue: An Analysis of the Intention Requirement in Australia and South Africa' (n 630) 56–82; Paweł Janowski, 'Doktryna „substantial compliance" (merytorycznej zgodności) w anglosaskim prawie spadkowym, na przykładzie Australii i Nowej Zelandii' [2016] Ius et Administratio 73, 73–95; Langbein, 'Absorbing South Australia's Wills Act Dispensing Power in the United States: Emulation, Resistance, Expansion' (n 94) 1 ff.

636 Brook (n 50) 205–212; Tucker (n 94) 969–979; Horton, 'Partial Harmless Error For Wills: Evidence From California' (n 501) 2027 ff; Martin (n 55) 431 ff.

637 *Cf.* Flaks (n 203).

638 Załucki, 'Forma testamentu w perspektywie rekodyfikacji polskiego prawa spadkowego. Czas na rewolucję?' (n 35).

639 Załucki, 'Evidentiary Function of the Provisions on the Form of Wills in the Contemporary Succession Law. Is the Complete Abandonment of Formalism Possible?' (n 45).

640 Uniform Electronic Wills Act was approved by The National Conference of Commissioners in July 2019. *Cf.* Hirsch, 'Technology Adrift: In Search of a Role for Electronic Wills' (n 83).

641 *Cf.* Banta (n 48); Dubravka Klasiček (n 368).

wills[642], in legal systems that decided to make legislative changes, not all the formalities were abandoned, following the principle that complete abandonment of wills formalities is not possible.[643]Those of the formalities which were not affected during the changes also serve primarily the evidentiary function. The role of formalities is therefore still relevant, although it is possible to imagine more relaxed formalities in the future. However, a reform under which the provisions on the form of wills will cease to perform the evidentiary function does not seem possible. Provisions based on the doctrine of *substantial compliance* and its variations, as well as other mechanisms to relax the formal rigour of wills formalities, do not and will not change this state of affairs.

3. The channelling function of the wills formalities regulations

The recognition by individual legislators of the solution according to which testation should be formal over the years has developed, among others, certain tools in which bequeathers disposed of property in case of death.[644] The development of law in this field has led to the creation of a certain standard, a common criterion determining the most desirable characteristics of human behaviour during the act of testation.[645] This is one of the reasons why it is commonly accepted that while the final result of testation should be a carrier of the testator's intent, which is an expression of the evidentiary function of the provisions on the form of wills, the testation procedure should fall within a certain framework set by the provisions of the law, which means that the provisions on the form also perform a function referred to as standardization or channelling function.[646] Such a concept is found in both *civil law* and *common law* countries, where precedent law is known to be the primary source of law rather than the acts passed by parliaments. In the area of succession law, however, this is not the case and it is the provisions of the law that are only the starting point

---

642 *Cf.* Horton and Weisbord (n 52).

643 Załucki, 'Evidentiary Function of the Provisions on the Form of Wills in the Contemporary Succession Law. Is the Complete Abandonment of Formalism Possible?' (n 45).

644 *Cf.* Roscoe Pound, 'The Role of the Will in Law' (1954) 68 Harvard Law Review 1.

645 Roger Kerridge, *Hawkins on the Construction of Wills* (Sweet & Maxwell 2000) 19 ff.

646 Peart (n 98) 31 ff.

for court precedents. It is therefore the provisions of the law that provide the framework for the legal action of the will, modelling the tools that can be used by the testator to plan the fate of his estate after death. This is the case, for example, in France where the *Code civil* lists an enumerating catalogue of will forms (Art. 970-976),[647] this is the case of Switzerland where the legal system contain the catalogue of will forms provided for in the *Zivilgesetzbuch* (Art. 498),[648] this is the case in the Canadian province of British Columbia for which the catalogue of testamentary *mortis causa* dispositions is provided for in the *Wills, Estates and Succession Act* (Section 37-40),[649] or the law of the American State of Minnesota (Section 524.2-504 *Minnesota Statutes*).[650] This is also the case of almost all countries in the world. The main purpose of this is to ensure consistency between the content that the testator determined at the time of making his will and the content that will be reproduced after his death and have legal effect. Many believe that this is precisely what is needed to ensure, as far as possible, that the testation process is unified, so that the testator can use the instruments available to him routinely and quickly. In other words, the introduction of a specific model of *mortis causa* legal acts can provide an appropriate level of quality, safety and convenience.[651]

The formal requirements of a will can therefore serve to structure the testation procedure.[652] Individual legislators do not allow for arbitrary behaviour of testators; they require them to use forms of wills designed by the legislature. That is why the regulations concerning the form of a will are absolutely binding.[653] The rule in this respect is that any deviation from the requirements imposed by the provisions of the law, and thus formal defects, result in the invalidity of the disposition in case of death.[654] Although, as it is known and was already explained, individual legislators have been looking for intermediate solutions for some time, the vast ma-

---

647 Malaurie and Brenner (n 21) 287 ff.
648 Breitschmid, 'Testament und Erbvertrag - Formprobleme: Die Einsatzmöglichkeiten für die Nachlassplanung im Lichte neuerer Rechtsentwicklungen' (n 119) 274 ff.
649 Peter W Bogardus, Mary B Hamilton and Sadie L Wetzel, *Wills and Personal Planning Precedents. An Annotated Guide* (The Continuing Legal Education Society of British Columbia 2020) passim.
650 *Cf.* Frerichs and Kovacevic (n 307).
651 Załucki, *Videotestament. Prawo spadkowe wobec nowych technologii* (n 33) 178.
652 Lois J MacLean, *Rectification and Validation of Wills and Codicils* (LESA 2015) 3.
653 Fernández (n 92).
654 Röthel (n 113).

jority of legal systems are "punishable" by nullity in the event that a disposition of property upon death is made in a manner that violates the rules on form (*ad solemnitatem*). This is typical, for example, of continental Europe.[655]

As I have already explained,[656] the requirements for the testation process related to the security of legal transactions might be seen as being in conflict with the private law principle of autonomy of will and independence of legal entities in making decisions. In the succession law however, the principle of autonomy of will is manifested in the principle of freedom to dispose of property in case of death, which includes, among others, the freedom of testation.[657] The doctrine indicates that the freedom of testation should be understood as the scope of the testator's powers to dispose of his estate in case of death.[658] This is a certain legally protected possibility of making effective dispositions of property upon death, a fragment of the autonomy of the will of legal entities that involves the freedom to make such a legal act as a last will and the possibility to include in there various dispositions of the testator's property effective at the time of his death.[659]

It has to be reminded that the freedom of testation, as well as the right to succession, is now guaranteed in individual states on a constitutional level.[660] Moreover, it should be regarded as a derivative of the public subjective law - the right to property.[661] It is in this context, among other things, that legislators decide to raise the principle of succession protection to constitutional status.[662] It is not merely a question of protecting the future heir, but rather the situation of the person who has the property or

---

655 Schmoeckel and Otte (n 590) passim.

656 Załucki, *Videotestament. Prawo spadkowe wobec nowych technologii* (n 33) 179 ff.

657 Kevin Noble Maillard, 'The Color of Testamentary Freedom' (2014) 62 SMU Law Review 1783.

658 Eike Götz Hosemann, 'Protecting Freedom of Testation: A Proposal for Law Reform' (2014) 47 University of Michigan Journal of Law Reform 419.

659 Alberto Maria Benedetti, 'Notas sobre la prohibición del testamento conjunto: Sobre la validez de los mirror wills' [2015] Revista de Derecho Privado 59.

660 Jan Peter Schmidt, 'Grundlagen der Testierfähigkeit in Deutschland und Europa' (2012) 220 Rabels Zeitschrift für ausländisches und internationales Privatrecht 1022.

661 Renate Barbaix and Alain-Laurent Verbeke, *Beginselen erfrecht* (die Keure 2012) 15 ff.

662 Andrzej Mączyński, 'Prawo dziedziczenia i jego ochrona w świetle orzecznictwa Trybunału Konstytucyjnego' in Marek Zubik (ed), *Minikomentarz dla Maksiprofesora. Księga jubileuszowa profesora Leszka Garlickiego* (Wydawnictwo Sejmowe 2017) 322 ff.

other right of proprietary nature that can be inherited.[663] In this respect, it is doubtful whether the statutory requirement imposing on the testator the obligation to choose one of the statutory forms for drawing up the testation act, and thus breaking with the principle of freedom of form of legal acts, is constitutionally legitimate.

These considerations are all the more justified in that the possible denial of the form rules as violating the constitutional right of property would have to result in legislative changes in the area of wills formalities. Although there are opinions according to which the principle of freedom of form of legal acts is not a component of the principle of autonomy of will, but only a general rule of private law of a constructional nature, and due to this basis it is not possible to seek any relation between the two values in this respect, this opinions do not seem justified. In fact, it can be assumed that overly strict requirements as to form, making it impossible to make a will in practice, would unduly interfere with the principle of the testator's autonomy of will, without allowing the realization of his *mortis causa* intent.[664]

The constitutional understanding of the right to succession, expressed for obvious reasons primarily in the continental legal orders, against the background of such provisions as Articles 21 and 64 of the *Polish Constitution*,[665] Article 11 paragraph 1 of the *Czech Constitution*,[666] Article 14 paragraph 1 of the *German Constitution*[667] or Article 33 paragraph 1 of the *Spanish Constitution*,[668] is, among other things, an order to take into account the intent of the owner as the basic determining factor for the fate of the succession, where excessive interference by the legislature or other public authorities in the sovereignty of the last will is to be regarded as an infringement of the right to succession.[669] The jurisprudence of the Polish

---

663 Załucki, *Videotestament. Prawo spadkowe wobec nowych technologii* (n 33) 180.

664 ibid.

665 *Cf.* Andrzej Mączyński, 'Konstytucyjne prawo dziedziczenia' in Wojciech Popiołek, Maciej Szpunar and Leszek Ogiegło (eds), *Rozprawy prawnicze. Księga pamiątkowa Profesora Maksymiliana Pazdana* (Zakamycze 2005).

666 *Cf.* Katerina Ronovska, 'Civil Law in the Czech Republic : Tendencies of Development (Some Notes on the Proposal of the New Civil Code)' [2008] European Review of Private Law 111.

667 Solzbach (n 60) 104 ff.

668 Antoni Vaquer Aloy, 'Freedom of Testation, Compulsory Share and Disinheritance Based on Lack of Family Relationship' in M Anderson and E Arroyo I Amayuelas (eds), *The Law of Succession: Testamentary Freedom. European Perspectives* (Europa Law Publishing 2009) 2 ff.

669 Załucki, *Videotestament. Prawo spadkowe wobec nowych technologii* (n 33) 180.

Constitutional Tribunal can serve as an example. According to its view, the legislators should establish regulations subsidiary to the statutory succession, assuming at the same time a certain type of testamentary dispositions, create a mechanism taking into account the freedom to dispose of the *mortis causa* estate so that the intent of the testator is of primary importance, not the rules established by the legislator.[670]

In this light, when the provisions on the form of wills are treated as a kind of mechanism for the standardization of dispositions of property upon death, it is necessary to ensure that they can be a guarantee of the testator's last intent.[671] The certainty of circulation, as one of the reasons for the introduction of the obligation to observe the special form, may also serve to protect the execution of the testator's will.[672] Without a minimum of legal certainty, the will expressed by the testator could not be protected at all and could be exposed to the danger of distortion. Total freedom in this area could therefore lead to a situation in which the testator would not be certain to carry out his *mortis causa* disposition. It therefore seems desirable to maintain a certain standard of disposition in the event of death.[673] The paradox, therefore, is that the limitation of the autonomy of the will by the rules of form means at the same time a guarantee of the realization of that autonomy. The absence of a minimum standard for dispositions of property upon death in terms of legal certainty would increase the testator's freedom, but this freedom would prove useless in practice, due to the lack of protection.[674] Hence, on the one hand, legal certainty and security of legal transactions may be a limitation of the freedom of testation and, on the other hand, an instrument for the exercise of that freedom. Everything depends on a specific statutory solution. The legislator, when introducing the obligation to observe a form specific for testation activities, must propose such a solution which will appropriately combine the two above values: legal certainty of legal circulation and the bequeather's will autonomy. The wills formalities should be shaped in such a way that a statistical testator can easily use it, without the need for legal expertise.[675]

This approach, as one might think, is precisely the right one for the creators of the doctrine of *substantial compliance* and the solutions based on it,

---

670 K 23/98, [1999] 2 OTK ZU 25.

671 Marsal Guillamet (n 635) passim.

672 Lon L Fuller, 'Consideration and Form' (1941) 1 Columbia Law Review 799, 799 ff.

673 Gulliver and Tilson (n 34) 5 ff.

674 Załucki, *Videotestament. Prawo spadkowe wobec nowych technologii* (n 33) 181.

675 *Cf.* Ponath (n 105) 242 ff.

applied in practice. Those legislators who have decided to introduce one of the variations of the doctrine of *substantial compliance* are primarily concerned with ensuring that the will of the testator is properly reflected.[676] At the same time, they ensure that there is clear and convincing evidence of testation in the case of informal wills where the testator's fantasy or lack of knowledge has resulted in the testator's use of a medium which is not provided for this type of legal action by the law.[677] Solutions such as the *harmless error* or the *dispensing power* are predictable solutions, which are also based on a specific standard, which is implemented in practice by the courts. As a matter of principle, the *harmless error* and the *dispensing power* in determining whether a will has been prepared validly in a given case are based on a writing or its derivative, refer to essential elements of a form of a will. There is no room for absolute discretion, the court must rely on the existing standard, which, among other things, is developed in case law.[678]

Regulations are therefore designed to enable succession by way of an informal will, but not at any cost, but only if the other criteria provided by law are met. In the context of solutions created in Australia, Canada, the United States of America or South Africa, as well as some solutions observed in European countries, it has to be explained that they are based on the search mechanism for elements of a will provided by the law.[679] This search may indicate that the testator had a testamentary intent and wanted to make a will, but was unable to or couldn't do so. Finding such elements, such as the testator's own handwriting or an e-mail marked as his last will, may suggest a willingness to comply with the rules of form and lead to the will being considered valid.[680] If there were no specific standards for this legal action, if the legislator did not indicate what elements should be expected for this legal action, or what elements shape this legal action, then it would not be possible to determine whether such an action

---

676 *Cf.* John H Langbein, 'Defects of Form in the Execution of Wills: Australian and Other Experience with the Substantial Compliance Doctrine', *American/Australian/New Zealand Law: Parallels and Contrasts (Papers presented in Sydney, Australia, from 11-16 August 1980 at a meeting between the American Bar Association, Law Council of Australia, New Zealand Law Society, to commemorate the bicentenar* (1980).

677 *Cf.* du Toit, 'Remedying Formal Irregularities in Wills: A Comparative Analysis of Testamentary Rescue in Canada and South Africa' (n 7).

678 Langbein, 'Absorbing South Australia's Wills Act Dispensing Power in the United States: Emulation, Resistance, Expansion' (n 94) 3 ff.

679 Purser and Cockburn (n 55) 46 ff.

680 Załucki, 'About the Need to Adjust the Regulations Regarding the Form of Will to the Modern Requirements' (n 14) 3 ff.

was a last will in practice. Therefore, even where the formal requirements of wills are treated relatively mildly, and are not based on the beliefs of *strict compliance*, some paradigm of a last will is necessary, to which the authority applying the law, and earlier the testator, could refer.[681] This is why, for example, in the Israeli law the court searches for "static formalities" of a will (Section 25 of the *Israeli Succession Law* (חוק הירושה)),[682] in South Australia the court examines if a document is a will with "no reasonable doubt" (Section 12(2) of the *Wills Act*),[683] and in New Zealand it looks for the document to express the deceased intentions (Section 14 of the *Wills Act*).[684] In this sense, standardisation is indispensable.

The above can be seen in the case law of individual countries. The channelling function was described, for example in one of the judgements of Manitoba's court. It was stated there that the main purpose or function of the formality requirements of the law is, *inter alia*, the channelling function in which the formal requirements result in a degree of uniformity in the organization, language and content of most wills.[685] This view is shared by other courts, deciding on the validity of certain documents executed contrary to the legal requirements. As it is known, there are number of requirements for a will to be valid and where the requirements are not all met, there is an opportunity to challenge the will.[686] The standards resulting from the provisions of the law allow, among others, to determine whether the testator acted with sufficient discernment and willingness to make a will *(animus testandi)*.[687] Testamentary intent, or *"animus testandi"*, is a key ingredient in any testamentary document. The court, when the will is challenged, has to determine it, and the closer to the statutory standard by a certain disposition, the bigger chances for it to be validated.[688] This was outlined, for example, in the recent case from British Columbia, where the court has emphasized that the best evidence of whether a writing was intended to be a testamentary act is the document itself.[689] As can be seen, in this sense the formalities mean that a will provides a well-de-

---

681 *Cf.* Melanie B Leslie, 'Frustration of Intent in the Wealth Transmission Process' (2014) 2 Oñati Socio-Legal Series 283.
682 Menashe (n 54).
683 Lester (n 230).
684 Peart and Kelly (n 98).
685 George v. Daily, [1997] 15 E.T.R. (2) 1.
686 Barret v. Bem, [20120 EWCA 52.
687 Costa v Public Trustee [2007] NSWSC 1271.
688 Estate of Thomas S. Souther, [2012] 25 Quinnipiac Probate Law Journal 161.
689 Quinn Estate v. Rydland, [2019] BCCA 91.

fined means of passing property on death and testators are channelled towards a well-understood, standard method of accomplishing their ends.[690]

The next goal of standardizing the forms of will, as can be judged, is to prevent the testator's last will from being distorted, to prevent its falsification.[691] Establishing by the legislator the requirement of observing the special form of a will in the form specified by the legislator is to guarantee the authenticity of the will, allow for identification of the testator and reconstruction of his last will.[692] In this respect, the standardization function of the provisions on the form of testamentary dispositions largely coincides with the evidentiary function. These functions complement each other. Legislators should therefore avoid such forms that do not allow the testator's intentions to be reconstructed in a way that borders on the certainty that the will revealed in a given case belongs to the testator.[693] Certainly, this requirement may be fulfilled by the necessity of the testator's own handwritten signature or the participation in testation of third parties, especially those performing official functions, which may be encountered under certain statutory solutions. It is also these requirements that are emphasized in systems that know the solution based on the doctrine of *substantial compliance*. Some variations of this doctrine require strict existence of such elements of the will (as the Colorado's approach),[694] without which it is impossible to consider informal wills valid. The requirements of "clear and convincing evidence"[695] or "beyond reasonable doubt"[696] and the search for "essential elements"[697] should also be considered as fulfilling the objective of reconstructing the testator's last will.

One of the purposes of legislators' use of the construction of forms of will may also be the desire to define a standard of wording used in such activities. Over the years of using various forms of testamentation, a specific language has developed, a terminology that is basically only suitable for

---

690 Law Commission, *Making a Will. Consultation Paper 231* (The Law Commission 2017) 74.
691 Gwiazdomorski (n 43).
692 Grundmann (n 61) 442 ff.
693 Ponath (n 105) 158 ff.
694 Miller, 'How Harmless Is Harmless? An In-Depth Look Into the Harmless Error Rule' (n 472) 12.
695 Sherwin (n 364).
696 Johnson (n 262) 10 ff.
697 Maxton (n 38) 94 ff.

mortis causa legal acts.[698] The style of dispositions of property upon death is fundamentally different from that of other legal acts.[699] The availability of specific normative models results in practice in a relatively high similarity of the statements of individual testators, their official-legal style or even an attempt to imitate statutory formulations.[700] The content of individual wills drawn up in practice very often contains formulas such as: "I declare that I want to appoint upon my death", "this is my last will" or "in the event of my death, I will transfer my property", etc.[701] For this reason, it is argued, among other things, that one of the objectives pursued by the channelling function of the regulations on the form of wills is a linguistic objective, which is related, for example, to facilitating the demonstration of the testator's intention in a given case because of the testator's use of typical words appropriate for *mortis causa* dispositions.[702] It should be added that in the doctrine there are voices about the possibility of performing the channelling function of testation by reducing testation activities to filling in a generally available form, prepared by the legislator and attached e.g. to annual tax returns. This is supposed to simplify the making of wills in practice, increase the number of people using *mortis causa* instruments or facilitate possible changes in the testator's last will. Already today, there are various websites offering specific forms suggesting that filling them out may allow the testator to more properly implement his will in case of death. And although their status is unclear, perhaps this is one of the ways that could be used in the future to ensure the realization of the intent expressed *mortis causa*.[703] Undoubtedly, most of the mechanisms based on the concept of *substantial compliance* also touch upon the problem of increasing public interest in the mechanisms of succession law, or even the

---

698 Scott T Jarboe, 'Interpreting a Testator's Intent from the Language of Her Will: A Descriptive Linguistic Approach' (2002) 80 Washington University Law Quarterly 1365.

699 Karen J Sneddon, 'Speaking For the Dead: Voice in Last Wills and Testaments' (2011) 85 St. John's Law Review 684.

700 *Cf.* Paola Fontana and others, 'Handwriting as a Gauge of Cognitive Status: A Novel Forensic Tool for Posthumous Evaluation of Testamentary Capacity' (2008) 29 Neurological Sciences 257; Mark Glover, 'Minimizing Probate-Error Risk' (2016) 49 University of Michigan Journal of Law Reform 335.

701 Champine (n 132); Adam J Hirsch, 'Incomplete Wills' (2013) 111 Michigan Law Review 1423; Anna Koziczak, 'Oznaki emocji w testamencie a jego autentyczność' (2012) 277 Problemy Kryminalistyki 30 ff.

702 Peter T Wendel, 'Setting the Record Straight: The "Flexible Strict Compliance" Approach to the Wills Act Formalities' (2016) 95 Oregon Law Review 50 ff.

703 Załucki, *Videotestament. Prawo spadkowe wobec nowych technologii* (n 33) 183.

validity of wills already drawn up in such an unusual way. Certainly these are also steps towards simplifying the standards of drafting wills.

The doctrine of succession law also argues that the standardization of dispositions of property upon death may be relevant in circumstances where the legal awareness of society is not high. Then, the use of instruments that are more or less similar to each other makes it possible to standardize the testation of individual persons who, without specific legal knowledge, will refer to already used instruments or, more likely, use the knowledge of persons with such knowledge.[704] This is also certainly the way to simplify the practice, which otherwise would have to deal with an unlimited number of problems, which would be very difficult to solve. Certain minimum formal requirements make it possible to determine whether a given activity was intended to be the testator's will, i.e. whether it contains a declaration of last will expressed upon death.[705] Therefore, such a minimum standard of wills formalities is desirable and is currently being implemented in practice. While legislators require specific ways of making wills, it is increasingly accepted that a deviation from those specific ways of making wills should be effective if it contains evidence that the testator acted with the testamentary intention. The possibility of stating such circumstances therefore detaches the declaration of will from a particular way of expressing it, makes the declaration independent, and allows the estate to be passed on based on it, which, however, would not be possible if there was no standard of wills formalities.[706]

In the above contexts the provisions on the form of will and the solution to relax the rigour of wills formalities realize a standardization function. Without the existence of a standard in this respect, there would be no free testation understood as the testator's unrestricted act of determining his successors in title.[707] Consequently, the channelling function of wills formalities regulations, traditionally recognized in succession law, plays an important role even today. The provisions on the form of a will, complemented by solutions based on the doctrine of *substantial compliance* and its variations, or other mechanisms to mitigate the rigour of formal requirements, do not deviate from standardization despite the technological

---

704 *Cf.* Patti (n 6).
705 Langbein, 'Substantial Compliance with the Wills Act' (n 10) 494 ff.
706 *Cf.* Iris J Goodwin, 'Access to Justice: What to Do about the Law of Wills' [2016] Wisconsin Law Review 947, 947 ff.
707 *Cf.* Susanna Blumenthal, 'The Deviance of the Will: Policing the Bounds of Testamentary Freedom in Nineteenth-Century America' (2006) 119 Harvard Law Review 959, 963 ff.

changes that have emerged over the years. This function complements the evidentiary function of form regulations, and its implementation in the law of succession allows to search for the existence of the testator's intention based on elements which can be called essential elements of wills formalities.[708] The lack of a standard in the succession law that would specify the basis of a will as a legal act allowing to dispose of property upon death would make it impossible to use this legal instrument. The indication of the *essentialia negotii* of a last will in the law makes it possible to dispose of property in case of death by means of this instrument, putting aside the issue of whether the testator has actually drawn up a will in a given case, not to mention the issue of validity of such an activity.[709] It is only the actual existence of an instrument drawn up for the purpose of disposing of the estate in the event of death based on a statutory model that may give rise to further reflection on the practical implications of such an instrument, including its validity. The provisions around the statutory model of a will may provide for who may use this instrument and under what circumstances.[710] Without a statutory model of a last will, it would not make sense to have such provisions, and a will could not be an alternative to other titles of succession in case of death.[711] Such solutions should therefore also exist in the future.

4. The cautionary function of the wills formalities regulations

One of the most important elements of testation activities is the intent and awareness of testation.[712] As constitutive components of this activity they influence its validity.[713] The testator must be aware and willing to make a disposition in case of death, and demonstrate that the behaviour he undertakes constitutes the drawing up of a will.[714] The legal science, defining *animus testandi*, indicates that the lack of this element in the testator's statement must lead to the conclusion that the testator's conduct does not con-

---

708 Patricia Critchley, 'Privileged Wills and Testamentary Formalities: A Time to Die?' (1999) 58 Cambridge Law Journal 49, 52 ff.
709 *Cf.* Niedośpiał (n 622) 177 ff.
710 *Cf.* Hirsch, 'Incomplete Wills' (n 701) 1443 ff.
711 *Cf.* Croucher (n 97).
712 Reid K Weisbord, David Horton and Stephen K Urice, *Wills, Trusts and Estates. The Essentials* (Wolters Kluwer 2018) passim.
713 Esquivel and Acuna (n 56) 194 ff.
714 Franz Gschnitzer, *Erbrecht* (Springer 1964) 22 ff.

stitute a will.[715] Therefore, also in this area, the regulations on the form of a will play an important role. Their task is also to make the testator aware of the seriousness of the action being performed. It is not a question of the testator's intention to draw up an act of last will in a particular form, but rather, in general, of his intention to cause the *mortis causa* effects of his disposition.[716] This can be seen not only in the *strict compliance* countries,[717] but also in the *substantial compliance* model,[718] as well as in other countries familiar with mechanisms to relax the rigour of wills formalities. *Harmless error, dispensing power, favor testamenti* - all of these doctrines are based on the intention of a testator as one of the most important factors in determining whether a document constitutes a valid will.

The testamentary intention is an element of the act of testation that many consider the cornerstone of *mortis causa* dispositions.[719] The lack of *animus testandi* leads to the invalidity of *mortis causa* dispositions.[720] This intention must be distinguished from the capacity to make a will, which may be a subject to certain limitations, especially of a mental nature.[721] In the case of *animus testandi*, it is the bequeather's desire that his decisions regarding the fate of his estate become effective upon his death.[722] The two elements complement each other. The testator must not only have the intent to dispose of his estate in case of death, but must also be able to express his intent in a way that is consistent with his desires and understandable to his surroundings. The regulations on the form of a will may therefore also serve to make arrangements of this kind. This can be seen, for example, in the South Australian approach, as well as in the provisions of the *Civil Code of Quebec*. The first example shows a need for a search by the court of the testamentary intentions of the deceased person to satisfy the court that there can be no reasonable doubt that the deceased intended the document to constitute a will (Section 12(2) of the South Australia *Wills*

---

715 Bernhard Eccher, *Bürgerliches Recht. Band VI. Erbrecht* (Springer 2010) 50 ff.
716 Piotr Stec and Mariusz Załucki, *Podstawy prawa cywilnego z umowami w administracji* (Difin 2011) 349 ff.
717 Eccher (n 57) 52.
718 Sitkoff and Dukeminier (n 37) passim.
719 Atkinson (n 28) passim.
720 Renate Barbaix and Alain-Laurent Verbeke, *Kernbegrippen erfrecht en giften* (Intersentia 2013) 134 ff.
721 Stephen Lynch, 'Wills and Estates: Succession Law and Testamentry Capacity' in RG Beran (ed), *Legal and Forensic Medicine* (Springer 2013) 1473 ff.
722 Lynch (n 721).

Act).[723] The second example requires for a will not only to meet essential elements of a will but also to unquestionably and unequivocally contain the last wishes of the deceased (Art. 714 of the *Civil Code of Quebec*).[724] Both regulations require a search for testamentary intent in order to determine will's validity. Similar solutions can be found in other countries. It is the essence and rationale that lies behind wills formalities regulations, even if it is not expressed *verba legis*, as for example, in the Polish *Kodeks cywilny*. Despite the lack of an unambiguous legal regulation requiring the assessment of whether the testator had *animus testandi* in a given case, it is assumed in Polish practice that the content of the will must clearly indicate *animus testandi* - the intent to dispose in case of death.[725] Therefore, as a *mortis causa* legal act, a will is to a certain extent subject to more stringent rules than *inter vivos* acts. This is expressed in particular in the requirement for the testator to act *cum animo testandi*.[726] The intention to create a will (*animus testandi*) has to be aimed at and aware of a legal act done upon death. *Animus testandi* is a specific requirement and should be searched at a specific person, for a specific moment. Therefore, the testator has to include, with his consciousness, the fact of regulating the fate of his property for the time after his death (with consequences after his death). The testator often, as is evident from the observation of everyday life, wonders, cites divergent projects, makes various variants of his dispositions in case of death, which he then rejects, changes, and sometimes does not finish, and therefore considers projects that are not yet a reflection of his last intent. Often there may be difficulties in determining the caesura between the project of his last will and its full, final expression. To put it another way, the question of assessing whether the deceased, when drawing up a particular document, had testamentary intent at all, can and often does cause difficulties in practice.[727] Therefore, the wills formalities must be structured in such a way as to make it possible to evaluate the existence of testamentary intent after the death of the testator. In this respect, the doctrines of *substantial compliance, harmless error, dispensing power* or *favor testamenti* seem to allow for such an assessment.

Cautionary function is most readable in connection with the drafting of these wills, where a certain role is assigned to an official person, such as a

---

723 White (n 7) 56–60.
724 Martin (n 55) 431 ff.
725 III CZP 78/72, [1973] 12 OSNCP 207.
726 Pabin (n 31) 101.
727 Wolak (n 535) 2.

notary.[728] In this case, it may be the task of the official to make sure that the testator has the intent to make a disposition of property upon death, and that he is sufficiently aware of and understands the meaning of his conduct.

Such a solution can be found, for example, in the Polish law on notaries, where when performing notarial activities, the notary is obliged to ensure that the rights and legitimate interests of the parties and other persons for whom the activity may cause legal effects, as well as to provide the parties with the necessary explanations concerning the performed notarial activity. In case of significant doubts the notary should refuse to perform the notarial act (Art. 86 et seq. of the *Prawo o notariacie*).[729] The often emphasized goal of this form of will is to ensure consistency between the content of the will and the intent of the testator, which will become effective at the moment of his death. The form of a will is to give the testator - in this respect - a high probability of security. Therefore, when drawing up a will, the testator must be aware of the consequences of his disposition after his death.[730] The participation of a notary, or presence of another official person certainly facilitates this. Similarly, in the case of solutions based on the doctrine of *substantial compliance*, the requirement of "clear and convincing evidence" or the "beyond reasonable doubt" standard etc. are also steps towards the implementation of the cautionary function of the wills formalities regulations.

However, not all known forms of wills are based on so-called "professional" advice. While the participation of a lawyer with special qualifications may protect the testator from doing something he did not intend to do, the vast majority of wills functioning in practice are wills drawn up without the participation of such a person and not of a public character.[731] In such cases, the testamentary intent may be evidenced by the content of the will. The use of words and phrases in a document drawn up to indicate that it is a will, including, among others, terms such as "after my death", "in case of death", "my last will", "if I die", etc., may suggest that the document in question was conceived as a *mortis causa* disposition. However,

728 Holmes (n 261) 511 ff.

729 Maksymilian Pazdan, 'Czynności notarialne w międzynarodowym prawie spadkowym' (1998) 8 Rejent 99, 99–115.

730 Ciotola, 'Le testateur et son clone inavoué, le juge : clone difforme ou conforme dans la recherche des intentions du testateur : le juge et l'interprétation des volontés du testateur' (n 53) 239–301.

731 Osajda, 'Wpływ rozwoju techniki na uregulowanie formy testamentu - rozważania de lege ferenda' (n 540) 50–67.

this cannot guarantee the existence of *animus testandi*. Also, the place where the document is stored, including, for example, the previous will, may suggest the existence of the testator's testamentary intent. The determination of the existence of this premise is so important that in practice the found document may turn out to be only a project of disposition upon death. The provisions of the law of succession should be constructed in such a way as to preclude the possibility of such an action from producing legal effects.[732]

The cautionary function (sometimes referred to as the warning function) of the provisions on the form of a will is also connected with the concept based on the statement that in the law of succession it is necessary to counteract the testator's rash behaviour. Therefore, the obligation to observe the form is aimed at indicating to the testator that the activity performed by him does not belong to ordinary everyday activities, is not an activity undertaken cyclically or causing insignificant legal effects. Hence, the provisions on the form of a will may and should encourage the testator to think about the potential effects, evoking a sense of a kind of responsibility.[733] Therefore, a declaration of intent is required to be made in a certain way, and after the testator's death, the standard of proving the circumstances of testation is high. Otherwise, there would be too great of a risk that many ill-considered decisions or unfinished draft wills would have to be considered as valid dispositions.

The implementation of this function into the law of succession may be troublesome in practice, especially since the existing forms of will make it possible to create an appropriate disposition many years before death. In the case of private wills, a number of evidentiary difficulties arise in practice with regard to establishing a possible *animus testandi*. Too rigorous approach to this problem may result in the invalidity of the will, which is often too negative effect in a given succession case. Rigorism leading to the annulment of the testator's last will is not, especially in recent times, treated as an indispensable element of the view of *mortis causa* dispositions. It is increasingly accepted that the form of a will cannot be understood as an obstacle to reflecting the testator's last will. Hence, a number of mechanisms, where the lack of fulfilment of the formal requirements of the will when the existence of *animus testandi* is obvious allows the will to be maintained.[734] Under these assumptions, the bequeather's warning resulting

---

732 Załucki, *Videotestament. Prawo spadkowe wobec nowych technologii* (n 33) 186.
733 Grundmann (n 61) 448.
734 Langbein, 'Substantial Compliance with the Wills Act' (n 10) 495 ff.

from the regulations on the form of the will can be understood as an instrument to determine, in an appropriate proceeding concerning the validity of the will, whether the bequeather treated the document he drew up as his last will legally binding. The testator must want and be aware of that he makes a *mortis causa* declaration. In case of a doubt, it is up to the authority assessing the effectiveness of the existing disposition in the succession case (usually a probate court) to determine this.[735]

Doubts about the bequeather's testamentary intention usually occur in practice in cases of using testamentary forms known to the succession law, but the testation activity is not traditional.[736] This may be the case when, while drawing up a holographic will, a deceased writes his intention in a letter addressed to some addressee, and thus he does not draw up a traditional document which can be quoted as a "will"', as well as when the deceased uses tools that he is convinced of its legality (e.g. a will drawn up in a text message), even though, according to the regulations in force in this respect, they may not produce legal effects. It is then up to the legislator and law enforcement authorities to resolve the dilemma of how far to deviate from the formal requirements when the testamentary intent appears to be unquestionable.[737] In general, however, the derogations related to the cautionary function are not common. The testator's last intent reflection is the most important task of the will, and this cannot be done without establishing that the testator had the testamentary intent, understood the circumstances and anticipated the consequences of his disposition. The lack of requirements as to the form of the will would conceal the danger of the testator taking ill-considered actions. This is probably why most legal systems relaxing formal requirements require some testation elements that are considered "essential" in a given legal system for the validity of an informal will. For example, New Zealand requires that a given document "appear to be a will" (section 14(1) of the *Wills Act*),[738] New Jersey law indicates the possibility of validation when "the decedent intended the document or writing to constitute the decedent's will" (§ 3B:3-3 *New Jersey Revised Statutes*)[739] or Israeli law emphasizes the necessity of "fundamental parts of a will" (section 25 of the *Israeli Succession Law* חוק הירושה).[740]

---

735 *Cf.* Peart and Kelly (n 98) 78.

736 Załucki, *Videotestament. Prawo spadkowe wobec nowych technologii* (n 33) 188.

737 John H Langbein, 'Crumbling of the Wills Act: Australians Point the Way' (1979) 65 American Bar Association Journal 1192.

738 Peart and Kelly (n 98) 83–85.

739 Sasso (n 30) 176.

740 Flaks (n 203) passim.

Therefore, in the context of the cautionary function of the provisions on the form of will, it is indicated that even a small formal requirement, such as the obligation to preserve the declaration of intent on any medium, requires the testator to take a minimum of care.[741] The materialization of the declaration of last intent, apart from the fact that it allows to determine its content, makes it possible to get acquainted with its content at any time, what increases the bequeather's knowledge of his legal situation, thus reducing the conflicting nature of turnover. The necessity to fulfil the technical conditions of a given form of will, even if they are a few, has the effect of delaying the submission of an appropriate declaration.[742] It gives the testator time to think about it, it helps him to understand the importance and the definite nature of the declaration made, despite the later possibility of revoking the will. In this respect, the bequeather's special form of action also provides protection against him.

Common forms of wills, including holographic wills, generally implement the above assumptions. While in the case of public wills, it is typical to have the testator's awareness of the *mortis causa* act, certain doubts may be raised in the case of private wills, where this is not necessarily obvious. Nevertheless, the mere requirement to keep the form, which serves primarily to consolidate the testator's declaration of intent, serves precisely to protect the testator from making an accidental declaration.[743] This is, as it may be assumed, the main warning task of the regulations on the form of wills.[744] This task is also realized by the recent anti-rigorous wills formalities provisions based on the doctrine of *substantial compliance* and its variations. In individual systems of this kind, the provisions of the law indicate the need to search for certain formalities, which are to show, among other things, that the testator acted with the proper intent and proper discernment. The relaxation of formal requirements does not therefore mean the loss of this element of examining the testation.

The above shows that the cautionary function of the wills formalities plays an important role in practice, and the legislation in force in this respect is not indifferent to it. In systems of *strict compliance* and *substantial compliance*, the issue of the existence of *animus testandi* is one of the most important elements of the *post factum* assessment of a succession by a par-

---

741 Langbein, 'Substantial Compliance with the Wills Act' (n 10) 495 ff.
742 Załucki, *Videotestament. Prawo spadkowe wobec nowych technologii* (n 33) 188–189.
743 Sasso (n 30) 170.
744 Vukotic (n 377) 478.

ticular court, and therefore the statutory structure must make it possible. *Ex ante* construction is to make the testator aware of the circumstances in which he finds himself and to counteract the randomness and uncertainty of testation. It is therefore undoubtedly a function related to the evidentiary and standardization function of the wills formalities.[745] In the future law of succession, this function should also be taken into account, and possible statutory provisions must take into account the possibility of establishing after the testator's death that he acted with the awareness of drawing up the will.

5. The protective function of the wills formalities regulations

The existing solutions in the area of succession law can and often do serve other purposes as well. One important objective in this respect is also to protect the testator and other persons, including the testator's relatives, from dispositions that are not made freely by him. Some regulations on the substantive validity of the will may pursue this goal.[746] Among the various requirements that are placed on legal transactions, the specific statutory solutions are those concerning the behaviour of the person performing the legal transaction of interest.[747] It is known that the will of a person performing a legal action must be freely undertaken and expressed in such a way as to produce certain legal effects.[748] The personal qualifications on which the ability of a given subject to cause effects in the sphere of private law depends on the legislator who usually associates them with specific qualities of a given person, such as age and appropriate mental development. It is no different under the law of succession, where *mortis causa* acts can be performed only by persons who have the ability to do so.[749] In the case of a will, this is the so-called "testamentary capacity", i.e. an attribute

---

745 Hardin (n 127) 1145–1190.

746 *Cf.* Penelope Reed, 'Challenges to Wills' [2012] Private Client Business 109.

747 *Cf.* Rescigno (n 583).

748 Jacek Wierciński, 'Sporządzenie testamentu w stanie wyłączającym świadome powzięcie decyzji i wyrażenie woli w praktyce notarialnej' [2011] Przegląd Sądowy 7.

749 *Cf.* Lawrence A Frolik, 'The Strange Interplay of Testamentary Capacity and the Doctrine of Undue Influence. Are We Protecting Older Testators or Overriding Individual Preferences?' (2001) 24 International Journal of Law and Psychiatry 253.

granted to an individual by a legal norm to make and revoke a will.[750] Against this background, various solutions are possible, which to a greater or lesser extent link the testamentary capacity with the requirement that the testator has full legal capacity.[751]

For a will to be valid, it is generally also required that the testator's intent was made freely, consciously and without any interference. A testator capable of testation, which is the starting point for assessing the validity of the will,[752] should therefore be aware of the situation of making a will and have a testation intent.[753] A condition in which the testator cannot make his last will consciously and freely and therefore, for whatever reason, excluding the conscious or free decision and expression of will, must result in the invalidity of the disposition.[754] Individual legislators have therefore developed mechanisms to protect the testator. Among these solutions, the ones that stand out are those concerning the defects of the declaration of intent and the negative consequences associated with the disruption of the testator's intent.[755] These regulations usually also apply to other defects in the declaration of intent, including errors and threats.[756] Legislators usually decide to specifically regulate this issue in the area of succession law, regardless of the general provisions for all legal acts. This is currently the case, for example, under the German law (§ 2078 and § 2229 section 4 of the *Bürgerliches Gesetzbuch*)[757] or French law (Article 901 of the French *Code civil*).[758] It is also characteristic of Polish law (Article 945 of the *Kodeks cywilny*).[759] The catalogue of legally relevant defects of the declaration of intent, which a will may be affected with, is generally closed. When

---

750 Miriam Anderson, 'La capacitat per a testar de qui té habitualment disminuïda la capacitat natural: l'art. 116 del Codi de Successions' (2009) 2009 InDret 1.

751 Lynch (n 721).

752 Kenneth I Shulman, Carole A Cohen and Ian Hull, 'Psychiatric Issues in Retrospective Challenges of Testamentary Capacity' (2005) 20 International Journal of Geriatric Psychiatry 63.

753 Julian Rivers and Roger Kerridge, 'The Construction of Wills' (2000) 116 Law Quarterly Review 287.

754 Kerridge (n 645) 19 ff.

755 *Cf.* Andrzej Mączyński, 'Wpływ wad oświadczenia woli na ważność testamentu' (1991) 1991 Rejent 24.

756 *Cf.* Scalise (n 582) 41 ff.

757 *Cf.* Leipold, *Erbrecht* (n 594) 89 ff.

758 Malaurie and Brenner (n 21) 190 ff.

759 Mączyński, 'Wpływ wad oświadczenia woli na ważność testamentu' (n 755) 24 ff.

a testator's declaration of intent is affected by a defect, it usually means its invalidity. This invalidity usually occurs *ipso iure*.[760]

Apart from those related to the testator's person and the process of testation, the requirements of substantive validity of a will include the content of a will.[761] This is because it is also important for determining whether a will may have certain legal effects. Generally speaking, it is connected with the idea that a will contrary to public order, the law or good faith should not have legal effects. In this respect, one may point out, for example, the prohibition in Polish law to include certain dispositions in the will, such as the limitation of the spouse's right to use the apartment and household facilities after the opening of the inheritance (Article 923 § 1 of the *Kodeks cywilny*) or the prohibition in Italian law to prepare one will by more than one testator (Article 989 of the Italian *Codice civile*).[762]

Such protective purposes may also be achieved by the provisions on the form of a will. In particular, those forms which are connected with the participation of third parties accompanying the testamentary activities allow to counteract a situation in which the testator's intention is not free.[763] The freedom of testation, which means, among other things, autonomy in making of *mortis causa* dispositions without the influence of third parties, is an important value which legislators have decided to protect. In some legal systems, it is connected, among others, with the ban on making joint wills, where there is a fear that the influence of the other testator will violate the freedom to dispose of the property at the discretion of the testator. According to the prevailing opinion in this respect, in the case of a joint will, therefore, to some extent, there is a violation of the unilateral declaration of intent and the principle that the testator's declaration is based on his intent fully freely taken.[764] Therefore, in the opinion of many, only those persons who are not interested in the content of a specific disposition, even if they are not concerned about the potential financial benefits related to it, can and should create a guarantee of the testator's free decision.[765]

---

760 Niedośpiał (n 622).

761 Załucki, *Videotestament. Prawo spadkowe wobec nowych technologii* (n 33) 32 ff.

762 Benedetti (n 659) 60–70.

763 Aloy (n 17) 10–11.

764 Stefano Pagliantini, *Causa e motivi del regolamento testamentario* (Jovene 2000) 74.

765 *Cf.* Joseph Laufer, 'Flexible Restraints on Testamentary Freedom-a Report on Decedents' Family Maintenance Legislation' (1954) 79 Harvard Law Review 277.

The regulations on the form of a will are therefore familiar with situations in which the declaration of intent is made before a third party, often a body of public trust, which is intended precisely to provide not only reliable proof of the testation, but also the lack of influence on the testator of other people. Hence, public wills, which can be found in many legal systems, where it is generally believed that the participation of an official person in the process of declaring the last will by the testator is a guarantee of undisturbed course of making the testator's declaration.[766] In this case, it is not a matter of shaping the contents of the will, giving it an appropriate legal meaning in accordance with the testator's will, as it may be the case with the channelling function, but of ensuring that the final form of the will statement understandable by the testator is not influenced by third parties. In this sense, official persons can also be treated as witnesses of the *mortis causa* disposition, which sometimes leads to them being described as qualified witnesses.[767]

The participation of ordinary witnesses in testation activities can also have the same meaning. The presence of people who do not have any function, but can be a source of proof of the circumstances of testation is a very popular requirement of the wills formalities regulations.[768] And although this requirement is increasingly being waived in the case of public wills (an official person is sufficient), in the case of private wills witnesses still play a role, although there is also a tendency to eliminate the requirement of their presence when making wills. Where the regulations on the form of wills require the participation of witnesses, there are usually regulations that require the witnesses of a will to meet certain formal criteria, including full legal capacity, use of sight, speech and writing, and understanding of the language spoken by the testator.[769] This is justified inasmuch as it is the task of the witness of the will to ensure that the intent expressed by the testator will be accurately reproduced after the death of the testator. A witness is the depositary of this will and is to ensure its faithful transmission. This function therefore determines the basic characteristics that a testimonial witness must possess. In addition, there are other limitations in the various legal systems, including the regulations that the person for whom

---

766 *Cf.* Agustín Ibarra García de Quevedo, 'La forrnalización del testamento público abierto' (1996) 14 Revista Colegio de Notarios 1.

767 *Cf.* Alvin E Evans, 'The Competency of Testamentary Witnesses' (1927) 25 Michigan Law Review 238.

768 Catherine Rendell, *Law of Succession* (Macmillan 1997) 38 ff.

769 Gareth Miller, *The Machinery of Succession* (Darmouth 1996) passim.

the will provides any benefit cannot be a witness when drawing up a will. Neither may they be witnesses: the person's spouse, his first- and second-class relatives or affinities and persons in a relationship of adoption. Such regulation can be met, for example, in the Polish law (Art. 957 § 1 of the *Kodeks cywilny*).[770]

It should be added that the concepts of forms of a will using the presence of people other than the testator are also intended to protect against the destruction or concealment of the will. While the succession laws of individual countries provide for sanctions for this type of action by certain persons which, after all, is annihilating the testator's intent, such protection cannot always be effective. It is not always clear whether the testator has drawn up a will, and if he has done so, where the will is located and what its content is. The presence of third parties during the drafting of the will therefore makes it possible to reveal the testator's will and to counteract pathological events.[771] The lawmakers, while observing the principle of the freedom of testation in order to guarantee the authenticity of the will and to obtain maximum certainty that the testator's declaration of intent at the time of making the will was free from defects, therefore use instruments which create conditions for determining the probability of the testation and its contents. It should be noted in this respect that personal sources of evidence do not always lead to the desired goals. This can be seen especially in the case of oral wills, which were questioned for many reasons for their validity, which were misjudged in Poland, abolished in Austria, for example, and remodelled in other legal systems.[772]

The formal requirements for wills can and usually are therefore used as a way for the legislator to protect the testator.[773] Various instruments that support this provide such protection either directly or indirectly. Guaranteeing legal certainty, the testator's intent and its finality is an objective that many legislators believe should be achieved in succession law.[774] Understanding this objective may, in extreme cases, lead to an attempt to impose solutions that make it difficult to revoke the will if the circumstances on the basis of which the testator made the disposition in the event of death change. There are solutions in the world that make it difficult or

---

770 Jan Gwiazdomorski and Andrzej Mączyński, *Prawo spadkowe w zarysie* (Państwowe Wydawnictwo Naukowe 1985) passim.
771 Załucki, *Videotestament. Prawo spadkowe wobec nowych technologii* (n 33) 192.
772 *Cf.* Borysiak (n 626); Welser, 'Die Reform des österreichischen Erbrechts' (n 87).
773 Gulliver and Tilson (n 34) 9 ff.
774 Langbein, 'Substantial Compliance with the Wills Act' (n 10).

even impossible to revoke a will drawn up in one form with a will in another form. The example given in the doctrine is connected with the drawing up of a notarial will, which then, under the influence of an impulse, is revoked by a less formalised will, e.g. with a handwritten will.[775] According to some opinions, the regulations on the form of a will should prevent such dispositions and provide that a possible revocation of a notarial will should take place only in another notarial will. This idea has gained supporters in some European countries. Poland can serve as an example, where - according to this concept - this kind of regulation protects the testator, especially when, as an elderly person limited by his own awkwardness, he is under the influence of relatives for whom no benefits were provided for in a previously drafted will.[776] In this way, the protective function may complement the channelling function of the will form regulations, since on the one hand it counteracts hasty decisions made by the testator, making sure that his will is not disturbed by a momentary strong impulse from a person who may have a significant influence on the testator.

In this regard, however, it should be pointed out that the protective function has been criticized from the very beginning of its perception in succession law[777]. Among other things, it was pointed out that it is difficult to justify in modern times. It was alleged that there are forms which, by definition, do not protect the testator properly, such as the holographic form. It was argued, among other things, that it is difficult to provide relatively strong proof that the person signing the declaration of last intent actually did so.[778] Similar allegations were made against other forms of will, including the above mentioned form of an oral will. This does not mean, however, that the regulations on the form of a will are defective or useless. Rather, it is a clear signal that deviations from the formal rules in favour of the functionalism of succession law are possible and, moreover, necessary[779]. In the law of succession, it is desirable that the intent of the testator be reconstructed after his death, while at the same time maintaining the

---

775 Załucki, *Videotestament. Prawo spadkowe wobec nowych technologii* (n 33) 193–194.

776 Fryderyk Zoll, 'Czy odwołalność testamentu zawsze powinna być nieograniczona' in Marlena Pecyna, Małgorzata Podrecka and Jerzy Pisuliński (eds), *Rozprawy cywilistyczne. Księga pamiatkowa dedeykowana Profesorowi Edwardowi Drozdowi* (Lexis Nexis 2013).

777 Gulliver and Tilson (n 34) 9–10.

778 Clowney (n 129) 58; Brown (n 107) 93 ff.

779 Załucki, *Videotestament. Prawo spadkowe wobec nowych technologii* (n 33) 194–195.

security of circulation, i.e., preventing the occurrence in circulation of dispositions of uncertain origin made in unclear circumstances with doubts as to their authorship. The task of the provisions on the form of a will is then to ensure that the testator's will is properly reflected. This can also be the case with types of *mortis causa* dispositions that potentially pose some risk to the realisation of these values. The conflict that exists between the freedom of testation and its reflection and the safety of legal trade should be resolved with due respect for the assumption that it is not the observance of formal requirements but the realization of the testator's intent that is important enough to strive for its realization, sometimes precisely against formal requirements.

This idea is the guiding principle for all solutions to mitigate formal requirements, including those based on the doctrine of *substantial compliance* and its variations. However, a functional approach to the law of succession does not mean that the testator's protection is waived.[780] In essence, *substantial compliance* solutions serve to reflect the testator's last will, but not at any cost. There must be certainty, supported by clear and convincing evidence, beyond any doubt, that in a given succession the testator's last will was expressed unconditionally and absolutely. If looking, for example, at the requirements of American states with the doctrine of *harmless error*, it can be seen that in practice, the courts pay attention to whether the testator actually had the testamentary intent and whether the process of free testation was in any way compromised (e.g., *Estate of Wiltfong* in Colorado[781] or the *Estate of Smoke* in Michigan[782]). Formal errors are saved as long as there is evidence of the testator's free will. The same can be found in different *substantial compliance-type* solutions. South Africa can serve as another example. In *Macdonald* the court was examining whether the security measures with regard to the computer file containing a will were breached and only after it has been established that this has not happened, found a will valid.[783] In *Van der Merwe* the court finding an informal will valid has highlighted that it was only possible because the true intention of the drafter of an informal document was self-evident.[784] The same can be

---

780 *Cf.* Duncan Kennedy, 'From the Will Theory to the Principle of Private Autonomy: Lon Fuller's "Consideration and Form"' (2000) 100 Columbia Law Review 94.
781 Re Estate of Wiltfong, [2006] 148 P.3d 465.
782 Re Estate of Smoke, [2007] Michigan Court of Appeals 273114.
783 MacDonald v. The Master, [2002] South African Law Reports 64.
784 Van der Merwe v. Master of the High Court & Another, [2010] ZASCA 99.

found in another case – *Ex Parte Maurice*.[785] A similar position was also expressed, for example, in the Canadian Province of Matinoba where only a single requirement has to be satisfied in order for a court to exercise the dispensation power: the document in question must embody the deceased's testamentary intentions.[786] In this context, the testator can be considered to be protected.

Therefore, systems based on the doctrine of *substantial compliance* or its variations in addition to the intent of testation also pay attention to, among other things, the age of the testator, errors or other circumstances surrounding testation (e.g. *Estate of Richards* in California[787]). It comes from the above that these solutions can also have a protective function, and their task is, among other things, to prove that the testator, when expressing his last will, was completely uninhibited.

In such circumstances, against the background of the solutions found in individual countries, the protective function of the provisions on the form of wills has played and continues to play an important role. Today and in the future, it is and will be important to determine whether the testator acted intentionally and his will was undisturbed. The form rules (wills formalities) thus support the provisions on the substantive validity of the will, and in principle it is difficult to imagine the need to change this. At least to a minimum, this goal of wills formalities should continue to be pursued.

In the light of the above, it can be assumed that the provisions on the form of a will still have four basic functions: evidentiary, channelling, cautionary, protective. Each of these functions has a different role, and the introduction of solutions aimed at relaxing the rigor of wills formalities into the law of succession does not preclude the existence of these functions. On the contrary, the protection of the testator, the predictability and repeatability of his action, the possibility of proving that he has acted with testamentary intent and *animus testandi* and that he was aware of the consequences of his action as a result of the introduction of solutions based on the doctrine of *substantial compliance* or its variations are strengthened. In this case, in the succession proceedings, the elements that are examined (with such a high degree of probability) cause that the role of relaxation of wills formalities is at the same time a mechanism to search for the exis-

---

785 Ex Parte Maurice, [1985] 2 SA 713.
786 *Cf.* du Toit, 'Remedying Formal Irregularities in Wills: A Comparative Analysis of Testamentary Rescue in Canada and South Africa' (n 7).
787 Re Estate of Richards, [2011] B226261.

tence of the testator's last intent, which normally does not necessarily have to happen. The relaxation concerns only technical issues, not the proof of intent of the testator. The latter is to be preserved and restored after his death, and these requirements are not a subject to any mitigation. The need to determine, with clear and convincing evidence or beyond reasonable doubt, that testamentary intent occurs, strengthens the role of the provisions on wills formalities.

(5) Functional wills formalities. Proposal of a model solution based on testamentary intent

1. Introductory remarks

The considerations presented so far show that the traditional and formal approach to the issue of the form of a will is now a relict, with individual legislators tending to maintain the validity of the last will even if the manner of its expression does not meet formal requirements. Despite the different mechanisms, the functions of the provisions on the form of a will are still preserved and the medium of the last will has the primary role of proving that a testation has taken place. The presentation of current trends in the development of the law in the area of succession law, against the background of standards known in succession law for many years and consequences of failure to comply with the wills formalities, as long as the presentation of some "cures" to rescue an informal last will, both in theory and practice of functioning of these solutions, unequivocally indicates the need for a modern, informalized look at the process of testation. Having analysed the traditional view and meaning of the functions of the form of a will against the background of the modern, informal solutions which are appearing more and more boldly in selected legal systems and which aim to reflect the last intention at the expense of formal requirements,[788] it has become necessary to advocate the need to build succession law around these solutions. It is therefore now the time to consider whether it is possible to reconcile in a single legal instrument the seemingly extreme values of *strict compliance* and *substantial compliance* so that testamentary succession is based on the testator's actual intention, while at the same time satisfying the functions of these rules and allowing informal wills to remain in force.

It may be argued that a way to solve the problem of the inadequacy of the rules on the form of wills to modern times, allowing for the flexibility of these rules while preserving their functions, may be introducing into

---

788 Ronald J JR Scalise, 'Will Formalities in Louisiana: Yesterday, Today, and Tomorrow' (2020) 80 Louisiana Law Review 1334; Horton and Weisbord (n 52); Bridget J Crawford, Kelly Purser and Tina Cockburn, 'Post-Pandemic Wills' (2021) 2021 University of Chicago Legal Forum.

the legal system only a general definition of the form of wills and the associated minimum requirements for such a disposition (last will).[789] The latter could consist only of the necessity to preserve the testator's declaration of will, but without indicating a specific type of form and manner of preservation, while at the same time obliging the authority applying the law (court) to determine whether a given testator's declaration includes the testator's disposition *mortis causa* of his estate.[790] This is because the preservation of the testator's last will and its reflection, and not his authentication, is the most important task of the regulations on the form of the wills; without preservation of the testator's will, there will be no will after his death. The way in which this will is preserved is of secondary importance, as evidenced, for example, by the diversity of regulations on form in different legal systems or loosening of rules in connection with the COVID-19 pandemic. Legislators place emphasis above all on the material element (medium), not on the way in which the last will is manifested.[791] Under such an assumption, the problems concerning the forms of wills currently existing in individual legal systems would no longer play a significant role; the facts whether the testator makes a declaration of last will in the presence of an official, notary or witnesses, just as whether he makes a declaration orally or in writing would become essentially irrelevant.[792]

With this in mind, I will consider why a functional approach should replace strict formalism and will then analyse in detail the above proposal and justify how such a functional approach could work in the practice of succession law in different countries.

2. Replacing strict formalism by a functional approach

The discussion so far has shown that the practice of succession law has frequently had to deal with last wills that are informal in nature. This informality is a feature that is becoming increasingly common with the development of new technologies. Testators are generally unaware of the wording of the applicable rules of succession law but are happy to use technology to express their last will. They are unconcerned about the applicable

---

789 Załucki, 'Forma testamentu w perspektywie rekodyfikacji polskiego prawa spadkowego. Czas na rewolucję?' (n 35) 45.
790 ibid.
791 ibid.
792 Dubravka Klasiček (n 368) 45.

rules, wrongly believing that this is not necessary. We know of attempts to make a last will on a record player,[793] DVD,[794] by sending an e-mail[795] or a text message.[796] Probably still to come, or at least there is no case law available on this, wills in cloud computing, blockchain technology or other technological boons, not necessarily already known.[797] The law is unable to keep up with this kind of human activity. Past experience in individual countries has shown that it is necessary to preserve the testator's last will in order to be able to reconstruct it some time after the death of its author. However, legislators are not unanimous as to how this preservation should take place.[798] Some are still using purely traditional solutions, the models of which are over two thousand years old. Others try to find solutions that keep up with modern challenges and make relatively modern instruments available for the purpose of preserving the last will, based for example on digital technologies. Such innovations have had varying degrees of success; an unsuccessful example being the 2001 proposal by the US State of Nevada, the world's first statutorily defined form of electronic will which, however, failed to enjoy any popularity and had to be redesigned by the legislature.[799] Others have rejected modern forms of wills, such as the Florida once did,[800] another US state, on the grounds that it could lead to too much use of Florida's jurisdiction by people from other areas.[801] So there is no single coherent policy, no single pattern that would allow similar instruments to be used throughout the world.[802] Such solutions would, however, seem tempting.

In addition to the above, the question of the form of the will is an issue which is, however, at a different stage of development in the various legal systems.[803] While the traditional instruments are similar in many legal sys-

---

793 *Cf.* Estate of Robert G. Reed, [1981] 672 P.2d 829 (WY).

794 *Cf.* Mellino v. Wnuk, [2013] Queensland Supreme Court 336.

795 *Cf.* Mahlo v. Hehir. [2011] Queensland Supreme Court 243.

796 *Cf.* Nichol v. Nichol, [2017] Queensland Supreme Court 220.

797 Crawford (n 82); Shah and others (n 82) 407 ff.

798 Zimmermann (n 22) 471 ff.

799 Hirsch, 'Technology Adrift: In Search of a Role for Electronic Wills' (n 83) 846; Gerry W Beyer and Katherine V. Peters, 'Sign on the [Electronic] Dotted Line: The Rise of the Electronic Will' (2019) 1 Wills Trusts & Estates Law eJournal.

800 Na Crous, *A Comparative Study of the Legal Status of Electronic Wills* (North West University 2019) 35.

801 ibid. However, the law was finally enacted.

802 *Cf.* Sasso (n 30) 169 ff.

803 Reid, De Waal and Zimmermann (n 31) passim.

tems, some of the detailed solutions vary considerably.[804] This has been a significant problem in recent times. The divergence between the different systems of succession law has major practical consequences, particularly in connection with so-called cross-border successions.[805] This phenomenon occurs mainly where a testator holds his estate in several countries (jurisdictions).[806] This raises the question of which law (the law of which country) should be regarded as applicable to the succession, including for instance for the assessment of whether the last will has been drawn up correctly and will produce the intended legal effects, and therefore for the assessment of its formal and substantive validity.[807] As regards the formal validity of a will, it should be pointed out that it is theoretically possible, and frequently encountered in practice, for a testator to draw up a will in a form which is unknown in the legislation which will be applicable under private international law to his succession. There are at least several possible solutions to this situation.[808] Since these problems were recognised some time ago, they have led, among other things, to certain international instruments which attempt to remove the boundaries between the national systems of succession law.[809]

In this respect, it should be pointed out that on 5 October 1961 the Hague Convention on the Conflicts of Laws relating to the Form of Testamentary Dispositions was adopted. Its aim was to facilitate the maintenance of the validity of wills.[810] In order to be formally valid, a will had to be drawn up in a form which complied with the requirements of the internal law of the place where it was made, of the nationality of the testator at the time when the will was made or died, of the testator's domicile or habitual residence or of the location of immovable property (Article 1 of the Convention). The practical operation of the Convention has been and con-

---

804 Crawford (n 36) 270 ff.

805 Mariusz Załucki, 'The Future of Succession Law in the EU. A Proposal' in C Santos Botelho and F da Silva Veiga (eds), *Future Law* (2018) 582 ff.

806 Andrzej Mączyński, *Dziedziczenie testamentowe w prawie prywatnym międzynarodowym. Ustawowe i konwencyjne unormowanie problematyki formy* (Uniwersytet Jagielloński 1976) 16 ff.

807 Raventos (n 519).

808 *Cf.* Jeffrey Talpis, 'Freedom of Cross-Border Estate Planning: Anticipated Problems' (2016) 22 Trusts & Trustees 119, 119–131.

809 Mariusz Załucki, *Uniform European Inheritance Law. Myth, Dream or Reality of the Future* (AFM Publishing House 2015) 79 ff.

810 *Cf.* Donald G Casswell, 'The Conflict of Laws Rules Governing the Formal Validity of Wills: Past Developments and Suggested Reform' (1977) 15 Osgoode Hal Law Journal 165.

tinues to be extremely useful for testators with assets in more than one country, as it makes it possible to dispose of these assets by means of a single will.[811] However, the practical application of the Convention rules is complicated.

Another step towards an attempt to harmonise the issue of the form of a will was taken at an international conference held in 1973 in Washington. It adopted the Convention providing a Uniform Law on the form of international will. The Convention introduces a new form of will into the national law of the States Parties: the international will.[812] An international will is a written testament, written in any language by hand or by any other means, not necessarily by the testator, who, in the presence of two witnesses and a person empowered to act in connection with the drafting of the international will declares that the document presented is his will, and is then signed by the testator, the witnesses and the person empowered. Like the 1961 Hague Convention, the purpose of this convention is to ensure that the last wills of testators are respected as far as possible. The difference, however, lies in the fact that the Washington Convention provides for an additional form of will - the international will. The application of this form in specific cases makes it unnecessary to seek the law applicable to the assessment of the validity of the testator's last will. However, the effectiveness of this instrument is not great, as it is not particularly popular.[813]

Over the years there have also been various regional attempts to harmonise the various systems of succession law, including the issue of the form of a will. An example of this type of activity is the American *Uniform Probate Code* of 1969, which has been amended several times, introducing, *inter alia*, a proposal to unify provisions concerning the form of a will in the territory of the United States of America.[814] The current wording of § 2-502 of the *Uniform Probate Code* distinguishes between two forms of

---

811 Andrzej Maczynski, 'La revocation du testament ' a la lumiere de la loi sur le droit international prive et de la Convention de La Haye sur les conflits de lois en matiere de forme des dispositions testamentaires' 19 Polish Yearbook of International Law 85.

812 *Cf.* Jack N Sibley, 'Convention Poviding a Uniform Law on the Form on an International Will: Problems with State Probate Law' (1974) 4 Georgia Journal of International and Comparative Law 422.

813 Załucki, *Uniform European Inheritance Law. Myth, Dream or Reality of the Future* (n 809) 90.

814 *Cf.* Lawrence W Waggoner, 'The Revised Uniform Probate Code' (1994) 5 Trust & Estates 18.

wills: a written will executed in the presence of witnesses or a notary public and a holographic will.[815] This regulation, however, constitutes a kind of "background" to the legislation on succession law. Of particular importance is the provision of § 2-503 of the *Uniform Probate Code* introducing the so-called *"harmless error"* rule.[816] As the doctrine points out, the formal requirements imposed on wills since the time of this provision are therefore not of an essential nature; they are merely a guide.[817] According to this solution, the most important thing is the testamentary intention, regardless of its form.[818] Although not all state legislatures in the United States of America have chosen to adopt the solutions proposed in the *Uniform Probate Code*, they provide valuable comparative material, particularly in the context of a regulation which allows for the validity of a will which does not meet all the formal requirements of the law. The same can be said about other variations of the *substantial compliance* doctrine, however they are not widely harmonized. The existing differences raise many questions.

Attempts to harmonise succession law have also been made in the European Union.[819] Although initially the matter was considered to be outside the competence of the EU legislature, after the European Union set itself the objective of maintaining and developing an area of freedom, security and justice in which the free movement of persons is ensured (Art. 3 par. 2 TEU) it became necessary, in order for such an area to function properly, to adopt private law measures with cross-border implications.[820] This was necessary for the proper functioning of the common market, as the international conventions known so far did not solve the problems of cross-border succession. Work on a European instrument in matters of succession was therefore announced as early as 1998 in the so-called Vienna Action Plan, and the current result is the *EU Succession Regulation* No. 650/2012.[821]

---

815 Mann (n 7).

816 Bonfield (n 260).

817 *Cf.* Miller, 'Reforming the Formal Requirements for the Execution of a Will' (n 90); Miller, 'How Harmless Is Harmless? An In-Depth Look Into the Harmless Error Rule' (n 472); Crawford (n 36).

818 Wendel, 'Wills Act Compliance and the Harmless Error Approach: Flawed Narrative Equals Flawed Analysis?' (n 122).

819 Alain-Laurent Verbeke and Yves-Henri Leleu, 'Harmonization of the Law of Succession in Europe' in AS Hartkamp and others (eds), *Towards a European Civil Code* (Kluwer Law International 2011) 459–479.

820 Elise Goossens and Alain-Laurent Verbeke, 'De Europese Erfrechtverordening' [2012] Themis 105.

821 Paul Lagarde, 'Les principes de base du nouveau du règlement européen sur les successions' [2012] Revue Critique de Droit International Privé 691.

This instrument primarily regulates issues of private international law, and in this context also concerns the forms of testamentary dispositions, but only written ones. The Regulation explicitly excludes its application to the formal validity of oral dispositions of property upon death (Article 1(2)(f)), while it regulates the form of dispositions of property upon death made in writing (Article 27).[822] The provision of Art. 27 of the Regulation provides that a disposition of property upon death made in writing shall be valid as regards form if its form complies with the law: a) of the State in which the disposition was made or the agreement as to succession concluded; b) of a State whose nationality the testator or at least one of the persons whose succession is concerned by an agreement as to succession possessed, either at the time when the disposition was made or the agreement concluded, or at the time of death; c) of a State in which the testator or at least one of the persons whose succession is concerned by an agreement as to succession had his domicile, either at the time when the disposition was made or the agreement concluded, or at the time of death; d) of the State in which the testator or at least one of the persons whose succession is concerned by the agreement as to succession had his habitual residence, either at the time when the disposition was made or the agreement concluded, or at the time of death; e) in so far as immovable property is concerned, of the State in which that property is located.[823] It should be added, however, that pursuant to Article 75 of the Regulation, the States Parties to the Hague Convention on the Conflicts of Laws relating to the Form of Testamentary Dispositions continue to apply the provisions of that Convention instead of Article 27 of the Regulation. So far, however, Regulation has not prompted any wider reflection, either academic or jurisprudential, in the context of wills formalities.

In addition to the above, European doctrine is beginning to discuss the need for a uniform substantive law of succession in the European Union, highlighting the ineffectiveness of harmonisation in the area of private international law alone.[824] One of the proposals in this debate is the adoption in future of a single law on succession for the countries of the Euro-

---

822 Tito Ballarino, 'Il nuovo regolamento europe sulle successioni' [2013] Rivista di Diritto Internazionale 1116.

823 Katarzyna Anna Dadańska and Krzysztof Kubasik, 'Forma rozrządzeń na wypadek śmierci po wejściu w życie Rozporządzenia Parlamentu Europejskiego i Rady (UE) nr 650/2012 z dnia 4 lipca 2012 roku' [2014] Problemy Prawa Prywatnego Międzynarodowego 9.

824 Laura-Dumitrana Rath-Boşca, Loredana Mirela Barmoş and Ioana Andreea Stănescu, 'The Need to Harmonize the Laws of the European Union Regarding

pean Union and, as part of this law, uniform rules on the form of a will based on the construction of a holographic will, an international will or any other.[825] Over the years, testamentary succession has thus evolved throughout the world according to the needs of society. This development is thought to be linked to an important worldwide trend. Namely, testamentary succession is the preferred means by which property passes to another person after the death of an individual.[826] The forms of wills and the rules governing them should make it possible, indeed encourage, an individual to make a last will. However, only legislation that is effective, forgiving of innocent mistakes, will be able to meet the needs of society. The degree of complexity of the various legal solutions, including doubts as to the applicability or otherwise of particular international conventions, is undoubtedly one of the stimuli for the further search for a solution that would make it possible to achieve the objective of increased use of the last will as an instrument of succession planning. Therefore, wills formalities regulations need modernisation.[827] Ideally, this modernisation should be of a universal nature, allowing the same approach in different legal systems. It seems that such a possibility exists.

As it has been argued so far, the provisions on the form of a last will have four basic functions. While preserving these functions, it is not only possible to take a rigorous approach, but also a flexible one which will still ensure that the provisions on the form of a last will achieve all their objectives. Reliable proof of the testator's intentions, acting without pressure from third parties and with a purpose, while at the same time the testator understands the seriousness of the act being performed, are values which should not be departed from when designing solutions for testamentary succession. However, in order for these values to function properly in practice and for the succession to be based on the testator's true will, it is necessary to create flexible rules which take account of the testator's state of knowledge and habits. If the testator wishes to use a particular method to record the last will and testator's intentions in such a way as to give effect

---

the Succesion Law' [2016] Agora International Journal of Economical Sciences 35.

825 Załucki, *Uniform European Inheritance Law. Myth, Dream or Reality of the Future* (n 809) passim.

826 *Cf.* Harris (n 622).

827 Renzo E Saavedra Velazco, 'El Anteproyecto de Reforma al Código Civil y los negocios juridicos mortis causa' (2019) 64 Actualidad Civil 43; Załucki, 'About the Need to Adjust the Regulations Regarding the Form of Will to the Modern Requirements' (n 14).

to these values, the law should not limit it. In doing so, it encroaches upon the sphere of freedom of disposal of property, protected at the constitutional level, which, as is well known, means that the legislator must ensure such instruments that will allow the last will to be reflected after the testator's death.[828] Forcing the testator to use for this purpose only, for instance, the services of a notary seems to be an over-reaching restriction that certainly does not realise the principle of freedom of will. For this reason, legislators should seek instruments that implement the freedom of testation and, at the same time, all the values that guide testamentary succession. The way in which the testator's last will is recorded should be irrelevant and technologically indifferent, depending only on whether it allows the testator's last will to be preserved in a secure manner and whether it can be reconstructed after the testator's death. Whether this medium is a piece of paper or a computer cloud, and whether the testator's will is expressed orally or manually or in any other manner, should be irrelevant. Only then it is possible to speak of a desire on the part of the legislator to reflect the testator's real will and to create mechanisms enabling it to be carried out.[829] This is the route to be taken by the various systems of succession law.

In this context, it should also be noted that a testator who draws up a private will is usually convinced that he knows what he has done and thinks that he has done it in no uncertain terms[830]. Ironically, however, these supposedly clear formulations may be interpreted quite differently in the course of legal proceedings. On the other hand, a testator who entrusts the drafting of a will to a professional may - no matter how long individual provisions are explained to him - not be able to understand their meaning. Again, ironically, such a will cannot usually adequately express his desires as to how his estate should be distributed.[831] The relationship between words and intention thus appears to be one of the most significant problems of will interpretation.[832] In fact, it is a question of solving two differ-

---

828 Rzewuski, 'Formalisation of the Testament in the Light of the Favor Testamenti Principle' (n 48).

829 *Cf.*, however: Roger Kerridge and others, *Making a Will* (Society of Legal Scholars 2017).

830 Mark Glover, 'A Taxonomy of Testamentary Intent' (2016) 23 George Mason Law Review 269.

831 Pierre Ciotola, 'Des principes usuels d'interprétation des testaments et les décisions rendues en 2007' (2018) 110 Revue du notariat 37.

832 Karen J Sneddon, 'In the Name of God, Amen. Language in Last Wills and Testaments' (2011) 29 Quinnioac Law Review 665.

ent problems: the problem of discovering the testator's desires, that is to say of ascertaining the deceased's intention, and the problem of neutrally bringing them to fruition. The primary task of interpreting a will is to ascertain and give effect as fully as possible to the intention of the deceased.[833] The construction of provisions of the law of succession should make such interpretation possible. Where in a given case it is undoubtedly that the testator acted with *animus testandi*, it should be the task of the authority applying the law and settling the succession to reflect his wishes and not to emphasise the existence of formalism. The law must allow for this. Therefore, replacing strict formalism with a flexible approach is a necessary further development of succession law. Continuing to adhere strictly to formal requirements at the expense of the testator's true but informal intention appears to be incorrect. The development of new technologies will only reinforce the incorrectness of the formalistic approach to succession law. A flexible approach is needed, introducing a mechanism that will once and for all allow succession law to become predictable, technologically independent, regardless of the legislator's perception of the changes taking place, treating the last will as the main instrument for transferring property in the event of death. How to achieve it?

3. Solution to reconcile functional approach and formalism

On the basis of the initial assumptions that the statutory provision concerning the form of a will should be technologically irrelevant, serve to record the testator's last will, allow the last will to be reconstructed some time after the testator's death and fulfil the four basic functions of this type of provision (evidentiary, channelling, cautionary, protective), having due regard to the testator's intention, it is possible to formulate a proposal for a universal statutory provision that would reconcile the requirements and values indicated. The main problem in applying the law of succession in practice is the serious divergences between legal systems, which, in the case of a testator living in several jurisdictions, can be confusing in the context of the valid preparation of a disposition of property upon death. There is convincing evidence, supported by doctrine and case law and discussed so far, that the starting point for any instrument to reflect the testator's last will is a tool to convey the testator's actual last intention, irrespective of how it is recorded. Mechanisms based on the doctrine of *substantial compli-*

---

833 Joseph Warren, 'Interpretation of Wills' (1936) 49 Harvard Law Review 689.

ance and its variations, as well as other internationally known methods of mitigating formal requirements, are generally agreed to the effect that an essential element of the validity of a will is a recorded *animus testandi* with testator's declaration of intention. The same is also true for the *strict compliance* jurisdictions. Regardless of whether the testator made a will in Australia, New Zealand, Canada, South Africa, the United States of America, England, the Netherlands, France, Austria, Germany or Poland, the element which always appears as a legal requirement of a will is the testator's declaration of last will (intention) and its preservation. In view of the fact that a will is generally drawn up some considerable time before the testator's death, the form in which it is recorded must allow the last will to be reproduced some time after the testator's death. As a rule, all legal systems which regard the will as an instrument for disposing of property in the event of death place the emphasis on this part of testamentary succession. However, the implementation of the act of preservation varies from one legal system to another, although in many cases the differences are not fundamental. Nevertheless, current reality can and does lead to situations in which a will validly drawn up in one country is deemed invalid in another. This is due to the fact that different legislators have a different approach to the issue of form and some of them are more flexible than others. Such a state of affairs seems undesirable, particularly as the foundation of the legal arrangements for testamentary succession is the same everywhere. As a matter of principle, testamentary succession as a process does not differ, and one would think, should not differ, from the death of a testator in Europe or in America or Australia. There are, of course, differences in the process of acquiring succession to all the rights and obligations of the deceased, but these should not be decisive in matters as fundamental as wills. There can be no doubt, however, that the most appropriate solution for ensuring legal certainty in succession law would be a global uniformity of all succession procedures, but this is clearly not possible in the current state of affairs, both because of the different traditions and customs and simply because of the different needs of certain societies. This does not mean, however, that mechanisms cannot already be developed to bring such uniformity closer. In the context of testamentary succession this is possible because, in fact, the practice of *strict compliance* and *substantial compliance* has more and more in common. This is also recognised by the doctrine, which is increasingly bold in its search for solutions conducive to the maintenance of wills (as valid wills). Of course, this is also a consequence of the judicial activity of the courts, which, seeing the injustice of certain normative solutions, are looking for various ways to resolve the resulting impasse.

One example of this is the law in the Canadian province of Ontario, where the need for a greater latitude in validating or rectifying an improperly prepared will was recently raised, and where a person making a will is formally required to meet all of the legislated formalities relating to the making of a will (*strict compliance*). Despite this state of affairs and the unambiguous wording of the provisions of the law (section 3-4 of the *Succession Law Reform Act*), the courts have tried to mitigate the effects of the law. For example, in *Sisson v. Park Street Baptist Church* the court has stated that "the absence of legislation on point should not stop the court from developing the *common law* where there has been *substantial compliance* given that the dangers which two witnesses are to guard against does not exist".[834] This view was recalled, *inter alia*, in the 2020 discussion about the future of the testamentary succession in this province, taking into consideration whether it is time for Ontario to change from *strict compliance* to a *substantial compliance* regime for wills legislation.[835] The discussion still continues and of course Ontario is not the only example of it. However, it is another incentive to think about comprehensive reform of wills formalities, and to take the needs of testators into account in designing the wills formalities law.[836] Thus, even in the countries that are already familiar with the doctrine of *substantial compliance*, there is a need for further legislative changes, and solutions based on the doctrine of *substantial compliance* and its variations are only one possibility.

Another possibility, which seems more reasonable at the moment, is to modify the current provisions on the form of the will in order to remove their characteristics as being dependent on any method of making and preserving the last will. The law should be flexible in this respect and require, in order for the will to be valid, that the last will be made and preserved in such a way as to enable it to be reproduced after the testator's death, but it should not prescribe a particular manner of making the declaration and

---

834 *Sisson v. Park Street Baptist Church*, [1998] 71 O.T.C. 35 (GD).

835 James Jacuta, 'Is Substantial Compliance in Ontario's Future?' (2020) <https://hullandhull.com/2020/08/is-substantial-compliance-in-ontarios-future/> accessed 21 January 2021.

836 Andrea Hill and Turkstra Mazza, 'Strict versus Substantial Compliance with Statutory Formalities for Wills' (2020) <https://www.hamiltonlaw.on.ca/Web/About-the-HLA/HLA-Journal-Articles/Estates---Trusts-Journal-Artices/Estates_Law_News_Strict_versus_Substantial.aspx> accessed 21 January 2021.

the means of preserving it.[837] That should be irrelevant. Irrespective of whether a testator chooses to use the written or handwritten technique, to make a declaration of intent to an official person, to record the last will in the cloud or using blockchain technology, or in any other way, as long as it is possible to recreate the testator's last will after his death and such action allows the importance of the four essential functions of a will to be fully taken into account, such way of preparing a testator's disposition of property upon death, should be permitted.[838]

The main argument why this kind of proposal seems to be a more appropriate solution than the widespread adaptation of the doctrine of *substantial compliance* or variations thereof is linked to the fact that the latter solutions depend on the existence of various forms of will, or a certain form of will, which the testator is unable to satisfy by making a will, so they are made to rectify mistakes.[839] The idea behind this proposal, however, is to eliminate mistakes at the very first stage of drafting a will, when decisions are made on how to make a last will and how to preserve it. There is no convincing evidence that this has to be done in any of the ways indicated in the current legislation, which are usually by holographic means or with the participation of an official person or witnesses. Any other way is equally good, as long as the basic functions and values of dispositions upon death are reflected. Moreover, solutions based on the doctrine of *substantial compliance* usually serve to rescue only those forms that were the basis for the drafting of a will in Anglo-Saxon countries, and therefore aim primarily to remedy the shortcomings of writing or witnessing a will, which does not seem to be sufficient at present.[840] While the requirement to keep the form of a will shall continue to appear in the law, it is difficult to reduce it to a mere requirement of writing or witnessing a will, when any other form of preservation of a testamentary intent shall be sufficient, if it meets all the necessary standards. For this reason, a variation on the regulation of the form of a will may consist of a combination of both models: *strict compliance* and *substantial compliance*. On the one hand, certain

---

837 Załucki, 'Forma testamentu w perspektywie rekodyfikacji polskiego prawa spad-kowego. Czas na rewolucję?' (n 35) 46–47.

838 However, see: Victoria J Haneman, 'The Disruptive Potential of Blockchain in the Law of Wills' [2020] Trust & Estates 2.

839 du Toit, 'Remedying Formal Irregularities in Wills: A Comparative Analysis of Testamentary Rescue in Canada and South Africa' (n 7).

840 See, for example, the abovementioned case law form the United States of America. *Cf.* Dorman (n 134); Horton, 'Partial Harmless Error For Wills: Evidence From California' (n 501).

minimum formalities should be required, while, on the other, the primary objective should be to reflect the testator's last intention,[841] as convincingly expressed. This can be done more easily and precisely than through the use of an additional, supplementary mechanism such as one of the mechanisms for rectifying wills based on the doctrine of *substantial compliance*.

In such a model of testamentary succession the emphasis would be differently distributed. The burden of proof that we are dealing with a testament would be transferred to another dimension. Assuming that such a solution would continue to perform the functions indicated for the forms of wills, the question arises about the possibility of constructing a model of testamentary succession in such a way as to enable free testation while providing reliable evidence of the testator's intentions and circumstances of creating a will, unifying the process of passing the inheritance estate to the heirs, making the testator aware of the seriousness of the action he is performing and protecting him against external pressures, while being at the same time a flexible solution and taking into account the needs of the changing society.[842]

It seems that the implementation of such model testamentary succession regulations would depend on the configuration of the proposed solution. If the future statutory regulation in this area were to be shaped in general terms, what seems necessary and appropriate, the provision on the obligation to comply with the form of a wills could read as follows:

> "*The testator may create a will in such a way that he expresses his testamentary intention by any conduct which reveals his declaration of will sufficiently, and his declaration is preserved on any medium which makes it possible to reflect it in a way which allows the person making this declaration to be identified*".

Then, in principle, the other provisions contained in the individual laws on the form of wills (providing for types of wills form) would be redundant. In this case, there would be no need for further development of the provisions on form and no need to consider whether the current opportunities created for legislators should be supplemented in the light of technological change and the needs of society. This proposal reconciles the *strict compliance* doctrine with the *substantial compliance* doctrine, and causes that no other regulations concerning testamentary formalities shall be nec-

---

841 Crawford (n 36) 294.
842 This idea combines all the basic functions of the provisions on the form of a will, see: Gulliver and Tilson (n 34) 2 ff.

essary to ensure that the testator's intentions are carried out.[843] The evaluation of the testator's performance would become a one-stage assessment. After such a change, a will would still be a formalised legal act, although this formalism would not refer to any particular type of testamentary form, but would allow for the testator's freedom of choice in this regard, requiring only the preservation of a declaration of will in virtually any way. It may be a solution that enables the last will, which, under many circumstances, should be regarded as having been expressed unequivocally but in contravention of the law, and therefore often invalid under the current rules.

Such a regulation, which requires the documenting of a declaration of testamentary intention in order for it to have certain legal effects, would refer to the approach found in some legal systems, to treating a document as a message of human will,[844] which feature is to be its intellectual content, i.e. the content (information) including the declaration of will, which must be preserved in such a way that it can be reflected after the testator's death, regardless of the type of medium on which the preservation is based.[845] Such a change is part of the trend of an informal view of today's private law relations.[846] In this light, the content of a will could therefore be freely disclosed (verbally, with graphic signs, sound, image), but it would have to be preserved, on any medium (paper, electronic information carrier) and by any means (pen, computer, tablet). However, the limit of this neutrality would be set by the evidential function of the document, which requires that the way in which the content is stored should allow it to be preserved and reflected.

In order for the information containing the declaration of testamentary intention ("content") to be reflected, it must be properly stored in the medium. Only the two elements together, i.e. the reflectable information and the medium, constitute a document, in this case a will. Thus, information without a medium alone would not be a testament, just like an information-less medium. Thus, the form of wills proposed in this way would be a form with a lower degree of formalisation than the handwritten form or other forms known at present, but it does not exclude the use of the holographic form, as well as other current forms. The courts could still

---

843 *Cf.* Gray (n 130) 340 ff.
844 Szostek (n 601) 26 ff.
845 Dvoenosova (n 611).
846 Thomas Nachbar, 'Form and Formalism' (2018) 1 University of Virginia School of Law Public Law and Legal Theory Research Paper Series 36 ff.

monitor whether the testator's declaration of will is intended to create legal effects in the area of succession (*animus testandi*), thus ensuring the evidentiary and protective function of the regulations on form. The obligation to preserve the declaration of will would, in turn, constitute the execution of the protective function of the provisions on form, and it could be discussed whether the regulation designed in this way would perform also the chanelling function. As a rule, the transfer of assets to the heirs as a result of the testator's will would still take place according to the concept of will as an alternative to statutory inheritance or other instruments known under the succession law; there would also be an obligation to preserve the testator's last will, which at least indirectly performs the indicated function. Even if this was not the case, it does not seem that the unification of the process of passing the estate to the heirs - which is the task of the form regulations in this case - would be such a strong obstacle that the proposed solution should be rejected immediately. After all, the proposed norm could be complemented by further provisions, such as the obligation to mark the testator's declaration of testamentary intention in time or space, as well as - even if a third party preserves the declaration of will (if such a solution is allowed) - by provisions concerning the suitability of witnesses to participate in creating the will or possible requirements for other persons. It may also be tempting to apply a solution known for example from Dutch law, which assumes that a will is invalidated by the action of a person having a legal interest in it, rather than being automatically invalid.

This would, I think, minimize the negative effects of informalisation of current solutions, and reconcile the *strict* and the *substantial* concepts of wills formalities. The most important value in succession law would still be to reflect the will of the testator, to graciously refer to *animus testandi* and testator's intent,[847] while preserving all the functions of the wills formalities regulations and using the unquestionable *favor testamenti* rule as a tool to reflect the last will.[848] This would achieve the goal of increasing the availability of succession planning tools. This availability will be independent of pandemics or other unforeseeable external circumstances that may occur in the future.[849]

It is therefore in this context and to this extent that changes to the law of succession should be called for. Legislation based on the concept of *strict compliance*, which customarily provides for a broad catalogue of possible

---

847 Langbein, 'Substantial Compliance with the Wills Act' (n 10) passim.
848 Aloy (n 17) 11 ff.
849 Purser, Cockburn and Crawford (n 9) 13 ff.

forms of will, would not need to give further consideration to the legitimacy of introducing electronic or blockchain-based wills.[850] The proposed solution would make it possible for wills to be drawn up in this way as well. In the first place, the proposed solution therefore has the advantage of making the provisions on the form of wills technologically neutral. Whether it is a handwritten will, a witnessed will, an official will or a video will, the proposed wording of the provisions on the form of wills would enable all of them to be validly drawn up. In principle, there is also no need to "cure" the declaration of last will, on the basis of the *substantial compliance* and similar solutions, as the proposal would introduce a high degree of discretion and neutrality in terms of the testator's actions to transfer his estate upon death. Such arrangements could also be dispensed with, thereby eliminating, among other things, the conflicts which can arise in some jurisdictions as a result of the application of such provisions. This can be seen, for example, in a case decided recently in the United States of America, where on December 16, 2020, the Supreme Court of Ohio's decision in the case *Estate of Shaffer*[851] reversed the Sixth District Court of Appeals and settled ambiguity pertaining to a witness's ability to inherit under a will. The ambiguity at issue was between the "interested-witness rule" (section 2107.15 of Ohio Revised Code) and the "*harmless error* rule" (section 2107.24 of Ohio Revised Code). The interested-witness rule voids any gift in a will made to a person who is one of the witnesses to the will.[852] The *Shaffer* decision addressed whether this rule applies to wills whose validity relies on the *harmless error* rule.[853] The probate court rejected the application to admit the will to probate. The second instance court reversed and found the will could be admitted to probate under the *harmless error* rule stating that the gift to the beneficiary-witness did not need to be voided by the interested-witness rule because the *harmless error* rule empowered the probate court to "evaluate the credibility of the interested witness and weigh the evidence." However, in reversing the appellate decision, the Supreme Court of Ohio held the interested-witness rule applies both to wills executed in compliance with section 2107.03 of Ohio Revised

---

850 Hirsch, 'Technology Adrift: In Search of a Role for Electronic Wills' (n 83) 846 ff; Röthel (n 1) 62 ff.
851 Re Estate of Shaffer, [2019] Supreme Court of Ohio 0364.
852 Adrian S McGee, 'Revisiting Ohio's Harmless Error Statute - Saving Grace or Unintended Loophole?' (2019) 29 Probate Journal of Ohio 233.
853 *Cf.* Matthew Hochstetler, 'Where There's a "Will," There's a Way: The Harmless-Error Rule, Interested-Witness Rule, and In Re Estate of Shaffer' (2020) 30 Ohio Probate Law Journal 202.

Code and those submitted pursuant to the *harmless error* rule. There are certainly many examples of similar doubts about the application of the doctrine of *substantial compliance* and its variations,[854] while the statutory solution shall be intended to simplify the system of testamentary succession, not to complicate it. A one-stage assessment of the validity of dispositions of property upon death would seem to be a more efficient solution, especially since in the Ohio's case it seems more desirable to keep the will in force as a valid will, since the purpose of the legislation is to reflect the will of the testator in the first place (and it seems that the approach of the second instance court leaving this matter to be assessed in the succession proceedings is a turn toward that direction).

The proposed solution should also not be regarded as a complete informalisation of the will. A total departure from formalism could lead to a blurring of the boundaries between valid and invalid wills, between a will and a draft or other document.[855] The proposed solution runs no such risk. The wording of the proposed provision, with its emphasis on the testator's expression of a testamentary intention manifested by his conduct, the possibility of identifying the testator and of reconstructing the last will after his death, as mandatory requirements in any will, should prove sufficient to establish with a degree of probability verging on certainty that there is a last will in the case in question. Comparing this solution with the provisions currently in force regarding, for example, the validity of oral or holographic wills, the proposal seems to entail no bigger risks than the provisions already in force.[856] It certainly brings a breath of fresh air to models based on ancient models. By means of the proposal, the possibility of seeking to uphold the testator's last will and testator's actual will appears wider. The drafting of wills would become simpler and formal obstacles would no longer constitute a barrier to the assessment of whether a will is valid in substance, i.e. made with the *animus testandi*. It is this last element that is the most important in a testamentary succession, just as the reflection of the testator's last will is the most important value of succession law to be pursued. Such a proposal also ensures the widest possible freedom of testation, enabling the testator to freely dispose of his property upon death.

---

854 *Cf*, e.g.: Wendel, 'Wills Act Compliance and the Harmless Error Approach: Flawed Narrative Equals Flawed Analysis?' (n 122) 361–363.

855 Holmes (n 261).

856 Brown (n 107).

In assessing the reasons why the doctrine of *strict compliance* and its variations persists in the various jurisdictions rejecting the doctrine of *substantial compliance*, including the assumption that the formalities of execution ensure, *inter alia*, that the "will was executed by the person purporting to be the testator and prevents a ne'er-do-well from impersonating the testator or someone from forging the testator's signature",[857] it can be accepted that the presented solution will also counteract this risk. The basis for assessing whether there is a will would be to determine whether, in the particular case, the testator expressed his testamentary intention. A similar consideration can be given to the levelling of the threat of fraud, undue influence and coercion. Although, of course, such action cannot be ruled out in the case of certain methods of making a last will, this is also characteristic of current forms of will (e.g. holographic).[858] The obligation to express and preserve a last intent would also create the possibility of enhancing the testator's appreciation of the importance of the action being performed.

The testator's intention, as a result of the proposed amendment, would become a fundamental element of the testamentary process, the reflection of which would not be hindered by unnecessary formalism.[859] The conflict of intention v. formalism would be resolved in favour of intention, with the proviso that without a minimum of formality it would not be possible to recreate the intention. In such a case, i.e. without any formal successful attempt to preserve the intention, it would not be possible to speak of a will at all. In order to consider that there is a will in a given succession case the intention of the testator and the minimum formalities described as "revealing declaration of will sufficiently" and "preserving declaration of will on a medium which makes it possible to reflect".

In this light, the proposed solution would appear to be capable of becoming a stand-alone provision governing the form of a will, being a flexible approach to the wills formalities, taking into account the interests of society and performing all the functions which the law of succession envisages for the provisions on the form of a will. It has the ability to reconcile

---

857 *Cf.* Charles Wagner, 'Have Ontario's Courts Dispensed with Strict Compliance with the Formalities of Execution?' (2012) <https://www.wagnersidlofsky.com/have-ontarios-courts-dispensed-with-strict-compliance-with-the-formalities-of-execution> accessed 21 January 2021.

858 However, as may be thought, extrinsic evidence can help to solve these problems if they arise. These arrangements shall, to a large extent, depend on the active involvement of the parties to the proceedings concerned.

859 Marsal Guillamet (n 635) 2 ff.

two seemingly contradictory approaches, i.e. *strict compliance* and *substantial compliance*.

4. Towards functional wills formalities

The considerations so far have shown that it is possible to design a single legal instrument which would have the effect of increasing the influence of the intent of the testator on the succession. This instrument would be technologically independent and essentially based on testamentary intent, a value of paramount importance in succession law.[860] There is no doubt that a solution such as the one proposed would allow a respite from the excessive formalism of the current statutory solutions dealing with wills formalities, while taking into account the hitherto known and acknowledged important functions of provisions of this kind. By introducing the proposed instrument, the legislator would strike a balance between formalism and intention, adapting the rules of succession law to the times and requirements of society.[861] Against this background, the problems of the place where the signature is affixed, where witnesses are revealed or where the last will is declared and around whom etc. would give way to an examination of whether, in a given case, we are dealing with the real last intention of the testator, expressed in a convincing manner. Such a solution seems desirable.

In order to make this kind of change to the succession law, it is worth considering whether it is possible on a wider scale, whether it has a universal dimension, or whether it is intended solely for one legal system. When analysing the issue of the form of a will against the background of selected legislations, it should be noted that it is being increasingly frequently argued that an important feature to be met by the regulations on form is to enable the testator's last will to be reproduced as accurately as possible. Hence, in some legal systems, a certain relaxation as regards form may already be observed, particularly in situations where the determination of the testator's will by evidence external to the will is beyond doubt. In this connection, it should be reminded that there is a general trend worldwide towards the informalisation of testamentary dispositions, as presented above. It is accepted that the reflection of the testator's last will, rather

---

860 Eccher (n 57) 47 ff; Wendel, *Wills, Trusts, and Estates* (n 26) 146 ff.
861 Anne Alstott, 'Family Values and the Law of Inheritance' (2009) 7 Socioeconomic Review 145.

than the requirements as to form, is one of the main priorities of modern succession law. In this direction, it should therefore be noted that testamentary dispositions are increasingly being made in such forms as to allow the testator's will to be carried out without raising doubts as to the authenticity of the *mortis causa* disposition in question, and only afterwards should the rigours concerning non-compliance with the form be formulated.[862] For this reason, the proposed amendment appears to be in line with this type of trend, both in *strict* and *substantial* compliance approaches. Therefore it seems like it is able to be accepted on a wider scale, not only in one legal system. The proposal is intended to be uniform and capable of implementation to any legal system. It is designed to be universal.

In assessing the scope of the required changes in the law of succession of any country, it appears sufficient to frame the provisions on the form of a will in such a way as to give them the shape proposed here, while dispensing with the other provisions on the form of a will which appear in the various legislations (i.e. the provisions on holographic wills, the provisions on official wills, etc.). As a model of provisions on the form of a will, the proposed solution is capable of replacing the existing solutions in this area. There is no need to place it alongside the current forms of will, as the proposal would allow wills to be validly drawn up in each of these forms. The proposal is self-sustaining. It is also intended to be used in any legal system that recognizes the idea of wills formalities and its functions.

The proposed solution is therefore not a rule proposed for an international instrument, but rather a model rule to be emulated, similar in nature to those used in some model legal systems, such as the *Uniform Probate Code* or an analogous act, in which it could be successfully introduced. In this respect, one would rather count on so-called spontaneous harmonisation in practice,[863] i.e. a situation in which one legislator decided on a revolution of this kind and others followed suit.[864] Looking at the current legislations in this area, it seems that this should be another step in adapting the law of succession to the requirements of modern times. A step that seems necessary and is able to revolutionize the current law on testamentary succession.

I therefore propose that the provisions on the form of a will, regardless of longitude and latitude, should be given the wording proposed here. The

---

862 du Toit (n 99) 159 ff.
863 *Cf.* Beckert (n 24).
864 Stefan Leible, *Wege zu einem Europäischen Privatrecht* (Universitat Bayreuth 2001) 19 ff.

model of the form of a will indicated and designed here can function independently in practice (or perhaps be supplemented by elements such as marking a disposition in time and space which I propose to settle in academic discussion). It would make inheritance law more socially friendly. The need is to reflect testators will as much as possible[865] and this seems a proper instrument to achieve this goal.

Under the new arrangements, the technical conditions of a will would become a solution based explicitly on testamentary intention. The testator, before drawing up the will, should decide on a medium preserving the declaration of his last will. Then, after the declaration is expressed, the testamentary act should end and the will stored in any medium should share the fate of the other forms already known, i.e. be preserved in some way. Such a will would enter normal legal circulation and would be subject to the same rules as those currently in force. It could therefore be revoked, modified or deposited etc.[866] One of the elements of the proceedings for the probate of the estate would be to reflect the contents of the will and, if this were possible, such a will would potentially be eligible for assessment as to whether it contained all the other necessary elements. There's no need for more formalities, since this model solution realize all the basic functions of the wills formalities regulations.

When considering the above, let's try to look at the proposed solution from the perspective of different legislations and decide whether it can fit into them. In this respect, of course, it would be extremely difficult to trace the fate of the proposed provision on a large scale, but it seems sufficient to focus on a few selected legal systems that approach the problems of wills formalities differently. Examples are the legislation of Poland and the legislation of the Canadian province of Ontario (variations of *strict compliance*) and the legislations of the American state of Ohio and the Australian state of New South Wales (variations of *substantial compliance*). From the perspective of these solutions, a will executed by a testator using a smartphone will be assessed,[867] assuming that it meets all other requirements for validity and that the only doubt concerns its form. The choice of this method of preparing a will seems to be all the more appropriate given that the smartphone is nowadays one of the most frequently used tools for

---

865 Cobas Cobiella and de Joz Latorre (n 92).

866 Rivers and Kerridge (n 753).

867 By a smartphone will I mean a will registered by means of this device, irrespective of the manner in which the testator makes his last will declaration (one can imagine it to be done by oral, textual, audio, video, etc. declaration).

interpersonal communication and one can imagine the desire to use it also for legal succession purposes.

Starting with the Polish law, it should be noted that this form of a will is not covered by the current legal regime, as it is not a holographic will (Article 949 of the *Kodeks cywilny*), a notarial will (Article 950 of the *Kodeks cywilny*) or an allographic will (Article 951 *Kodeks cywilny*), nor does it come under the heading of specific wills (Articles 952-954 of the *Kodeks cywilny*). In the current state of normative law, the preparation of such a will (smartphone will) would lead to its invalidity (art. 958 of the *Kodeks cywilny*).[868] After the introduction into Polish law of the provision that should replace the provisions indicated above: *"The testator may create a will in such a way that he expresses his testamentary intention by any conduct which reveals his declaration of will sufficiently, and his declaration is preserved on any medium which makes it possible to reflect it in a way which allows the person making this declaration to be identified"*, the situation would change. What would be assessed under this provision would be primarily the manner of expression of the testamentary intention and the possibility of its reflection after the testator's death. This expression could take a variety of forms (e.g. oral, textual, video). In this respect, there would be no obstacle to considering such a will made on a smartphone, irrespective of the manner in which the last will was expressed, as valid.

Similarly, under current Canadian Ontario law, a smartphone will would be considered invalid. According to the Section 3 of the *Succession Law Reform Act* 1990 (Chapter 26), a will is valid only when it is in writing. It can be either attested by witnesses (Section 4) or holograph (Section 6).[869] Against this background, making a will on a smartphone does not appear to be sufficient to meet the validity requirement. It is only with the introduction of the new provision in the proposed wording would a will made on a smartphone be capable of being upheld.

According to the Ohio's law, except oral wills, every will to be valid shall be in writing and attested, but may be handwritten or typewritten (*Ohio Revised Code* section 2107.03). Also, an oral will, made in the last sickness, shall be valid in respect to personal property if reduced to writing and subscribed by two competent disinterested witnesses within ten days after the speaking of the testamentary words (*Ohio Revised Code* section 2107.60).[870] Against this background, it would seem that a will made on a smartphone

---

868 *Cf.* Gwiazdomorski and Mączyński (n 530) 113.
869 *Cf.* Jacuta (n 835).
870 *Cf.* McGee (n 852).

would also be invalid. Nevertheless, Ohio's law has a solution based on the *harmless error* rule whereby if a document that is executed that purports to be a will is not executed in compliance with the requirements of section 2107.03 of the Revised Code, that document shall be treated as if it had been executed as a will in compliance with the requirements of that section if a probate court, after holding a hearing, finds that the proponent of the document as a purported will has established, by clear and convincing evidence, all of the following: (1) The decedent prepared the document or caused the document to be prepared; (2) The decedent signed the document and intended the document to constitute the decedent's will; (3) The decedent signed the document in the conscious presence of two or more witnesses (*Ohio Revised Code* section 2107.60).[871] Here too, however, doubts would arise as to whether witnesses were present at the time of the testamentary act, which the example does not assume, and which would therefore most likely result in the invalidity of the will prepared on a smartphone. Only if the proposed solution were incorporated into local law would the outcome of the case be different and the will prepared on a smartphone be deemed valid.

The *Succession Act* 2006 of the Australian state of New South Wales provides for wills to be valid that it is made in writing and signed by the testator or by some other person in the presence of and at the direction of the testator, and the signature is made or acknowledged by the testator in the presence of two or more witnesses present at the same time and at least two of those witnesses attest and sign the will in the presence of the testator (Section 6 of the *Succession Act* 2006). Against this background, it is difficult to make a positive assessment of the validity of a will made on a smartphone. However, the document, or part of the document, may form the deceased person's will if the court is satisfied that the person intended it to form his or her will (according to the *dispensing power* solution known to the New South Wales law – Section 8 of the *Succession Act* 2006).[872] By making such an assessment against the background of a will made on a smartphone, the possibility of it being considered validly made will arise, one would think. Finally, there is a document stored on a smartphone. To this end, the court would have to determine whether the document found contains the testator's intentions, whether it was prepared in compliance with the requirements and whether the testator intended to dispose of his estate on death in this way. A similar result could also be achieved by in-

---

871   ibid.
872   *Cf.* White (n 7).

troducing the solution proposed here into the New South Wales law. It could then replace the provisions relating to the form of wills and their "rescue" mechanism under section 8 of the *Succession Act* 2006. The procedure for ascertaining the estate under the smartphone will, however, would be easier under the proposed provision and would end with the same result. Indeed, the assessment of the validity of the will would be a one-step procedure.

With the above in mind, when analysing the exemplary way in which a will might be prepared, in the light of the legal solutions currently in force around the world, a number of conclusions can be drawn. Firstly, in order to reflect such and similar needs of society, changes to the law would be necessary, which would have to consist in introducing technology-neutral solutions into the law of succession. Secondly, legislators would have to abandon the provisions currently in force, which exemplify the forms of wills currently allowed. Thirdly, solutions to "cure" informal wills based on the doctrine of *substantial compliance* and its variations would lose their relevance. Fourthly, the assessment in each case of whether a testator has made a valid will would become independent of the manner in which the testator has expressed his last intention. Fifthly, each assessment of whether the testator has made a valid will would become independent of the manner in which the last will was preserved. This alone shows that the proposed amendment is rather fundamental and would require a flexible approach to the problems of the form of a will. Some values would have to be reprioritised and testamentary intent, rather than formalism, put first. But this is what the future might look like, which could be judged by many as a revolution. In this "revolution" I am convinced that wills created on a smartphone should be admitted, as long as any other clear and convincing attempts made by a testator to preserve his last intention.

The revolution would exist in the fact that the manner in which the declaration of the last will was made and its preservation would now depend on the technological possibilities available and the imagination of the testator. Of course, to this extent, we should not expect testators to suddenly start using unknown solutions. Rather, the proposed provision is intended to maintain existing standards, but also to allow for the possibility of unusual solutions. Non-typicality is hardly a characteristic to be feared.[873] A testator who genuinely wants his will to be found and reconstructed after his death will tend to use traditional instruments. Tradition in this case, however, does not mean traditional instruments of succession law, but

---

873 Sneddon, 'Speaking For the Dead: Voice in Last Wills and Testaments' (n 699).

rather traditional instruments of communication. These, as we know, can vary and definitely do vary in practice.

Therefore, is the proposed solution really a revolution and, despite the fact that it may appear to be so at first glance, does it have a chance of success in practice? Everything in this regard depends on the objectives pursued by the specific law of succession. If the legislator considers it an indispensable element of the succession that the last will of the testator be reflected as fully as possible, this is the solution that meets this objective, while performing the basic functions inherent in a testate succession. In doing so, it recognises the same values on which the systems using the doctrine of *substantial compliance* and its variations or the systems using the doctrine of *strict compliance* are based, although it emphasises slightly different elements. The main objective of the law of succession, according to the solution proposed here, would be to base the testamentary succession unequivocally on testamentary intention. Would this really be a revolution?

Conclusions and Recommendations

The considerations carried out in this book prove that the current legal solutions shaping the form of a will are not perfect and have many times failed to meet the expectations of practice and society. Flexibility of succession law is a merit which should be pursued.[874] The competing values of the need to observe formal requirements on the one hand and the need to reflect the testator's last intent on the other[875] cannot today be resolved in favour of formalism. Formalism,[876] particularly when it is rigorous, can nullify the possibility of taking into account the testator's last intent, and the same aims as the aims of formalism can be achieved by other means.[877]

The 21st century, the era of new technologies, forces a modern outlook on law, including succession law.[878] Solutions considered until now to be basic and not in need of change, when confronted with reality, turn out to be inadequate to the needs of today's practice and society.[879] One such area is, as one might think, that of wills formalities. This is particularly noticeable in those countries that remain rather traditional in regulating this area and do not respond, or have not managed to respond to the needs of practice and society. The reality is, as can be seen with the naked eye, that more and more people are drawing up wills but doing so in a manner that does not comply with the legal requirements as regards last wills form.[880] Limiting the possibility of disposing of property on death to the holographic form of a will, wills in the presence of witnesses or wills made in the presence of public persons, as is usually the case in European legislation, is not an appropriate or desirable solution. In practice, there is a need to respond to the phenomenon of so-called informal wills, i.e. wills not prepared in accordance with the provisions on form, due to an error on the part of the

---

874 Orth (n 163) 73 ff.
875 du Toit (n 99) 159 ff.
876 Richard H Pildes, 'Forms of Formalism' (1999) 66 University of Chicago Law Review 607.
877 Fulli-Lemaire (n 575) 10 ff.
878 Crawford (n 36) 294.
879 Philipp Scholz, 'Digitales Testieren. Zur Verwendung digitaler Technologien beim eigenhändigen und Nottestament de lege lata et ferenda' [2019] Archiv Für Die Civilistische Praxis 100.
880 *Cf.* Slingo (n 323).

testator or his misconception of the actual legal situation. It is the reflection of this will, and not compliance with formal requirements, that is the most important task of the succession law rules.[881] It is a task that these rules must fulfil if they are to remove any doubt that the testator acted with testamentary intent and with the intention of making a disposition of property upon death.[882] The last will of the testator need not, however, be recorded merely by means of instruments which are currently recognised in the different legal systems. Any recording of the testator's last will, regardless of the means used, should be potentially admissible as a medium for this declaration, provided that it allows for its reconstruction in the future.

This was recognised a long time ago, but in the course of development of the law in this area the relevant changes can basically only be seen in the *common law* countries and only certain other states.[883] It is there that solutions operate that can be collectively referred to as the doctrine of *substantial compliance* and its variations, which successfully implement the postulate of reflection of the testator's last intent at the expense of formal requirements of dispositions upon death. These solutions, more broadly presented by John L. Langbein since 1975[884], and subsequently developed by many scholars and implemented in some succession regulations,[885] may constitute an interesting basis for further development of succession law in terms of wills formalities, especially in those countries that still remain solutions based on the primacy of formal requirements (which can be referred to as the *strict compliance* countries). However, these solutions are based on a model in which the law provides for specific forms of preparing a will, linked to a specific manner of making a declaration of intent and a specific manner of recording this declaration. Today it is more appropriate to dissociate the provisions on the form of a will from these specific ways

---

881 Shelly Kreiczer-Levy, 'Big Data and the Modern Family' (2019) 2019 Wisconsin Law Review 349.

882 Langbein, 'Substantial Compliance with the Wills Act' (n 10).

883 *Cf.* Menashe (n 54); Flaks (n 203).

884 *Cf.* Langbein, 'Substantial Compliance with the Wills Act' (n 10); Langbein, 'Defects of Form in the Execution of Wills: Australian and Other Experience with the Substantial Compliance Doctrine' (n 676); John H Langbein, 'The Nonprobate Revolution and the Future of the Law of Succession' (1984) 97 Harvard Law Review 1108; Langbein, 'Excusing Harmless Errors in the Execution of Wills: A Report on Australia's Tranquil Revolution in Probate Law' (n 42); Langbein, 'Absorbing South Australia's Wills Act Dispensing Power in the United States: Emulation, Resistance, Expansion' (n 94).

885 *Cf., e.g.:* Solzbach (n 60).

of making a declaration of intent and recording it. In this respect full freedom is required, including technological neutrality, of course taking into account the fact that any means must be capable of recording the declaration and reproducing it in the future, with the possibility of identifying the author of this declaration.

Taking into account the above, one may be tempted to draw some synthetic conclusions and proposals as to the future. Such a proposal is also part of this book. For I believe that in the future the provisions on the form of a will should be given the following wording:

> "*The testator may create a will in such a way that he expresses his testamentary intention by any conduct which reveals his declaration of will sufficiently, and his declaration is preserved on any medium which makes it possible to reflect it in a way which allows the person making this declaration to be identified*".

In this way it is possible to modify the current provisions on the form of a will in order to remove their characteristics as being dependent on any method of making and preserving the last will. The law would be flexible in this respect and require, in order for the will to be valid, that the last will be made and preserved in such a way as to enable it to be reproduced after the testator's death, but it would not prescribe a particular manner of making the declaration and the means of preserving it. Irrespective of whether a testator chooses to use the written or handwritten technique, to make a declaration of intent to an official person, to record the last will in the cloud or using blockchain technology, or in any other way, as long as it is possible to recreate the testator's last will after his death, such way of preparing a testator's disposition of property upon death, would be permitted. There will no longer be a phenomenon of informal will. This reflects the needs of practice and society.

Having regard to this proposal, the future law would allow for a free and discretionary construction of the declaration of the last will and the shaping of legal relations *mortis causa*.[886] It will make a room in succession law for the Internet, social media, smart phones and other benefits of new technologies[887] and will amend the forms of estate disposition coherent with the technological opportunities created by the emergence in recent years of a range of technological devices in almost every household, by

---

886 Mark Glover, 'Restraining Live Hand Control of Inheritance' (2020) 79 Maryland Law Review 329 ff.
887 Hall (n 81) 339–372.

making these rules technologically independent and therefore universal, something that cannot be said of them today. In this way, a functional mechanism of effective testation will be created. The set of provisions referred to as the wills formalities will be simplified and will allow practice to be shaped in a way that gives priority to the testamentary intention.[888] Formalism will only become a supporting tool and not the decisive factor for the disposal of property upon death.[889]

---

888 *Cf.* Banta (n 48).
889 *Cf.* Horton, 'Tomorrow's Inheritance: The Frontiers of Estate Planning Formalism' (n 261) 597.

Bibliography

Albery M, 'Coincidence and the Construction of Wills' (1963) 26 Modern Law Review 353

Alstott A, 'Family Values and the Law of Inheritance' (2009) 7 Socioeconomic Review 145

Anderson M, 'La capacitat per a testar de qui té habitualment disminuïda la capacitat natural: l'art. 116 del Codi de Successions' (2009) 2009 InDret 1

Atkinson TE, *Handbook of the Law of Wills and Other Principles of Succession: Including Intestacy and Administration of Decedents' Estates* (West Academic Publishing 1953)

Avenarius M, *BGB Kommentar* (Hans Prütting, Gerhard Wegen and Gerd Weinreich eds, Wolters Kluwer 2010)

Babusiaux U, *Römisches Erbrecht* (Böhlau Verlag 2015)

Ballarino T, 'Il nuovo regolamento europe sulle successioni' [2013] Rivista di Diritto Internazionale 1116

Banda TJA, *The Court's Power to Condone a Document in Terms of Section 2(3) and Section 2A of the Wills Act 7 of 1953: A Comparative Analysis and Recommendations* (University of Pretoria 2012)

Banta NM, 'Electronic Wills and Digital Assets: Reassessing Formality in the Digital Age' (2020) 71 Baylor Law Review 547

Barbaix R and Verbeke A-L, *Beginselen erfrecht* (die Keure 2012)

——, *Kernbegrippen erfrecht en giften* (Intersentia 2013)

Baron JB, 'Gifts, Bargains, and Form' (1998) 64 Indiana Law Journal 155

——, 'Irresolute Testators, Clear and Convincing Wills Law' (2016) 73 Washington & Lee Law Review 3

Bartsch H and Bartsch MB, *Das aktuelle Erbrecht* (Walhalla Fachverlag 2013)

Beaulne J, *La liquidation des successions* (Wilson & Lafleur 2002)

——, 'Bilan d'une première décennie en droit des successions' (2003) 105 Revue du notariat 271

Beckert J, 'The Longue Durée of Inheritance Law. Discourses and Institutional Development in France, Germany, and the United States since 1800' (2007) 48 European Journal of Sociology 79

Beinke U, *Der Formzwang beim privatschriftlichen Testament* (Philipps Universität Marburg 1988)

Benedetti AM, 'Notas sobre la prohibición del testamento conjunto: Sobre la validez de los mirror wills' [2015] Revista de Derecho Privado 59

Bérier FL de, *Law of Succession. Roman Legal Framework and Comparative Perspective* (Wolters Kluwer 2011)

Berti R and Zanetti S, 'La trasmissione mortis causa del patrimonio e dell'identità digitale: strumenti giuridici, operativi e prospettive de iure condendo' [2016] Law and Media Working Paper Series 1

Beyer GW, 'Video Requiem: Thy Will Be Done' (1985) 7 Trust & Estates 24

——, *What If Your Parrot Outlives You? Preparing for Your Bird's Future* (Phoenix Landing Foundation 2020)

Beyer GW and Hargrove CG, 'Digital Wills: Has the Time Come for Wills to Join the Digital Revolution' (2007) 33 Ohio NUL Rev. 865

Beyer GW and Peters K V., 'Sign on the [Electronic] Dotted Line: The Rise of the Electronic Will' (2019) 1 Wills Trusts & Estates Law eJournal

Bird GB, 'Sleight of Handwriting: The Holographic Will in California' (1981) 32 Hastings Law Journal 605

Blumenthal S, 'The Deviance of the Will: Policing the Bounds of Testamentary Freedom in Nineteenth-Century America' (2006) 119 Harvard Law Review 959

Bogardus PW, Hamilton MB and Wetzel SL, *Wills and Personal Planning Precedents. An Annotated Guide* (The Continuing Legal Education Society of British Columbia 2020)

Bonfield L, 'Reforming the Requirements for Due Execution of Wills: Some Guidance from the Past' (1996) 70 Tulane Law Review 1893

——, 'Reforming the Requirements for Due Execution of Wills: Some Guidance from the Past' (1996) 70 Tulane Law Review 1893

Borysiak W, *Funkcjonowanie w praktyce testamentu sporządzanego w formie ustnej (art. 952 k.c.)* (Instytut Wymiaru Sprawiedliwości 2014)

Breitschmid P, 'Testament und Erbvertrag - Formprobleme: Die Einsatzmöglichkeiten für die Nachlassplanung im Lichte neuerer Rechtsentwicklungen' in Peter Breitschmid (ed), *Testament und Erbvertrag* (Haupt 1991)

——, 'Revision der Formvorschriften des Testaments – Bemerkungen zur Umsetzung der «Initiative Guinand»' (1995) 1995 Zeitschrift des Bernischen Juristenvereins 179

——, 'Bericht zu den Konturen eines "zeitgemässen Erbrechts" zu Handen des Bundesamtes für Justiz zwecks Umsetzung der "Motion Gutzwiller"' (2014) Sonderheft Not@lex/succesio 7

British Columbia Law Institute, *Wills, Estates and Succession: A Modern Legal Framework* (2006)

Breuer A, 'Pellegrini v. Breitenbach. Power to Reform Innocent Mistakes in Wills' (2012) 26 Quinnipac Probate Law Journal 46

Brière G, *Traité de droit civil - Les successions* (Éditions Yvon Blais 1994)

——, 'Le projet de réforme du droit des successions' (1984) 15 Revue générale de droit 405

Brook J, 'To Dispense or Not to Dispense? A Comparison of Dispensing Powers and Their Judicial Application' (2018) 2018 Private Client Business 205

Brown RL, 'The Holograph Problem - The Case Against Holographic Wills' (2005) 74 Tennessee Law Review 93

Brox H and Walker W-D, *Erbrecht* (C H Beck 2018)

Burns F, 'Surviving Spouses, Surviving Children and the Reform of Total Intestacy Law in England and Scotland: Past, Present and Future' (2013) 33 Legal Studies 85

Busch E and Lobe M, *Das Bürgerliche Gesetzbuch mit besonderer Berücksichtigung der Rechtsprechung des Reichsgerichts* (De Gruyter 1928)

Casswell DG, 'The Conflict of Laws Rules Governing the Formal Validity of Wills: Past Developments and Suggested Reform' (1977) 15 Osgoode Hal Law Journal 165

Champine PR, 'My Will Be Done: Accommodating the Erring and the Atypical Testator' (2014) 80 Nebraska Law Review 388

Cicala C, 'Il formalismo testamentario. Il documento' in Giovanni Bonilini (ed), *Trattato di diritto delle successioni e delle donazioni. La successione testamentaria* (Giuffrè 2009)

Ciotola P, 'La vérification d'un testament sur disquette ou l'art de vers le formalisme testamentaire à la corbeille informatique' (1997) 4 Entracte 10

——, 'Le testateur et son clone inavoué, le juge: clone difforme ou conforme dans la recherche des intentions du testateur: le juge et l'interprétation des volontés du testateur' (2005) 107 La Reveue du Notariat 239

——, 'Des principes usuels d'interprétation des testaments et les décisions rendues en 2007' (2018) 110 Revue du notariat 37

Clougherty L, 'An Analysis of the National Advisory Committee on Uniform State Laws' Recommendation to Modify the Wills Act Formalities' (1991) 10 Probate Law Journal 283

Clowney S, 'In Their Own Hand: An Analysis of Holographic Wills and Homemade Willmaking' (2008) 43 Real Property, Probate and Trust Journal 27

Cobas Cobiella ME and de Joz Latorre C, 'La modernización del derecho de sucesiones. Algunas propuestas' (2007) 7 Cuestiones de Interés Jurídico 1

Coing H, 'Form und Billigkeit im moderne Privatrecht' (1965) 1965 Deutsche Notar-Zeitschfirt1 29

Cossío A, 'Dolo y captación en las disposiciones testamentarias' (1962) 1962 Anuario de Derecho Civil 277

Cottier M, 'Ein zeitgemässes erbrecht für die Schweiz: Bericht zur Motion 10.3524 Gutzwiller "Für Ein Zeitgemässes Erbrecht" zuhanden des Bundesamtes für Justiz' (2014) Sonderheft Not@lex/succesio 29

Coumaros N, *Le rôle de la volonté dans l'acte juridique* (Librarie du Recueil Sirey 1931)

Crawford BJ, 'Wills Formalities in the Twenty-First Century' (2019) 2019 Wisconsin Law Review 269

——, 'Blockchain Wills' (2020) 95 Indiana Law Journal 735

Crawford BJ, Purser K and Cockburn T, 'Post-Pandemic Wills' (2021) 2021 University of Chicago Legal Forum

Cristiani F, 'Nuove tecnologie e testamento: Presente e futuro' [2013] Diritto dell'informazione e dell'informatica 559

Critchley P, 'Privileged Wills and Testamentary Formalities: A Time to Die?' (1999) 58 Cambridge Law Journal 49

Croucher RF, 'Statutory Wills and Testamentary Freedom – Imagining the Testator's Intention in Anglo-Australia Law' (2007) 7 Oxford University Commonwealth Law Journal 241

Croucher RF and Vines P, *Succession: Families, Property and Death* (Lexis Nexis 2018)

Crous N, *A Comparative Study of the Legal Status of Electronic Wills* (North West University 2019)

Dadańska KA and Kubasik K, 'Forma rozrządzeń na wypadek śmierci po wejściu w życie Rozporządzenia Parlamentu Europejskiego i Rady (UE) nr 650/2012 z dnia 4 lipca 2012 roku' [2014] Problemy Prawa Prywatnego Międzynarodowego 9

Dainow J, 'Restricted Testation in New Zealand, Australia and Canada' (1938) 36 Michigan Law Review 1107

Danz E, 'Können Testamente mit Formfehlern aufrecht erhalten werden?' (1909) 1909 Deutsche Juristen Zeitung 281

Darwall S, 'The Value of Autonomy and Autonomy of the Will' (2006) 2006 Ethics 263

di Renzo Villata MG (ed), *Succession Law, Practice and Society in Europe across the Centuries* (Springer 2018)

Dorman JA, 'Stop Frustrating the Testator's Intent: Why the Connecticut Legislature Should Adopt the Harmless Error Rule' (2016) 30 Quinnipiac Probate Law Journal 36

Dunand J-P, 'Le testament oral en droit suisse et dans l'ancien droit neuchâtelois' in Jean Kellerhals, Dominique Manaï and Robert Roth (eds), *Pour un droit pluriel: études offertes au professeur Jean-François Perrin* (Helbing & Lichtenhahn 2002)

Dvoenosova GA, 'The Functions of a Document' (2013) 40 Scientific and Technical Information Processing 17

Dyląg Ł, 'Dokument a dokument a dokument elektroniczny w prawie cywilnym - pojęcie i istota desygnatu' [2011] Prawo Mediów Elektronicznych 8

Eccher B, *Bürgerliches Recht. Band VI. Erbrecht* (Springer 2010)

——, *Erbrecht* (Verlag Österreich 2016)

Echeverría JD, '¿Qué reformas cabe esperar en el derecho de sucesiones del Código civil? (Un ejercicio de prospectiva)' (2009) 3 El Cronista del Estado Social y Democrático de Derecho 26

Edwards HT, 'To Err Is Human, But Not Always Harmless: When Should Legal Error Be Tolerated?' (1995) 70 New York University Law Review 1167

Ellart CS-M, 'The Late Roman Law of Inheritance: The Testament of Five or Seven Witnesses' in Béatrice Caseau and Sabine R Huebner (eds), *Inheritance, Law and Religions in the Ancient and Mediaeval Worlds* (Association des amis du Centre d'histoire et civilisation de Byzance 2014)

Ellenberger J, 'Kommentar', *Palandt Bürgerliches Gesetzbuch Kommentar* (74th edn, CH Beck 2015)

Espino Bermell C, *El testamento ológrafo. La importancia de la escritura y la firma del testador. El cotejo pericial de letras (La prueba caligráfica)* (Universidad de Córdoba 2016)

Esquivel ME and Acuna ME, *Derecho sucesoral* (Universidad Libre 2011)

Essary M, 'Wich v. Fleming The Dilemma of a Harmless Defect in a Will' (1983) 35 Baylor Law Review 903

Evans AE, 'The Competency of Testamentary Witnesses' (1927) 25 Michigan Law Review 238

Evans S, 'Testators' Wishes; Dead or Alive: Is There a Difference?' (2013) 2013 Conveyance and Property Lawyer 481

Fernández FR, 'El testamento y la futura reforma del código civil en materia de discapacidad: Algunas reflexiones' (2009) 10 Actualidad Jurídica Iberoamericana 346

Flaks S, 'Excusing Harmless Error in Will Execution: The Israeli Experience' (2010) 3 Estate Planning and Community Property Law Journal 27

Fontana P and others, 'Handwriting as a Gauge of Cognitive Status: A Novel Forensic Tool for Posthumous Evaluation of Testamentary Capacity' (2008) 29 Neurological Sciences 257

Foster FH, 'Dark Side of Trusts: Challenges to Chinese Inheritance Law, The' (2003) 2 Washington University Global Studies Law Review 151

Frechette D, Zylberberg F and Raymond M, 'Canada - Quebec' in Louis Garb and John Wood (eds), *International Succession* (Oxford University Press 2010)

Frerichs MJ and Kovacevic E, 'What Could Be the Harm? Minnesota's Harmless Error Statute' (*Lexology*, 2020) <https://www.lexology.com/library/detail.aspx?g=74 e38c22-0717-4e2d-bc0f-3412e1ecd60f>

Friedman R, 'Proof and Effect of Mistake as to the Provisions of Wills' (1973) 38 Missouri Law Review 48

Friedmann LS, 'The Law Of The Living, The Law Of the Dead: Property, Succession, And Society' (1966) 1966 Wisconsin Law Review 340

Frolik LA, 'The Strange Interplay of Testamentary Capacity and the Doctrine of Undue Influence. Are We Protecting Older Testators or Overriding Individual Preferences?' (2001) 24 International Journal of Law and Psychiatry 253

Fuller LL, 'Consideration and Form' (1941) 1 Columbia Law Review 799

Fulli-Lemaire S, 'Le formalisme en droit patrimonial de la famille: regard comparatiste' (2016) 17 Max Planck Private Law Research Paper

Gardos P, 'Recodification of the Hungarian Civil Law' (2007) 2007 European Review of Private Law 707

Gary S, 'Adapting Intestacy Laws to Changing Families' (2000) 18 Law & Inequality: A Journal of Theory and Practice 1

——, 'Harmless Error: History of the Doctrine and Recent Cases from the U.S. and Australia', *Oregon State Bar CLE seminar Advanced Estate Planning 2019* (Oregon State Bar 2019)

Gee KB, 'Beyond Castro's Tablet Will: Exploring Electronic Will Cases Around the World and Re-Visiting Ohio's Harmless Error Statute' (2016) 26 Probate Journal of Ohio 149

Gernhuber J, 'Formnichtigkeit und Treu und Glauben', *Festschrift zum 70. Geburtstag von Walter Schmidt-Rimpler* (C F Müller 1956)

Gerver PHM, 'Het nieuwe erfrecht ingevoerd' [2003] Nederlands Juristenblad 72

Glendon MA, 'Fixed Rules and Discretion in Contemporary Family Law and Succession Law' (1986) 60 Tulane Law Review 1165

Glover M, 'The Therapeutic Function of Testamentary Formality' (2012) 185 Kansas Law Review 139

——, 'A Taxonomy of Testamentary Intent' (2016) 23 George Mason Law Review 269

——, 'Minimizing Probate-Error Risk' (2016) 49 University of Michigan Journal of Law Reform 335

——, 'A Social Welfare Theory of Inheritance Regulation' (2018) 2018 Utah Law Review 411

——, 'Restraining Live Hand Control of Inheritance' (2020) 79 Maryland Law Review

Goldberg JCP and Sitkoff RH, 'Torts and Estates: Remedying Wrongful Interference with Inheritance' (2013) 65 Stanford Law Review 335

Goodwin IJ, 'Access to Justice: What to Do about the Law of Wills' [2016] Wisconsin Law Review 947

Goossens E and Verbeke A-L, 'De Europese Erfrechtverordening' [2012] Themis 105

Górska K, *Zachowanie zwykłej formy pisemnej czynności prawnych* (C H Beck 2007)

Gray T, 'Succession Law: Reflections and Directions' (2019) 40 Adelaide Law Review 331

Greabe JM, 'The Riddle of Harmless Error Revisited' (2016) 54 Houston Law Review 59

Grochowski M, *Skutki braku zachowania formy szczególnej oświadczenia woli* (C H Beck 2017)

Gruchmann L, 'Die Entstehung des Testamentss-gesetzes vom 31. Juli 1938. Nationalsozialistische „Rechtserneuerung" und Reformkontinuität' (1985) 7 Zeitschrift für Neuere Rechtsgeschichte 53

Grundmann S, 'Favor Testamenti: Zu Formfreiheit und Formzwang bei bei privatschriftlichen Testamenten' (1987) 187 Archiv Für Die Civilistische Praxis 429

Gschnitzer F, *Erbrecht* (Springer 1964)

Gulliver AG and Tilson CJ, 'Classification of Gratuitous Transfers' (1941) 51 Yale Law Journal 1

Güre GY, 'No Paper? No Problem: Ushering in Electronic Wills Through California's "Harmless Error" Provision' (2016) 49 University of California Davis Law Review 1955

Gwiazdomorski J, 'Formy testamentu' (1966) 22 Nowe Prawo 713

Gwiazdomorski J and Mączyński A, *Prawo spadkowe w zarysie* (Państwowe Wydawnictwo Naukowe 1985)

Haines D, 'Informal Wills and the Uniform Legislation', *The Law Society of South Australia Succession Law Conference 2007* (The Law Society of Australia 2007)

Hall P, 'Welcoming E-Wills into the Mainstream: The Digital Communication of Testamentary Intent' (2019) 20 Nevada Law Journal 339

Haneman VJ, 'The Disruptive Potential of Blockchain in the Law of Wills' [2020] Trust & Estates 2

Hannah F and Mcgregor-Lowndes M, *From Testamentary Freedom to Testamentary Duty: Finding the Balance* (Queensland University of Technology 2008)

Hardin KA, 'An Analysis of The Virginia Wills Act Formalities and The Need For a Dispensing Power Statute in Virginia' (1993) 50 Washington & Lee Law Review 1145

Harris VM, 'The Importance of the Last Will and Testament' (1908) 25 Banking Law Journal 377

Häsemeyer L, *Die gesetzliche Form der Rechtsgeschäfte – objektive Ordnung und privatautonome Selbstbestimmung im formgebundenen Rechtsgeschäft* (Athenaeum 1971)

Hayton D, 'By-Passing Testamentary Formalities' (1987) 46 Cambridge Law Journal 215

Hedlund R, 'Introducing a Dispensing Power in English Succession Law' (2019) 25 Trusts & Trustees 722

Heiss H, *Formmängel und ihre Sanktionen. Eine privatrechtsvergleichende Untersuchung* (Mohr Siebeck 1999)

Hess B, *Intertemporales Privatrecht* (Mohr Siebeck 1998)

Hill A and Mazza T, 'Strict versus Substantial Compliance with Statutory Formalities for Wills' (2020) <https://www.hamiltonlaw.on.ca/Web/About-the-HLA/HLA-Journal-Articles/Estates---Trusts-Journal-Artices/Estates_Law_News_Strict_versus_Substantial.aspx> accessed 21 January 2021

von Hippel F, *Formalismus und Rechtsdogmatik: dargestellt am beispiel der 'errichtung' des zeugenlosen schrifttestaments (eigenhändiges testament; testament olographe)* (Hanseatische Verlagsanstalt 1935)

Hirsch AJ, 'Inheritance and Inconsistency' (1996) 57 Ohio State Law Journal1 1057

——, 'Incomplete Wills' (2013) 111 Michigan Law Review 1423

——, 'Technology Adrift: In Search of a Role for Electronic Wills' (2020) 61 Boston College Law Review 828

Hochstetler M, 'Where There's a "Will," There's a Way: The Harmless-Error Rule, Interested-Witness Rule, and In Re Estate of Shaffer' (2020) 30 Ohio Probate Law Journal 202

Hoeren T, 'Der Tod und das Internet. Rechtliche fragenzur verwendung von E-Mail- und WWW-Acounts nach dem Tode des Inhabers' (2005) 2005 Neue Juristiche Wochenschrift 2113

Holmes G, 'Testamentary Formalism in Louisiana: Curing Notarial Will Defects Through a Likelihood-of-Fraud Analysis' (2014) 75 Louisiana Law Review 511

Horton D, 'Wills Law on the Ground' (2015) 62 UCLA Law Review 1094

——, 'Tomorrow's Inheritance: The Frontiers of Estate Planning Formalism' (2017) 58 Boston College Law Review 540

——, 'Partial Harmless Error For Wills: Evidence From California' (2018) 103 Iowa Law Review 2027

Horton D and Weisbord RK, 'COVID-19 and Formal Wills' [2020] Stanford Law Review Online 1

Hosemann EG, 'Protecting Freedom of Testation: A Proposal for Law Reform' (2014) 47 University of Michigan Journal of Law Reform 419

Huebner R, *History of Germanic Private Law* (1918)

Hurlburt WH, 'Electronic Wills and Powers of Attorney: Has Their Day Come', *The Uniform Law Conference of Canada, Proceedings of 83rd Annual Meeting* (The Uniform Law Conference of Canada 2001)

Ibañez SB and others, *Testamento digital* (Ricardo Oliva Leon and Sonsoles Valero Barcelo eds, Juristas con Futuro 2016)

Institute ALR, 'Wills: Non-Compliance with Formalities' (2001) 20 Estates, Trusts & Pensions Journal

Israel Misrad ha-Mishpatim, A Succession Bill for Israel: Text and Explanatory Notes, translated in Harvard Law School-Israel Cooperative Research on Israel's Legal Development (1952)

Jacuta J, 'Is Substantial Compliance in Ontario's Future?' (2020) <https://hullandhull.com/2020/08/is-substantial-compliance-in-ontarios-future/> accessed 21 January 2021

Janowski P, 'Doktryna „substantial compliance" (merytorycznej zgodności) w anglosaskim prawie spadkowym, na przykładzie Australii i Nowej Zelandii' [2016] Ius et Administratio 73

Jarboe ST, 'Interpreting a Testator's Intent from the Language of Her Will: A Descriptive Linguistic Approach' (2002) 80 Washington University Law Quarterly 1365

Jayme E, 'Party Autonomy in International Succession and Family Law: New Tendencies' (2009) 11 Yearbook of Private International Law 1

Johnson JR, 'Dispensing with Wills' Act Formalities for Substantively Valid Wills' (1992) 18 Virginia Bar Association Journal 10

Kasirer N, 'The "Judicial Will" Architecturally Considered' (1996) 99 Revue du notariat 3

——, 'From Written Record to Memory in the Law of Wills' (1998) 29 Ottawa Law Review 43

Keeton GW and Gower LCB, 'Freedom of Testation in English Law' (1934) 20 Iowa Law Review 326

Kennedy D, 'From the Will Theory to the Principle of Private Autonomy: Lon Fuller's "Consideration and Form"' (2000) 100 Columbia Law Review 94

Kerridge R, *Hawkins on the Construction of Wills* (Sweet & Maxwell 2000)

——, *Making a Will* (Society of Legal Scholars 2017)

Keuk B, *Der Erblasserwille post testamentum und die Auslegung des Testaments* (Röhrscheid 1965)

Klasiček D, '21 St Century Wills' (2019) 35 Pravni vjesnik 29

Kocot W, *Wpływ Internetu na prawo umów* (Lexis Nexis 2004)

Koziczak A, 'Oznaki emocji w testamencie a jego autentyczność' (2012) 277 Problemy Kryminalistyki

Krawczyk M, 'Testament własnoręczny w świetle regulacji kodeksowej , poglądów doktryny i orzecznictwa Sądu Najwyższego' (2009) 7 Zeszyty Naukowe 123

Kreiczer-Levy S, 'The Mandatory Nature of Inheritance' (2008) 53 The American Journal of Jurisprudence 105

——, 'Big Data and the Modern Family' (2019) 2019 Wisconsin Law Review 349

Lagarde P, 'Les principes de base du nouveau du règlement européen sur les successions' [2012] Revue Critique de Droit International Privé 691

Lang AG, 'Formality v. Intention - Wills in an Australian Supermarket' (1985) 15 Melbourne University Law Review 82

Langbein JH, 'Substantial Compliance with the Wills Act' (1975) 88 Harvard Law Review 489

——, 'Crumbling of the Wills Act: Australians Point the Way' (1979) 65 American Bar Association Journal 1192

——, 'Defects of Form in the Execution of Wills: Australian and Other Experience with the Substantial Complicance Doctrine', *American/Australian/New Zealand Law: Parallels and Contrasts (Papers presented in Sydney, Australia, from 11-16 August 1980 at a meeting between the American Bar Association, Law Council of Australia, New Zealand Law Society, to commemorate the bicentenar* (1980)

——, 'The Nonprobate Revolution and the Future of the Law of Succession' (1984) 97 Harvard Law Review 1108

——, 'Excusing Harmless Errors in the Execution of Wills: A Report on Australia's Tranquil Revolution in Probate Law' (1987) 87 Columbia Law Review 1

——, 'Absorbing South Australia's Wills Act Dispensing Power in the United States: Emulation, Resistance, Expansion' (2017) 38 Adelaide Law Review 1

Lange KW, *Erbrecht* (C H Beck 2017)

Lapuente SC, 'New Developments in the Spanish Law of Succession' (2007) 2007 InDret 2

Laufer J, 'Flexible Restraints on Testamentary Freedom-a Report on Decedents' Family Maintenance Legislation' (1954) 79 Harvard Law Review 277

Law Reform Commission of British Columbia, *Report on the Making and Revocation of Wills (LRC 52)* (1981)

Law Reform Commission of Western Australia, *Report on Wills: Substantial Compliance* (1985)

Law Reform Committee, *Making and Revocation of Wills* (1980)

Law Reform Committee of South Australia, *Twenty-Eight Report of the Law Reform Committee of South Australia to the Attorney-General Relating to the Reform of the Law on Intestacy and Wills* (1974)

Lee WA, 'Queensland Succession Act 1981' (1983) 3 Oxford Journal of Legal Studies 442

Lefebvre B, 'L'accroissement du pouvoir discrétionnaire du juge en matière de validation d'un testament informe : les enseignements de la cour d'appel' in Brigitte Lefebvre (ed), *Mélanges Roger Comtois* (Éditions Thémis 2007)

Leible S, *Wege zu einem Europäischen Privatrecht* (Universitat Bayreuth 2001)

Leipold D, 'Europa und das Erbrecht' in Gerhard Köbler, Meinhard Heinze and Wolfgang Hromadka (eds), *Europas universale rechtsordnungspolitische Aufgabe im Recht des dritten Jahrtausends. Festschrift für A. Söllner zum 70. Geburtstag* (C H Beck 2000)

——, 'Ist unser Erbrecht noch zeitgemäß?' (2010) 65 Juristen Zeitung 802

——, *Erbrecht* (Mohr Siebeck 2014)

Leslie MB, 'Frustration of Intent in the Wealth Transmission Process' (2014) 2 Oñati Socio-Legal Series 283

Lester S, 'Admitting Defective Wills to Probate, Twenty Years Later: New Evidence for the Adoption of the Harmless Error Rule' (2007) 42 Real Property, Probate and Trust Journal 577

Lindgren J, 'Abolishing the Attestation Requirement for Wills' (1990) 68 North Carolina Law Review 541

——, 'The Fall of Formalism' (1992) 55 Albany Law Review 1009

Liżyńska K, *Badanie autentyczności testamentu holograficznego* (Cyfrowa Biblioteka Prawnicza 2008)

Lynch S, 'Wills and Estates: Succession Law and Testamentry Capacity' in RG Beran (ed), *Legal and Forensic Medicine* (Springer 2013)

Maciejewska-Szałas M, *Forma pisemna i elektroniczna czynności prawnych. Studium prawnoporównawcze* (CH Beck 2014)

Mackie K, *Principles of Australian Succession Law* (3rd edn, Lexis Nexis 2017)

MacLean LJ, *Rectification and Validation of Wills and Codicils* (LESA 2015)

Mączynski A, 'La revocation du testament ' a la lumiere de la loi sur le droit international prive et de la Convention de La Haye sur les conflits de lois en matiere de forme des dispositions testamentaires' 19 Polish Yearbook of International Law 85

——, *Dziedziczenie testamentowe w prawie prywatnym międzynarodowym. Ustawowe i konwencyjne unormowanie problematyki formy* (Uniwersytet Jagielloński 1976)

——, 'Wpływ wad oświadczenia woli na ważność testamentu' (1991) 1991 Rejent 24

——, 'Konstytucyjne prawo dziedziczenia' in Wojciech Popiołek, Maciej Szpunar and Leszek Ogiegło (eds), *Rozprawy prawnicze. Księga pamiątkowa Profesora Maksymiliana Pazdana* (Zakamycze 2005)

——, 'Prawo dziedziczenia i jego ochrona w świetle orzecznictwa Trybunału Konstytucyjnego' in Marek Zubik (ed), *Minikomentarz dla Maksiprofesora. Księga jubileuszowa profesora Leszka Garlickiego* (Wydawnictwo Sejmowe 2017)

Maillard KN, 'The Color of Testamentary Freedom' (2014) 62 SMU Law Review 1783

Malaurie P and Brenner C, *Droit des successions et des libéralités* (8th edn, LGDJ Lextenso 2018)

Manitoba Law Reform Commission, *Report on 'the Wills Act' and the Doctrine of Substantial Compliance* (1980)

Mann BH, 'Formalities and Formalism in the Uniform Probate Code' (1994) 142 University of Pennsylvania Law Review 1033

Marsal Guillamet J, 'La Ineficàcia dels actes i disposicions d'última voluntat', *El Nou Dret successori del Codi Civil de Catalunya* (Documenta Universitaria 2012)

Martin J, 'La pertinence de l'article 714 du Code civil du Québec ou le paradoxe d'un formalisme sujet à la libre interprétation des tribunaux' (2018) 113 Revue du notariat 431

Marty-Nelson E and others, *Florida Wills, Trusts, and Estates. Cases and Materials* (Carolina Academic Press 2016)

Martyn JGR and others, *Theobald on Wills* (Thomson Reuters 2010)

Maxton JK, *Formalities, Mistake and Construction in the Law of Wills* (Uniersity of Canterbury 1982)

Mazeaud H, Mazeaud L and Mazeaud J, *Leçons de Droit Civil* (Editions Montchrestien 1999)

Mc Nary A, *The New Alberta Wills and Succession Act—What's In It?...And What's Out* (Legal Education Society of Alberta 2011)

McCrum MW, 'Wills – Execution – Witnesses' Signatures Located Only after Self-Proving Affidavit Do Not Satisfy Attestation Requirements' (1983) 15 St. Mary's Law Journal 219

McEniery B, 'Succession Law Keeping Pace with Changes in Technology and Community Expectations – Informal Wills' (2014) 12 Journal of New Business Ideas & Trends 1

McGee AS, 'Revisiting Ohio's Harmless Error Statute - Saving Grace or Unintended Loophole?' (2019) 29 Probate Journal of Ohio 233

Melnychuk KS, 'One Click Away: The Prospect of Electronic Wills in Saskatchewan' (2014) 77 Saskatchewan Law Review 27

Menashe D, 'Relaxed Formalism: The Validation of Flawed Wills' (2007) 40 Israel Law Review 119

Mentrek J, 'Estate Planning in a Digital World' [2009] Ohio Probate Law Journal 195

Merlini O de L, 'Los vicios de la voluntad testamentaria: Apuntes para una interpretación del articulo 673 del Código Civil' (2007) 2007 Revista General de Legislación y Jurisprudencia 50

Miller CD, 'Will Formality, Judicial Formalism, and Legislative Reform: An Examination of the New Uniform Probate Code "Harmless Error" Rule and the Movement Toward Amorphism' (1991) 43 Florida Law Review 167

Miller D, 'How Harmless Is Harmless? An In-Depth Look Into the Harmless Error Rule' [2013] ACTEC Foundation: Mary Moers Wenig Writing Competition Winners 1

Miller G, 'Reforming the Formal Requirements for the Execution of a Will' (1993) 8 Denning Law Journal 71

——, *The Machinery of Succession* (Darmouth 1996)

Miller JG, 'Substantial Compliance and the Execution of Wills' (1987) 9 International and Comparative Law Quarterly 343

du Mongh J, 'Het erfrecht van de langstlevende echtgenoot: de "Wet-Valkeniers" van 22 April 2003' (2004) 2004 Rechtskundig Weekblad 1521

Moreteau O, 'A Summary Reflection on the Future of Civil Codes in Europe ' in P Apathy and others (eds), *Festschrift fur Helmut Koziol zum 70. Geburtstag* (2010)

Muscheler K, 'Das eigenhändige Testament – gestern , heute und morgen' (2014) 2014 Successio - Zeitschrift für Erbrecht 24

Nachbar T, 'Form and Formalism' (2018) 1 University of Virginia School of Law Public Law and Legal Theory Research Paper Series

Nelson C and Stark J, 'Formalities and Formalism: A Critical Look at the Execution of Wills' (1978) 6 Pepperdine Law Review 331

Newbould J, 'Demand for Wills on the Rise as Coronavirus Fears Set in for Australians' *Money Magazine* (8 April 2020)

Niedośpiał M, *Testament. Zagadnienia ogólne testamentu w polskim prawie cywilnym* (Polski Dom Wydawniczy 'Ławica' 1993)

——, *Testament jako dokument prawny (zagadnienia dowodowe i procesowe testamentu)* (Biblioteka Jagiellońska 2019)

Olsson B, *Handläggning av testamente - från upprättande till skifte* (Stockholms Universitet 2014)

Olzen D, *Erbrecht* (De Gruyter 2005)

Ormiston WF, 'Formalities and Wills: A Plea for Caution' (1980) 54 Australian Law Journal 451

Orth J V., 'Wills Act Formalities: How Much Compliance Is Enough?' (2008) 43 Real Property, Probate and Trust Journal 73

Osajda K, 'Wpływ rozwoju techniki na uregulowanie formy testamentu - rozważania de lege ferenda' (2010) 2010 Rejent 50

——, 'Sposoby stwierdzenia treści testamentu ustnego' [2013] Monitor Prawniczy 463

——, 'Prawo spadkowe (w) przyszłości. Perspektywy rozwoju prawa spadkowego' (2019) 2019 Monitor Prawniczy 66

Otero Crespo M, 'La sucesión en los «bienes digitales». La respuesta plurilegislativa española' (2019) 6 Revista de Derecho Civil 89

Pabin A, 'Testament jako akt sformalizowany - uwagi w sprawie przyszłego ksztaltu regulacji dotyczących formy rozrządzeń testamentowych' (2016) 2016 Studia Prawnicze 91

Pagliantini S, *Causa e motivi del regolamento testamentario* (Jovene 2000)

Papadopoulos S, 'Electronic Wills with an Aura of Authenticity: Van Der Merwe v Master of the High Court and Another' (2012) 24 South African Mercantile Law Journal 93

Parker R, 'History of the Holograph Testament in the Civil Law' (1943) 3 Jurist 1

Patti S, 'Il testamento olografo nell'era digitale' (2014) 2014 Rivistra di dirittio civile 992

Pazdan M, 'Czynności notarialne w międzynarodowym prawie spadkowym' (1998) 8 Rejent 99

Peart N, 'Where There Is a Will, There Is a Way - A New Wills Act for New Zealand' (2007) 15 Waikato Law Review 26

Peart N and Kelly G, 'The Scope of the Validation Power in the Wills Act 2007' (2013) 2013 New Zealand Law Review 73

Pelletier Jr GA and Sonnenreich MR, 'A Comparative Analysis of Civil Law Succession' (1966) 11 Villanova Law Review 323

Perka M, 'Zasada favor testamenti w prawie spadkowym' [2017] Palestra 57

Piątowski JS and Kordasiewicz B, *Prawo spadkowe. Zarys wykładu* (Lexis Nexis 2011)

Pildes RH, 'Forms of Formalism' (1999) 66 University of Chicago Law Review 607

Ponath G, *Die Beschränkungen der Testierfreiheit durch das Testamentsrecht* (Zerb Verlag 2006)

Pound R, 'The Role of the Will in Law' (1954) 68 Harvard Law Review 1

Purser K and Cockburn T, 'Wills Formalities in the Twenty-First Century – Promoting Testamentary Intention in the Face of Societal Change and Advancements in Technology: An Australian Response to Professor Crawford' (2019) 2019 Wisconsin Law Review Forward 46

Purser K, Cockburn T and Crawford BJ, 'Wills Formalities beyond COVID-19; An Australian-United States Perspective' (2020) 9 UNSW Law Journal Forum 1

Québec Ministre de la Justice, *Commentaires du ministre de la Justice* (Les Publications du Québec 1993)

Queensland Law Reform Comission, *The Law Relating to Succession. Report No. 22* (1978)

——, *The Law Of Wills. Report No. 52* (1997)

Quevedo AIG de, 'La forrnalización del testamento público abierto' (1996) 14 Revista Colegio de Notarios 1

Radwański Z (ed), *System prawa prywatnego, vol. 2, Prawo cywilne - część ogólna* (C H Beck 2008)

Radzyner A, 'Inheritance from Uncle Sam: The American Influence on Israeli Succession Law' (2016) 4 Comparative Legal History 19

Rath-Boşca L-D, Barmoş LM and Stănescu IA, 'The Need to Harmonize the Laws of the European Union Regarding the Succesion Law' [2016] Agora International Journal of Economical Sciences 35

Raventos LA, 'The Formal Validity Of The Mortis Causa Provisions In The Regulations 650/2012 (EU): An Article on Spanish Law' (2016) 22 ILSA Journal of International & Comparative Law 515

Reed P, 'Challenges to Wills' [2012] Private Client Business 109

Reid KGC, De Waal MJ and Zimmermann R (eds), *Comparative Succession Law. Testamentary Formalities* (Oxford University Press 2011)

Reinhart G, *Das Verhältnis von Formnichtigkeit und Heilung des Formmangels im bürgerlichen Recht* (Universität Heidelberg 1969)

Rendell C, *Law of Succession* (Macmillan 1997)

Rescigno P, 'Ultime volontà e volontà della forma' (1987) 38 Vita Notarile 17

——, 'Il testatore anziano e la forma del testamento' [2017] Jus civile 382

Richemont HD, *Projet de loi portant réforme des successions et des libéralités (Rapport No. 343)* (Sénat de la République Française 2006)

Rivers J and Kerridge R, 'The Construction of Wills' (2000) 116 Law Quarterly Review 287

Robbins N, *New Zealand and the Holographic Will* (Victoria University of Wellington 2016)

Rogers M, 'If It Looks like a Will, There's a Way' (2017) 43 Lawtalk 32

Ronovska K, 'Civil Law in the Czech Republic: Tendencies of Development (Some Notes on the Proposal of the New Civil Code)' [2008] European Review of Private Law 111

Ropenga P, 'Testament by SMS' (2020) 2020 Alacriter - blog - Insights into contracts, intenational law, trusts and estates 1

Ross H, *Preserving Digital Materials* (Walter de Gruyter 2012)

Röthel A, *Ist unser Erbrecht noch zeitgemäß?* (C H Beck 2010)

——, 'Testamentsformen' (2014) 5 Juristische Ausbildung 475

Rudnicki J, 'Rola formy testamentu. Uwagi na tle porównawczym' (2013) 2 Forum Prawnicze 35

Ruggeri L, Kunda I and Winkler S (eds), *Family Property and Succession in EU Member States. National Reports on the Collected Data* (Sveučilište u Rijeci 2019)

Rzewuski M, 'Formalisation of the Testament in the Light of the Favor Testamenti Principle' (2013) 2013 Miľníky Práva v Stredoeurópskom Priestore 978

——, 'Wykładnia słusznościowa testamentu' [2014] Białostockie Studia Prawnicze 227

——, 'Konwersja testamentu' in Piotr Stec and Mariusz Załucki (eds), *50 lat kodeksu cywilnego. Perspektywy rekodyfikacji* (Wolters Kluwer 2015)

——, 'Wykładnia testamentu a okoliczności zewnętrzne towarzyszące testowaniu' (2015) 2015 Przegląd Sądowy 106

Safjan M, *System prawa prywatnego, vol. 1, Prawo cywilne - część ogólna* (Marek Safjan ed, C H Beck 2007)

Sagaut J-F, 'Présentation de la loi réformant le droit français des liberalités et des successions' (2010) 14 Electron. J. Comp. Law 1

Sanchez E V., 'Are We Ready for Electronic Wills' (2006) 206 Notes on Business Education 1

Sandoval JS, 'El testamento ológrafo en soporte digital y la firma biométrica' (2019) 2019 Boletín del Ministerio de Justicia 1

Sasso I, 'Will Formalities in the Digital Age: Some Comparative Remarks' (2018) 4 Italian Law Journal 169

Scalise RJJ, 'Undue Influence and the Law of Wills. A Comparative Analysis' (2008) 19 Duke Journal of Comparative and Intenational Law 41

——, 'Will Formalities in Louisiana: Yesterday, Today, and Tomorrow' (2020) 80 Louisiana Law Review 1334

Schapp J, *Methodenlehre und System des Rechts* (Mohr Siebeck 2009)

Schmidt JP, 'Grundlagen der Testierfähigkeit in Deutschland und Europa' (2012) 220 Rabels Zeitschrift für ausländisches und internationales Privatrecht 1022

Schmoeckel M and Otte G (eds), *Europäische Testamentsformen* (Nomos 2011)

Scholz P, 'Digitales Testieren. Zur Verwendung digitaler Technologien beim eigenhändigen und Nottestament de lege lata et ferenda' [2019] Archiv Für Die Civilistische Praxis 100

Shah JC and others, 'Crypto-Wills: Transferring Digital Assets by Maintaining Wills on the Blockchain' in Jagdish Chand Bansal and others (eds), *Communication and Intelligent Systems* (Springer 2020)

Sherwin E, 'Clear and Convincing Evidence of Testamentary Intent: The Search for a Compromise Between Formality and Adjudicative Justice' (2002) 34 Connecticut Law Review 453

Shulman KI, Cohen CA and Hull I, 'Psychiatric Issues in Retrospective Challenges of Testamentary Capacity' (2005) 20 International Journal of Geriatric Psychiatry 63

Sibley JN, 'Convention Poviding a Uniform Law on the Form on an International Will: Problems with State Probate Law' (1974) 4 Georgia Journal of International and Comparative Law 422

Sitkoff RH, 'Freedom of Disposition in American Succession Law' in Antoni Vaquer Aloy, María Paz Sánchez González, Esteve Bosch Capdevila (eds), *La libertad de testar y sus límites* (Marcial Pons 2018)

Sitkoff RH and Dukeminier J, *Wills, Trusts and Estates* (10th edn, Wolters Kluwer 2017)

Skowrońska-Bocian E, *Testament w prawie polskim* (Lexis Nexis 2004)

Slingo J, 'Coronavirus: Demand for Wills Jumps by 76%' *The Law Society Gazette* (31 March 2020)

Snail S and Hall N, 'Electronic Wills in South Africa' (2010) 7 Digital Evidence and Electronic Signature Law Review 67

Sneddon KJ, 'In the Name of God, Amen. Language in Last Wills and Testaments' (2011) 29 Quinnioac Law Review 665

——, 'Speaking For the Dead: Voice in Last Wills and Testaments' (2011) 85 St. John's Law Review 684

——, 'Not Your Mother's Will : Gender, Language, and Wills' (2015) 98 Marquette Law Review

Solzbach J, *Formstrenge bei Testamenten im deutsch–US–amerikanischen Vergleich* (Friedrich-Alexander- Universität Erlangen-Nürnberg 2016)

Sonnekus JC, 'Videotestamente naas skriftelike testamente' (1990) 1990 Tydskrif vir die Suid-Afrikaanse Reg 114

Spitzer M, 'Neues ze letzwilligen Verfügunen. Ein Beitrag zu Nottestament und Testierfähigkeit' (2006) 2006 Österreichische Notariats Zeitung 77

Stec P and Załucki M, *Podstawy prawa cywilnego z umowami w administracji* (Difin 2011)

Stern Y, 'The Testamentary Phenomenon in Ancient Rome' (2000) 49 Historia: Zeitschrift für Alte Geschichte 413

Szostek D, *Nowe ujęcie dokumentu w polskim prawie prywatnym ze szczególnym uwzględnieniem dokumentu w postaci elektronicznej* (C H Beck 2012)

Talpis J, 'Freedom of Cross-Border Estate Planning: Anticipated Problems' (2016) 22 Trusts & Trustees 119

Tamaruya M, 'Japanese Wealth Management and the Transformation of the Law of Trusts and Succession' (2019) 33 Trust Law International 147

Tampieri M, 'Formalismo testamentario e testamento olografo' (1998) 1998 Rivista del Notariato 119

Terner P, 'Perspectives of a European Law of Succession' (2007) 14 Maastricht Journal of European and Comparative Law 147

The Law Commission, *Making a Will. Consultation Paper 231* (The Law Commission 2017)

——, '*Making a Will*' Consultation Paper 231 (2017)

du Toit F, 'The Impact of Social and Economic Factors on Freedom of Testation in Roman and Roman-Dutch Law' (1999) 10 Stellenbosch Law Review 232

——, 'Testamentary Condonation in South Africa : A Pyrrhic Victory for Private Autonomy over Mandatory Formalism in the Law of Wills ?' in Alain-Laurent Verbeke and others (eds), *Confronting the Frontiers of Family and Succession Law. Liber Amicorum Walter Pintens* (Intersentia 2012)

——, 'Roman-Dutch Law in Modern South African Succession Law' (2014) 2014 Ars Aequi 278

——, 'Testamentary Rescue: An Analysis of the Intention Requirement in Australia and South Africa' [2014] Australian Property Law Journal 56

——, 'Remedying Formal Irregularities in Wills: A Comparative Analysis of Testamentary Rescue in Canada and South Africa' (2020) 20 Oxford University Commonwealth Law Journal 139

Traynor RJ, *The Riddle of Harmless Error* (Ohio University Press 1970)

Tucker RM, 'How Substantial Is Substantial? Compliance with the Louisiana Civil Code' s Requirements for Notarial Testaments' (2018) 92 Tulane Law Review 969

Uzcategui J, 'Application of the Harmless Error Doctrine in California and Beyond' (2015) 21 California Trusts & Estates Quarterly 1

Vaquer Aloy A, 'Freedom of Testation, Compulsory Share and Disinheritance Based on Lack of Family Relationship' in M Anderson and E Arroyo I Amayuelas (eds), *The Law of Succession: Testamentary Freedom. European Perspectives* (Europa Law Publishing 2009)

——, 'La protección del testador vulnerable' (2015) 68 Iuris Dictio 327

—— , 'La relajación de las solemnidades del testamento' (2016) 3 Revista de Derecho Civil 9

Velazco RES, 'El Anteproyecto de Reforma al Código Civil y los negocios juridicos mortis causa' (2019) 64 Actualidad Civil 43

Veloso Z, 'Testamentos – Nocoes Gerais, Formas ordinarias' in Domingos Franciulli Netto, Gilmar Ferreira Mendes and Ives G da Silva Martins Filho (eds), *O novo Codigo Civil: Estudos em Homenagem ao Prof Miguel Reale* (LTr 2003)

Verbeke A-L, 'Het nieuwe erfrecht international gestitueerd' [2003] Weekblad voor Privaatrecht, Notariat en Registratie 20

Verbeke A-L and Leleu Y-H, 'Harmonization of the Law of Succession in Europe' in AS Hartkamp and others (eds), *Towards a European Civil Code* (Kluwer Law International 2011)

Vukotic M, 'Importance of Will Execution Formalities in Serbian Law' in Bojan Milisavljevic, Tatjana Jevremovic Petrovic and Milos Zivkovic (eds), *Law and Transition* (University of Belgrade 2017)

Waggoner LW, 'The Revised Uniform Probate Code' (1994) 5 Trust & Estates 18

Wagner C, 'Have Ontario's Courts Dispensed with Strict Compliance with the Formalities of Execution?' (2012) <https://www.wagnersidlofsky.com/have-ontarios-courts-dispensed-with-strict-compliance-with-the-formalities-of-execution> accessed 21 January 2021

Wang H, Galligan MW and Kolodny JB, 'Modern Inheritance Develops in China' (2013) 2013 New York Law Journal 2

Warren J, 'Interpretation of Wills' (1936) 49 Harvard Law Review 689

Weisbord RK, 'Wills for Everyone: Helping Individuals Opt Out of Intestacy' (2013) 53 Boston College Law Review 877

Weisbord RK, Horton D and Urice SK, *Wills, Trusts and Estates. The Essentials* (Wolters Kluwer 2018)

Welser R, 'Die Reform des österreichischen Erbrechts', *Zivilrechtsgesetzgebung heute Festschrift Gerhard Hopf zum 65. Geburtstag* (Manz 2007)

——, 'Die Reform des österreichischen Erbrechts' (2012) 144 Österreichische Notariat Zeitung 249

——, 'Reformbedarf bei den letztwilligen Verfügungen' in Reinhold Geime, Rolf A Schütze and Thomas Garber (eds), *Europäische und internationale Dimension des Rechts: Festschrift für Daphne-Ariane Simotta* (Lexis Nexis 2012)

Wendel PT, 'Setting the Record Straight: The "Flexible Strict Compliance" Approach to the Wills Act Formalities' (2016) 95 Oregon Law Review

——, 'Wills Act Compliance and the Harmless Error Approach: Flawed Narrative Equals Flawed Analysis?' (2017) 95 Oregon Law Review 339

——, *Wills, Trusts, and Estates* (Wolters Kluwer 2018)

Westman T, *Tolking av testamente* (Stockholms Universitet 2013)

Weyer, 'Das eigenhändige Testament - Gedanken und Erfahrungen eines Nachlassrichters' (1935) 1935 Deutsche Notar-Zeitschfirt 348

White K, 'Dispensing Powers. Validating Testamentary Intentions in the Absence of Formal Compliance' [2000] Law Society Journal 56

Wiederkehr G and others, *Code Civil* (Dalloz 2014)

Wieling H, *Testamentsauslegung im Römischen Recht* (C H Beck 1972)

Wierciński J, 'Sporządzenie testamentu w stanie wyłączającym świadome powzięcie decyzji i wyrażenie woli w praktyce notarialnej' [2011] Przegląd Sądowy 7

——, 'Uwagi o zamiarze testowania (animus testandi)' (2012) 2012 Przegląd Sądowy 132

Wingerter A, *Die eigenhändige letztwillige Verfügung im Spannungsverhältnis zwischen Form und der Verwirklichung des Erblasserwillens* (Bayerischen Julius-Maximilians-Universität 1998)

Wójcik S, *System prawa cywilnego, vol. IV, Prawo spadkowe* (Józef Stanisław Piątowski ed, Ossolineum 1986)

Wójcik S and Zoll F, 'Testament' (2006) 2006 Studia Prawa Prywatnego 83

Wolak G, 'Animus testandi na tle orzecznictwa Sądu Najwyższego' (2015) 2015 Rejent 1

Wood-Bodley MC, 'MacDonald v. the Master: Computer Files and the Rescue Provision of the Wills Act' (2004) 121 South African Law Journal 34

Załucki M, 'Współczesne tendencje rozwoju ustawodawstwa testamentowego' (2012) 22 Roczniki Nauk Prawnych 23

——, *Uniform European Inheritance Law. Myth, Dream or Reality of the Future* (AFM Publishing House 2015)

——, 'Forma testamentu w perspektywie rekodyfikacji polskiego prawa spadkowego. Czas na rewolucję?' (2017) 72 Państwo i Prawo 31

——, 'Testament w prawie angielskim' in Piotr Kostański, Paweł Podrecki and Tomasz Targosz (eds), *Experentia docet. Księga jubileuszowa ofiarowana Pani Profesor Elżbiecie Traple* (Wolters Kluwer 2017)

——, 'Attempts to Harmonize the Inheritance Law in Europe: Past, Present, and Future' (2018) 103 Iowa Law Review 2318

——, 'The Future of Succession Law in the EU. A Proposal' in C Santos Botelho and F da Silva Veiga (eds), *Future Law* (2018)

——, *Videotestament. Prawo spadkowe wobec nowych technologii* (CH Beck 2018)

——, 'About the Need to Adjust the Regulations Regarding the Form of Will to the Modern Requirements' (2019) 6 The European Journal of Economics, Law and Politics 1

—— (ed), *Kodeks Cywilny. Komentarz* (C H Beck 2019)

——, 'A Few Remarks about the Future of Provisions on Making a Will Contrary to the Testamentary Formalities Law' (2020) 13 Cadernos de Dereito Actual 20

——, 'Evidentiary Function of the Provisions on the Form of Wills in the Contemporary Succession Law. Is the Complete Abandonment of Formalism Possible?' (2020) 26 Trusts & Trustees 814

——, 'Preparation of Wills in Times of COVID-19 Pandemic - Selected Observations' (2020) 45 Journal of Modern Science 143

Zerres T, *Bürgerliches Recht* (Springer 2019)

Zimmermann R, 'Testamentsformen :» Willkür « oder Ausdruck einer Rechtskultur?' (2012) 76 Rabels Zeitschrift für ausländisches und internationales Privatrecht 471

Zoll F, 'Czy odwołalność testamentu zawsze powinna być nieograniczona' in Marlena Pecyna, Małgorzata Podrecka and Jerzy Pisuliński (eds), *Rozprawy cywilistyczne. Księga pamiatkowa dedeykowana Profesorowi Edwardowi Drozdowi* (Lexis Nexis 2013)